Horace the Minstrel

Horace the Minstrel

A PRACTICAL *and*
AESTHETIC STUDY *of his*
AEOLIC VERSE

Noel A. Bonavia-Hunt, MA

Pembroke College, Oxford

Kineton: The Roundwood Press
1969

Set in 'Monotype' Caslon, series 128, and printed by
Gordon Norwood at The Roundwood Press Limited, Kineton,
in the County of Warwick. Bound by Henry Books at Oxford.

Made and Printed in Great Britain

To Michael Ramsey

Archbishop of Canterbury

this edition of

Horace the Minstrel

is humbly dedicated

by gracious permission

CONTENTS

Ad Quintum Horatium Flaccum   ix
Foreword   xi
Author's Preface   xiii
Editor's Note   xvii

Chapter I.   Horace and his Lyre
    i.   Was Horace a Musician?   1
    ii.   'For all the Music Could Do'.   27

Chapter II.   The Aeolic Odes:
    A.   Introduction   39
    B.   The Sapphic Ode   46
    C.   The Alcaic Ode   52
    D.   The Asclepiad Odes   61

Chapter III.   Composing in Horatian Metres   75

Chapter IV.   A Demonstration   101

Chapter V.   An Anthology   144

Select Bibliography   262

General Index   264

ACKNOWLEDGMENTS

PERMISSION TO INCLUDE extracts from *Testimentum Amoris* has been granted by The Society of Authors as the literary representative of the estate of the late Laurence Binyon.

Permission to include the extract from *A Shropshire Lad* has been granted by The Society of Authors as the literary representative of the estate of the late A. E. Housman, and Messrs. Jonathan Cape Limited, publishers of A. E. Housman's *Collected Poems*.

Permission to include the extract from *Reliquiae* by A. D. Godley (ed. C. R. L. Fletcher), has been granted by the Oxford University Press.

Permission to include the extract from *Ruthless Rhymes for Heartless Homes* by H. Graham has been given by the publishers, Messrs. Edward Arnold (Publishers) Limited.

The poem *To My Wood Merchant* by M. H. Longson is reprinted by permission of *Punch*.

Mr Laurence Swinyard's *Ode to J. E. Moeran* is reprinted by permission of Novello and Company, Limited.

Despite diligent search it has proved impossible to trace the owners of the copyrights of a number of works from which extracts have been quoted; to those authors, living or dead and their publishers, the editor of the present work is deeply grateful.

AD QUINTUM HORATIUM FLACCUM

"Visam Britannos hospitibus feros" :
oblivionis non metuens citae
sic, Flacce, dixisti perite
magna modis memorare magnis.

non gratiori pandimus advenae
nunc liberales ostia, qui novis
vulgamus inventis benignas
Pacis Amicitiaeque voces

totum per orbem. non tua vox tacet,
non visit Orcum plurima pars tui
quem Fama dilexit superstes
carmine nos lepido levantem.

quicunque et audens Aeolias avet
tentare Musas, sive fugacibus
artes per Orpheas libenter
divitiis meliora quaerit,

seu scandit altum discipulus pede
Pindum labanti, versibus e tuis
gazas honorandis beatas
adsiduo fodiat ligone.

N. A. B-H.

FOREWORD

THERE HAVE BEEN better poets than Horace. There have, at least to my way of thinking, been better Latin poets. To my own liking, Catullus, whose works, lost for a millennium, come down to us from a single archetype stuffed into a wine cask in his native Verona and miraculously rediscovered at the end of the Middle Age, is among them. But there is no poet who has had a more continuous fascination for urbane and civilised men and women than Horace. Moreover, there is none for some reason who has appealed more continuously to the cultivated English taste.

I am not qualified to criticise or appraise the thesis underlying the late Mr Bonavia-Hunt's "Horace the Minstrel," that Horace's Carmina were really sung in his own, presumably, light tenor voice, to the tune of a lyre plucked by his own little plump right thumb or at least his own plectrum, and not, as my pedagogues earnestly assured me, recited to an admiring audience of male companions after the last glass of Falernian; for I myself find nothing improbable in the theory, or even in the view (not advanced by the author) that he hired a pop group to sing them. What I am sure of is that the view is an attractive one and supported by an impressive armoury of musical and classical scholarship.

The second part of the book is an anthology of Horatian poems in several languages and many metres in the manner of Horace or translated from him, which lovers of lyric poetry will enjoy whatever their views of Horace's musical prowess. To all lovers of lyric poetry and classical learning this edition of Mr Bonavia-Hunt's book will be a valued acquisition to their library.

House of Commons   QUINTIN HOGG

PREFACE

RATHER MORE THAN ten years ago I wrote a Preface to this book for its first appearance. It is a great pleasure for me to find myself doing the same again for a second edition. For although the contents of this new edition have been entirely revised and very much expanded, yet the title of the book remains the same and still indicates the keynote of my maturer approach to the lyric verse of Horace. Nor has there been any change in the twin targets I have had in view from the very outset; namely, to present a reasoned case for my firm conviction that Horace wrote his Latin lyrics with the ear of a practical musician, and that some at least of them were written to be sung; secondly, to provide a compendious vade-mecum of what Americans, I believe, call *know-how*, with a view to encouraging the composing of modern Latin verse in Horatian vein and metre.

I write, however, as one whose real study of the poet did not begin until well after school and university days. As a VIth-former I had scraped no more than a nodding acquaintance with him, alas, but through no fault of my own. In those far-off days a tiny handful of familiar odes was all that most alumni were normally permitted to make contact with. Perhaps Victorian prudery had something to do with it. For I have a feeling somehow that with the powers-that-be even the Odes (let alone the Epodes, Satires and Epistles) were still regarded as not wholly 'quite nice', and potentially as unsuitable material to put before the young except in carefully vetted selections. In any case Latin verse composition for us was restricted to the usual hexameters and elegiacs, mostly on stereotyped and uninteresting themes. So much bias was there, in fact, in the exclusive direction of Virgil and Ovid that a trivial little episode is still fresh in my mind after more years than I care to remember. On some occasion or other a fellow disciple was asked to scan : *dulce et decorum est pro patria mori*. Bringing a truly marvellous ingenuity to the task he actually made an Ovidian "pentameter" out of it ![1]

For many years to my present regret I almost lost touch with Horace of the Carmina. I think really I owe it to a church organist friend and to another absurd incident that my thoughts were turned once again to Horace and to the music in his lyrics. For some reason this friend had his knife into that august body of Kensington Gore, London, the Royal College of Organists. I forget the reason for his displeasure and it matters not now. But one day he suddenly burst in on me with an impatient — "Odi profanum volgus et R.C.O." ! (The Arnoldian pronunciation of Latin usual in those days is of course necessary to the quip.) Strange to say, this did the trick. For no reason at all it started me off anew on a close study of the Odes ; and I found there what I had already begun to suspect — that there was a much more intimate connexion in them with music than the academic world had apparently realised. For generations past the literary aspect of course had been abundantly

---

[1] Evelyn Waugh's biography of Ronald Knox, p. 181 (Fontana paperback ed.) records a quotation from the report by Monsignor Knox on the history and condition of the Old Palace, Oxford, which Knox as Catholic University chaplain occupied for 13 years:

"In the old chapel stood a very imperfect list of Catholics who fell in the Great War: I had to remove this, because the quotation at the top *Dulce et decorum est pro patria mori* had been attributed by an oversight to Ovid."

explored and learnedly commented on from every angle, while the sonic properties of these works and the musical artistry, as such, apparent in their composition had, in Britain anyhow, escaped the detailed attention of editors; or so it seemed. There were plenty of experts around to assure us that the form and finish of the Carmina were above all criticism, but I do not recall any of them explaining just why and just how. This book now attempts to fill in some of the details.

But enough of personal reminiscence. On a broader front things have since improved; and today Horatian verse-writing is no longer the esoteric business of two or three specialists. Unhappily, there is still too big a gap in the technical and aesthetic equipment of modern composers (myself included) aspiring to write Horatian pastiche. Even today Latin Alcaics, Sapphics or Asclepiads win prizes or get published in the Sunday press and elsewhere despite the fact that, quite unnecessarily, they often fail to toe the Horatian line. Myself I have never regarded it as mere empty pedantry to insist on what might be called the good manners of Horatian style: these things can be learnt and learnt through the ear as well as through the eye and mind. Naturally, I very much hope that this book in its new edition will go far towards bridging the gap.

It only remains for me to pay my grateful and heartfelt tribute of thanks to helpers, past and present, in respect of both editions of this book: to Professor E. J. Wood of Leeds University, for his initial encouragement and active intervention at those stages where my foothold was perhaps not too sure; to my Birmingham barrister friend who compiled the Anthology now forming Chapter V of this edition; to my late brother Wilfrid, who had independently pursued his own enquiry into the mysteries of Horace's *numeri* and upon whose researches I was enabled to draw so fruitfully. As a *tour de force* his Alcaic rendering of Professor Arberry's literal translation of the original Rubá'iyát of Omar will appeal, especially to practitioners who will know only too well the truly appalling difficulties involved. To these good souls my debt is great. But for all their services to the book and myself it has to be recorded that the present edition could not have seen the light of day but for the enterprise of Mr Alan Treloar, M.A., now of the University of New England, Armidale, N.S.W., Australia, who without thought of reward save only that promised by the doing of the job itself has undertaken a general revision of the text. On the face of it, my obligation to his erudition and enthusiasm must always be of another order.

Benenden, Kent.   NOEL A. BONAVIA-HUNT

EDITOR'S NOTE

THE REV. NOEL A. BONAVIA-HUNT was actively interested in the preparation of this revised and enlarged edition of *Horace the Minstrel* throughout the last year or two of his life. When he died in August 1965 at the age of 82, the typescript draft was complete but for the last few pages. He had himself written the Preface, rewritten chapter I (*Horace and his Lyre*), revised other parts, and taken a close interest in the progress of the rest of the work. Fortunately, he was able to review the typescript of his own new contribution before he died. The editor would also take the opportunity of thanking Mr R. S. H. Capes, M.A. for his assistance in compiling the Index and in the reading and checking of proofs.

A.T.

Chapter One

Horace and his Lyre

«Señora, donde ay musica, no puede aver cosa mala»

I. WAS HORACE A MUSICIAN?

THE PURPOSE of this Section is to state the case for an affirmative answer to this question. Having done so, I leave it to the Opposition (the majority of scholars and scholiasts) to prove me wrong if it can. Nor do I make apology for any polemical note or for any gleams of mere commonsense that the reader may find in what I have to say.

In a nutshell my contentions are these: that Horace was an accomplished all-round amateur musician with a great love of the art and science of music; that he knew a good deal about it technically; that he not only could but did play the lyre competently; that music impregnates his lyric verse, deeply affecting its sonic qualities[1] and influencing even the drift of the thought at times; finally, that he wrote some at least (not all) of his Carmina for singing (with or

---

[1] *Cf.* Edward Lucie-Smith's report (in the *Sunday Times* of 25/7/65) of an interview with Basil Bunting, a contemporary poet, whom he describes as "intensely musical, and ... once a professional music critic." Bunting is reported as saying: "The essential thing about poetry is the sound it makes, the shapes you can make with the sound. Without the music of words there is no poetry. Anything else that's in it is secondary." And of technique he says: "Let it stay invisible. It's the effect on the reader that matters."

without instrumental accompaniment) and not merely for speech recitation.

The proving of this multiple proposition, if achieved, would lead somewhere, too: for it would leave something over for the student composer of to-day who aims to write convincingly in Horatian vein. What is the lesson for him here? Just this: he must try to make his own verse sound something like the sound of Horace's by paying more attention to music values than has hitherto been suspected as essential. Not every student has been gifted by nature with the master's exquisite ear, I know: few of us have it in such liberal measure. Nor are all of us musical in the narrower sense of the word. No matter; other things equal, this will be no fatal bar to our qualifying as good Horatian composers. Even if we cannot appreciate all the music in the diction of the master, we only need a sharp pair of ears to tell us that it has a certain verbal euphony of its own: how far we can assimilate this and reproduce something of it in our own work depends of course on ourselves. Some of the greatest poets in literature have been almost tone-deaf to organized music, but enormously aware of finest shades in the sound of words as such.

The Opposition's case can be stated very simply. It amounts to this: whenever you find references in Horace's works to his "playing the lyre" and the like, you are never to take them in a literal sense or at face value. They are purely a conventional figure of speech or poetic *cliché*. All he means is that he is composing lyric verse.

Although the Opposition does not quite go to the length of saying outright that 'vocal' words such as *cantare, carmen* and so on must always be interpreted figuratively, it has a strong bias in this direction. We are certainly meant to infer that no Horatian ode, with one exception, was ever designed to be sung by human voice or accompanied instrumentally. "The picture of Horace playing the lyre must be regarded as a fiction" — says R. Heinze.[1] *Er* (Horace) *sang seine Verse nicht, er rezitierte sie*, says the equally distinguished German commentator Wilamowitz[2] no less bluntly. And what goes for Horace himself ought, logically, to go for any one else on his behalf — Chloe, for instance.

I hope that I have put the Opposition case fairly, if in brief terms. I have tried to do so, and certainly with no unscholarly intent of fighting shy of anything known to me that might go to support it. But the awkward fact remains that it does so largely rest upon foundations that are negative : mostly scholiast tradition, one suspects. Nowhere does Horace say explicitly : "My Carmina were written to be recited, not to be sung; nor did I ever intend them to be accompanied by lyre or pipe. And don't run away with the idea that I used to play the lyre myself. I couldn't have done it if I'd tried."

Yet he does get pretty near at times to saying the other thing, as we shall see; and the only way the Opposition can parry the effect of the evidence against it is to persist in its 'figurative' strategy through thick and thin.

Before I pass to the attack I want to say at once that certain concessions have to be made. Assuredly we are not justified in taking up an extreme position over the key music-words and music-phrases. Neither side can afford to approach the matter as the lawyers do, so I am told, when they seek to construe a Statute of the Realm, and have to abide by Lord Wensleydale's famous Golden Rule. When we ourselves say in colloquial speech : "X loudly sang Y's

[1] *Vom Geist des Römertums*, 1960, 187 : *aber wir werden uns doch enstchließen müssen, das Bild des leierspielenden Horaz als Fiktion zu betrachten.*
[2] Quoted by E. Fraenkel in *Horace*, p. 404 n.3.

praises" we do not of course mean that X was to be heard lifting up his voice *fortissimo* in a *Lied* with words in praise of Y. On the other hand, 'Wine, Woman and Song' emphatically does not mean 'Wine, Woman and Verse Recitation'. It cuts both ways.

Thus to take one example from Horace against myself. In IV ii 33–34, when he urges Mark Antony's son Iullus to *concinere maiore plectro Caesarem*, it would be far-fetched to suppose that he thinks the bard ought to provide himself with an extra-thick plectral stick or quill for the purpose !¹

As against this, there are passages in Horace where a basic or literal interpretation of music-words would not merely be *not* absurd, but would in fact involve positive absurdity if a literal meaning were denied them. Not even the Opposition, I take it, would hold out for "black cares will be mitigated by recited verse" as a basic rendering of *minuentur atrae carmine curae* (IV xi 35–6).² This would be too silly. What is the context? Phyllis, the avowed last of his loves, is being coaxed by Horace to learn thoroughly (a strong word *condiscere*) some unspecified *modi*,³ and then give them back to him in her own *amanda voce*. She cannot have been an unmusical girl, or there would have been no point in getting her to learn and sing anything at all. Surely the implication is clear enough? He wants her to learn and practise up — not 'any old' *modi*, but some of his own Carmina *set to music*, and when she has done this to sing/play them back to him (*reddas*) like a modern tape-recorder.

---

¹ Yet in regard to *leviore plectro* (II i 40) Dr. J. Gow *ad loc*. notes with some force: 'the lighter plectrum would produce softer and more rapid notes in straying over the strings' (Horace, *Odes* ii, Cambridge University Press, 1928). *Cf.* also Ovid *Met.* x 150-2.

² *Cf.* Fraenkel, *Horace*, pp. 417–8.

³ For the meaning of *modi*, see p. 28 n.1.

By the same token it would be quite ridiculous to argue that the hypothetical ass in Sermo II iii 104, bought up a job lot of (?) "lyric poems" (*citharas*) instead of the actual musical instruments Horace so obviously means.[1] It will do the Opposition no good to protest that this is an extract from a 'prose' Sermo, not from one of the Carmina. As we shall see, one or two of the most trenchant proofs of my case come from the Hexameters : and, I agree, you cannot arbitrarily insist on a figurative interpretation in the middle of a 'prose' context just because the going gets too tough to be comfortable.

I must also of course concede that in certain passages of the Odes or Epodes relevant key words (mostly *carmina*) point in neither direction definitely : the effect of their evidence is ambivalent. When in IV viii 11–12, Horace writes :

gaudes carminibus; carmina possumus
donare . . . .

neither the Opposition nor I can pray *carmina* in aid of our respective cases. Or when he abruptly breaks off in III iii, at line 69, to say : *non hoc iocosae conveniet lyrae,* he could mean simply that descriptions of war and disaster belong properly not to light lyric poetry (which was 'up his street') but to epic (which was not). So too the key phrase in II xii 4 perhaps lies just inside the neutral zone, but only just. *Mollibus citharae modis,* if it is not purely another flowery way of saying 'lyric poetry', comes uncomfortably close to 'tender melody of the lyre' in a real sense — uncomfortably for the Opposition's case, that is.

---

[1] And if so, Horace does not want his old age to be without grace or the *cithara* in a real sense (I xxxi 20). This gives no trouble, if only we let the evidence lead us, and do not start from a cast-iron presumption that Horace could not and did not play the lyre. According to Quintilian, Socrates himself was not ashamed, even in his old age, to learn to play the lyre (I x 13).

If then I have succeeded in stating adequately the case for the other side and making all due concessions to it, it is now up to me to demolish it. I propose to start by considering the one ode of Horace known to have been composed for musical performance, known as a fact to have received it. I mean of course the *Carmen Saeculare*. It is much too late in the day to quibble over the musicality of this performance.

Under the Republic in B.C. 207 twenty-seven maidens (no boys) sang a Processional Song composed by Livius Andronicus for the ceremonial rites in propitiation of Juno. The historian Livy is quite explicit about this item in his account. He says they *carmen in Iunonem reginam canentes ibant*.[1] Not even Professor E. Fraenkel, who may be regarded as among the most eminent spokesmen for the Opposition, takes any point on the musicality of these 'vocal' words. Equally it is taken for granted on all hands that music of some sort went with the public performance of Horace's *Carmen* in June B.C. 17.[2]

This being so, then, the Opposition naturally has to be challenged immediately. "Seeing that you must admit this exception to your rule, is there not every good *a priori* reason for extending the list of exceptions? If one ode could be set to music, what was there to prevent a dozen others being treated similarly?"[3]

---

[1] XXVII 37 13.

[2] Dessau, *ILS* 5050 148–9.

[3] J. Perret, *Horace* (1959), pp. 102–3, observes pertinently that strophic composition is the form of poetry best fitted for a musical accompaniment, and asks whether the countless references to music in the *Odes* are merely a "façon de parler." He makes his own view clear in the following words: "Je me demande si l'anachronisme n'est pas au moins aussi grave à nous représenter Horace comme une sorte de Valéry ou de Mallarmé. Même à l'époque de la Renaissance, la poésie légère avait encore partie liée avec la musique ... Bien sûr, et dans l'Antiquité tout aussi bien, plus d'un lecteur a dû lire Horace ainsi que nous le lisons nous-mêmes; mais ne peut-on aussi lire à sa table les comédies de Molière et y trouver beaucoup

The only intelligible answer forthcoming seems to be this: "Yes, but other and previous odes were quite unsuitable for musical treatment".[1] Not perhaps a very convincing answer with, say, *Donec gratus eram* (III ix) staring us in the face as but one example admirably cut out for music.[2] I myself would also single out III xxviii (*Festo quid potius die*) as particularly apt.

Before going any further it must be stated that little trace of music that can be certified as indigenously Roman has come down to us. Indeed we know far more about the instruments used during the Golden and Silver Ages than about the music itself. We know that by Augustus' time a large number of Greeks had come to Rome in professional though often quite humble capacities, among them no doubt musicians with their own songs and instruments. We hear of a flute-girls' trade union in Sermo I ii 1. Imported slaves too would act as minstrels to rich *dilettanti* of Rome, and at great banquets would sing and accompany themselves on the lyre. There was also the music made by the priests in the worship of Cybele which had come to Rome during the second Punic War: such music had since become very popular in Rome. Horace himself in a passing reference alludes to the *testudo* being *amica* to the tables of the rich and

---

de plaisir? Qui voudrait en conclure que la représentation n'y ajoute rien, et qu' apparemment Molière a dû se désintéresser de cette question? Ainsi de la Musique pour Horace." He then refers to the evidence in Pliny (*Epp.* IV xix 4, VII iv 9) for the practice of improvising a lyre accompaniment or sung melody to a lyric text, which was apparently the normal practice even by an amateur who wished to give a poem "tout son lustre".

1 I xx, for instance (*Vile potabis*).

2 Of *Persicos odi* (I xxxviii), Rev. A. J. Macleane, M.A., Trinity (Cantab.), in his edition of *Quinti Horatii Flacci — Opera Omnia*, says: "The words were probably written as a song and set to music" (p. 84). In his commentary on I xii (*Quem virum* . . .) the same editor says: "The poem has much of the appearance of an ode for music" (p. 32).

the temples (III xi 6). But to what extent the music of these times was of Italian growth distinct from Greek traditions is hard to determine.

At all events Horace must have heard a good deal of music in his childhood — for he came from the Greek-speaking part of Italy — and still more so in his University days at Athens.[1] Even if Pindaric odes in their original setting were no longer publicly performed, he would have been there in time to hear rendered perhaps the Second Delphic Hymn amongst other things.[2] No doubt there were musical improvisations at supper parties too. It is quite unrealistic to suppose that to one of Horace's temperament it never occurred to try out lyre-playing for himself. Of course he did. He had no compunction about singing his Lalage outside the boundaries of his Sabine farm, regardless of what the 'locals' might think. He certainly did not recite verses about her at the top of his voice. Why the Opposition should jib at the notion of Horace playing the lyre I cannot imagine.

But to return to the musical background of the *Carmen Saeculare*: to what melody it was set, who composed that melody — whether Horace or another — history cannot now tell us for certain, unless or until another lucky strike somewhere turns up more information about the *Ludi*. The

---

[1] I accept it that a "gentleman's education" of Horace's day would include no music beyond elementary school singing. But a meagre academic training in music has never yet prevented a determined music-lover from equipping himself adequately for performance on a musical instrument or, for that matter, for creative composing, as of course in the classic case of Sir Edward Elgar. And *cf.* the case of Themistocles referred to by Quintilian (I x 19).

[2] Prof. W. B. Stanford of Dublin University and author of *The Sound of Greek* (CUP) writes: "On general principles it seems to me likely that some at least of Horace's odes were set to music, and that he could have heard Greek lyrics sung (or chanted with observance of the pitch-accent) in Athens. His diction is certainly highly vocalic."

late Isobel Henderson[1] thought that Horace would not have composed the musical setting for his own words : I take the opposite view. But whatever the tune was, and whoever its composer, it would have to be a simple and dignified one — simple, or it would have beaten the youngsters who had to sing it from memory ; dignified, to befit the time and place. Later in this chapter I give an imaginary reconstruction of it, and so will not anticipate myself further here.

Musically speaking, an unaccompanied double choir of 27 boys and 27 girls would not sound too impressive as a climax or conclusion to the great ceremonies, especially in an unenclosed space. It is interesting to read in Livy's account of the earlier Juno celebrations mentioned above that the maidens in procession *sonum vocis pulsu pedum modulantes incesserunt.*[2] In the absence of orchestral percussion, this would be better than nothing for marking the rhythmic beat. Mommsen thought that the *Carmen Saeculare* was likewise performed in procession : on the Palatine, others have held.[3] In any case on this very grand occasion only a large orchestra would have been able to make a big sound in the open air, as Handel knew so well. For this reason I think that there would be not only "strings" and "wood wind" but "brass" and certainly "percussion" in the shape of *scabellum.* This orchestra of course would not accompany the choirs *colla voce* at full strength so as to drown the voices and words. It is more likely that after an overture (ἐνδόσιμον) had concluded and so brought the choir in for the first 'bar' of the chorale, the voices would receive a very

---

1   Fellow of Somerville College, Oxford, and author of the splendid section on Greek music, *New Oxford History of Music*, Vol. i. Her opinion was communicated in a private letter.

2   *ibid.* 14.

3   This seems the natural interpretation of the official record, *cf.* Dessau, *ILS* 5050 139 and 148.

light *tibia* obbligato, with the Lesbian foot marked by *scabellum*, or it may be by occasional 'twangs' at strategic points from the big *citharae* like those from Horace's smaller *lyra* at choir-practice. Between the stanzas when the boys took over from the girls or *vice versa* there might well have been a short orchestral interlude and possibly even a flourish of trumpets before the final stanza, when both choirs combined to sing together.[1] This is not so fanciful a picture as it might seem. Musical instruments representing all these sections of the orchestra, as we should call them, could have been known to Horace.[2]

And here a parenthetical and slightly misplaced reflection. What is so curious about it all, I feel, is that nobody from the Opposition camp seems to have applied overmuch ordinary, everyday reasoning to the position of Horace himself in the composing of the *Carmen*. It seems quite incredible to me that he should be finding himself for the very first time in his poetic career *experimenting* with a sung

---

[1] Most scholars who have considered the matter take the view that the *Carmen Saeculare* was sung unaccompanied, or at most accompanied by a single *aulos* to keep the pitch. In the absence of positive evidence to this effect I cannot share this view. Its performance, on the contrary, was attended by the utmost pomp and circumstance, I think. As Professor Fraenkel reminds us, the *Carmen* itself was not built into the sacrifices and prayers then offered, and in this respect was an innovation. When it came to be sung, these had all been completed. If its performance, therefore, greatly enhanced the impression made by the celebrations, it did so as a thing apart. All the more reason, surely, why the services of the *collegium symphoniacorum* should have been enlisted to do justice to the finale of a great occasion. What can only be called a musical 'flop' could all too easily have resulted from the use of unduly thin and inadequate musical apparatus; and it is hard to believe that the orchestral forces were any inferior to those used, say, at one of Terence's Comedy performances. As for the choirs, I cannot help thinking that the boys were required to join in the singing — another innovation — instead of merely reciting prayers as in the earlier Juno ceremonies, largely for the same musical reasons, *viz.* to fill out the ensemble.

[2] The reader interested should further consult M. Gagé's *Recherches sur les jeux séculaires. Les Belles Lettres.* Paris (1934) pp. 45 *et seq.*

Sapphic ode for a supremely important Church-State occasion, if I may so term it.[1] Yet if the Opposition sticks to its guns and is right here, it must have been so. If no previous ode written by him had ever been designed for singing or had in fact been sung to music, this must have meant for him a very sharp, very decisive break with the past. Is there a tittle of evidence to show that he recognised it as such? I think not. Of course if in fact he had written odes for music many times before, his silence now becomes perfectly natural and understandable. The *Carmen Saeculare* job would only differ from previous jobs in being on a much bigger scale, with a double choir to sing it instead of individual soloists like himself, Chloe or Phyllis. So by that time he could take it all in his stride, having become an old hand at the game. I submit that on the evidence, negative as well as positive, Horace was *now just that*.

Who was the choirmaster? Not Horace at any rate, says the Opposition. Perhaps one of the XV priests, the *XV viri sacris faciundis* with musical qualifications. We will examine this point in some little detail.

No one could dispute that the two choirs of youngsters must have undergone a stiff course of training. Someone competent to do so must have made them practise their parts again and again until they had got them perfect. If the *Carmen* was to be 'accompanied', as I think it was, the instrumentalists would have to attend and take part in at least some of the rehearsals. With the Princeps, Agrippa, Maecenas and all the 'top brass' present in person on performance day, a hitch or breakdown would never do.

---

[1] Albeit Pasquali, *Orazio lirico*, p. 650 and n. 1, believes precisely this; and so does Burck (*Die Musik in Geschichte und Gegenwart* vi 1957 710–1), although he does not exclude the possibility that some odes were sung sooner or later after being written.

In this connexion, what exercises the Opposition mightily, I need hardly say, is the significance of verses 35–6 of IV vi,

Lesbium servate pedem meique
pollicis ictum.

How it has bothered the metaphorists! As we might expect, Professor Fraenkel rejects any literal rendering of these words: 'It is altogether unlikely', he writes, 'that Horace, a non-musician, should have undertaken the arduous task of rehearsing and conducting the performance of a choir of amateurs, and only an absolutely unambiguous piece of evidence could induce us to believe that such a thing did happen in the year B.C. 17'.[1]

He goes on to approve a comparison by the scholiast of Horace's *mei pollicis ictum* with Ovid's line:

reddidit icta suos pollice chorda sonos (*Fasti* ii 108).

Horace's plucking of the strings with his thumb 'forms part of the same metaphor', he adds.

Two question-begging *dicta* here. Why presume that Horace was a 'non-musician'? The evidence suggests otherwise. Non-professional musician no doubt; but why not a very gifted and accomplished amateur? Again, why presume the Ovid verse from the Arion story to be only metaphor? On the face of it it makes just a plain statement of fact that could hardly be more ordinary. Why this panicky rush for metaphorical cover every time there is a hint in the air of somebody striking a lyre? At this rate, poetic *cliché* could be pushed so far that it would be almost impossible, if a poet *did* actually play the lyre, for him to say so in classical Latin verse and ever get himself believed two thousand years later!

As for that 'absolutely unambiguous piece of evidence', this is rather what tends to be lacking where the occurrence

---

[1] *Horace*, pp. 403–4.

in question is so familiar and commonplace to those involved that nobody dreams of mentioning it expressly. We in Britain do not usually go out of our way to note in our family albums (for the benefit of posterity) that Sir Malcolm Sargent[1] conducts the B.B.C. Symphony Orchestra at Promenade concerts. In any given environment the more something is taken for granted, the less likely future historians will find in the records a direct statement deliberately made by some contemporary witness conveniently at the scene to make it. It is the *obiter dicta* that casually slip out from time to time and get preserved in permanent form somehow that make such telling circumstantial evidence. Everybody who was somebody in Rome at the time must have known that Horace had composed the *Carmen* and was training those teenagers from the upper crust to sing it on the great day : it was common talk.

Let us, however, leave open for the moment the question of who it was who acted as choirmaster, that is, trainer of the boys and girls. It does not follow that the same person would have to 'conduct' (in our modern sense) the choirs on performance day. Professor Fraenkel strongly doubts that there was a 'conductor' at all on that occasion. I am disposed to share his doubt. As mentioned above, it is more likely that the orchestra would play an overture, the conclusion of which would be the cue for the choir to begin the first note of the hymn. But to argue from the absence of conductor that Horace could not have *trained* the choir is not only bad logic but contrary to the indications of IV vi, which looks very much indeed like the occasion of a choir-practice.

Horace's lyre is not 'imaginary' at all (*pace* Mr Wilkinson).[2] At rehearsals it could take the place of the orchestra ;

---

[1] This was written of course before Sir Malcolm's death in October 1967 — *Ed*.

[2] *Golden Latin Artistry*, p. 92, footnote.

just as a church organist often uses a pianoforte in the vestry for practice with his trebles and altos rather than the organ in the church itself. Like Horace's lyre, the *pf* has more nimbleness and is better suited to emphasising accent, phrasing, rhythm, tempo and pitch for choir-training purposes.

Moreover, as every practitioner knows,[1] any teenage choir that has been properly trained and is keen to give of its best, is quite capable of singing a given anthem without any conductor to wave baton or hands.

If then, as I have suggested, we regard as separate and distinct the office of choir-trainer (χοροδιδάσκαλος) from that of conductor — Professor Fraenkel and others, as we have seen, confuse the two — no difficulty arises as to Horace's position in the matter. As composer of the *Carmen* and probably of its tune, as a perfectly competent amateur musician, he would be the best person to train the two choirs, and after consultation with the Princeps perhaps supervise in a general way the musical performance at the *Ludi*. The fallacy of Professor Fraenkel's contention, if I may say so, stems from reading too much into his own assumption that Horace was a non-musician; and then having satisfied himself from the evidence that there was no conductor, he has almost reasoned in reverse to a conclusion that Horace could not have trained the boys and girls to sing the *Carmen*. This will not do.

Again, we must attack what looks like a monstrous conspiracy of silence. For if Horace did not train the choirs, *who did?* Suetonius or Zosimus might (or might not) have mentioned Horace in a passing reference or aside, if he did. If he did not, you would have expected some explicit state-

---

[1] Perhaps in all modesty I may mention here that I myself have in my time trained three separate boys' choirs: N.A.B-H.

ment from somebody as to who in fact *was* responsible.[1]
Never was the identity of a Master of the King's Musick
wrapped in so much mystery ; or was it something that went
without saying?

Ovid again provides our next stopping-place. From exile
in Tomi he writes :

> Et tenuit nostras numerosus Horatius aures,
>   dum ferit Ausonia carmina culta lyra.
>
> *Tristia* IV x 49.

For the Opposition this will inevitably amount to more
metaphor, though it is a little surprising that Professor
Fraenkel in his monumental *Horace* does not even quote or
refer to the couplet at all.

The surrounding circumstances are worth examining
more closely. Ovid is here nostalgically recalling some of the
literary figures of his pre-exile Roman days : Propertius,
Ponticus, Bassus, Virgil, Tibullus, Gallus. Of the first
named he says :

> Saepe suos solitus recitare Propertius ignes
>
> (verse 45, *ibid.*)

Note particularly the word *recitare* :[2] it must mean exactly
what it means in English, "recite". Then comes what I
submit is a real body-blow for the Opposition : "Horace
the melodious (*numerosus*) charmed our ears while he *struck*
(*ferit*) sophisticated songs on his Italian lyre". *Ferit* of course
is the operative word. Ovid could just as easily have written
facit, movet, parit, canit and perhaps half a dozen other
possible verbs. Why *ferit*, unless he intends to convey just
that? Horace, the minstrel, could and did actually play the
lyre : *that is why.*

---

[1] *Viz.* that "Horace the known composer of the *Carmen Saeculare* did not,
however, train the juvenile choirs for the musical performance; that
training was done by X-tus".

[2] *Cf.* Horace's *Ars Poetica* 474; Sermo I iv 75.

Nor does the matter rest there. In line 59 (*ibid.*) Ovid tells us that his elegies in praise of his girl friend (Corinna, so called) were sung (*cantata*) through all Rome. As if to anticipate for our benefit the suggestion that this *cantata* is only another conventional *cliché*, in line 57 he expressly says that he read (*legi*) his youthful works to the people, when his beard had only been cut once or twice.

The combined effect of this evidence is all the more striking, when we recall that whereas Propertius, the *reciter* of red-hot love poetry, was a personal friend of Ovid's, there was no real love lost between Propertius and Horace, and little sympathy between Ovid and Horace.[1] So the couplet quoted above must have been a grudging tribute paid by one poet to a rival, who could perform *musical* feats beyond the powers of the other. In far-away Pontus it is the *music* of Horace's guitar-playing in Rome that leaves the most vivid impression on Ovid's memory, and he as good as says so. There is simply no room whatever for metaphor here : the burden of proving it falls fairly and squarely on the Opposition, and they have not discharged it.

On the subject of girl friends, I have already said something about Phyllis. It is by no accident that several of Horace's other girl friends had musical qualifications : he liked them not merely for their looks, but because they could sing and play to him. Licymnia and Neaera could both sing ; Chloe was a finished singer and lyrist as well ; Chia in IV xiii (whoever she was) besides having the bloom of youth on her side is *docta psallere* (accomplished in guitar-playing) also. The point is, it takes a person of fine musical discrimination to appreciate niceties in these special skills. Such a person manifestly Horace was.

---

[1] Ovid omits Horace's name from a list of entertaining poets (*AA* III 329-340).

I want now to give a few more quotations from the Carmina and Hexameter verse, with comments admittedly but inevitably tendentious. Some of these quotations will be more directly relevant to our main question, some less so. But all converge inexorably on the same point. Horace loved music and delighted in the sounds of organized musical utterance, both vocal and instrumental. With love usually goes a desire to know more about the thing loved, and a desire to involve oneself more actively in it. We may be sure that Horace came to have a first-hand, practical knowledge of the art and science of music as it was known in his day.

In this respect one clue of particular interest stands out. Notice the way in which he has an eye and ear for the smaller technical detail. Unlike our own Robert Browning in *Master Hughes of Saxe-Gotha* Horace gets his detail right. The *testudo* was *cava* (Epode xiv 11); it had seven *nervos*[1] (III xi 3); the *lyra* is *eburna* and *curva* (II xi 22 and III xxviii 11). It may have been the simplest "home" model which had only four strings; or indeed Horace's *quattuor chordis* may really denote the technical tetrachordal series (Sermo I iii 8). The contemporary Augustan-age *tibia* was fitted with brass collars over the stop-holes and was of large scale, emitting a sound rivalling in power that of the trumpet. Horace did not like it. He preferred the older style of *aulos*, of slender scale and with few stops, which used to accompany the Chorus (*Ars Poetica*, 202 *et seq.*). The new type, however, may well have formed part of the orchestra at the open-air performance of the *Carmen Saeculare*. The lyre-player is jeered at, says Horace, who keeps blundering on the same string (*ibid.* 355, 356). The string itself does not always give

---

[1] The legendary father-figure Terpander (*fl.* B.C. 670) is said to have increased the number of strings from four to seven.

the right note intended by the player's fingers : when he wants a flat, he very often gets a sharp. As a *citharoedus*[1] himself, Horace would know that much only too well! (*ibid.* 348, 349). A pleasant banquet can go on just as agreeably without any music. When the orchestra (*symphonia*)[2] between the courses plays out of tune (*discors*) it is as much an infliction on the diner as serving poppy seeds with Sardinian honey or providing unguent gone solid (*ibid.* 374). So it is indeed, but only for the diner who has a good musical ear. We cannot imagine Tennyson or Housman at dinner being disturbed by hearing wrong notes played, or the violas out of tune with the oboes : it is very much more likely that they would have noticed nothing musically amiss at all.

Nor must I forget to mention Epode ix 5–6, where Horace writes :

> sonante mixtum tibiis carmen lyra,
> hac Dorium, illis barbarum,

"while the lyre makes melody blended with the pipes, the lyre in Dorian, the pipes in foreign mode".[3] Provided we do not start from a presumption that Horace was a non-musician or near-ignoramus in matters musical, the technicalities behind this couplet are quite in line with what I have been urging. It is just what a Latin lyric poet (not a quasi-scientific Lucretius) who *did* know quite a lot about the Greek ἁρμονίαι or so-called modes would permit, just for once, to peep out.

In IV xv 30, we come across *Lydis remixto carmine tibiis*. Why were the *tibiae* 'Lydian' this time? Page suggests that this was no more than a conventional epithet deriving from

---

[1] That is, one who sings and accompanies himself on the lyre.

[2] Or, again technically, this might refer to the musical intervals of octave, fifth and fourth.

[3] That is, Phrygian.

the use made of them in the worship of Mother Cybele in Asia Minor. It may well be so, but I like to think that in the context of the quotation Horace was still being technically accurate. Although *tibiae* could be pretty noisy fellows (exceptionally so it seems in III xix 18–23), there is no reason musically why they should not play music in the Lydian τρόπος. After all, the mood itself of the ode is one of mellow retrospect, counting blessings and praising famous men. Cicero[1] tells us that it was an old Roman custom to do this at banquets to a background of *tibia* music.[2] The ode ends as it began on a musical note, but there is nothing to suggest that the *tibiae* in the final stanza had got out of hand.

Then what are we to make of another typical passage, this time with the Muses involved? Literally, I i 32–34 reads : " . . . . . . if neither Euterpe restrains the pipes, nor Polyhymnia shrinks from tuning the Lesbian guitar". Nothing here to disprove a purely figurative meaning for the music words, certainly. Is this one up for the Opposition?

In fact, we have not quite heard the conclusion of the matter. It is said that Euterpe was the Muse of Music, Polyhymnia of Hymnody. But I respectfully agree with Professor Fraenkel that it is a mistake to presume that Horace assigned any special function or department to the several Muses individually. Any one of them could stand in for any of the others, if necessary.[3] This is shown, I think, by all the pother that has arisen over the appearance of Melpomene in I xxiv 3, and even more so in III xxx 16. Why the alleged Muse of Tragedy in the very last line of what was originally intended to be Horace's *l'envoi*? The explanation is simple, I think, if one reads between the lines

---

[1] *TD* iv 2 3; *Brut.* 19 75.
[2] Quintilian adds lyres as well (I x 20).
[3] *Horace,* p. 281 n. 1.

of Professor Fraenkel's learned note.[1] I say 'reads between the lines', because the references he quotes come dangerously near to what (for him) is forbidden territory. If Melpomene was the mother of Thamyris, *this implies a close connexion with citharoedy*: (my italics). Jamot is quoted for the observation that *pendant longtemps Melpomène fut seulement la divinité du chant et de l'harmonie musicale*. Quite so. Peek infers from traces on the monument at Thespiae being discussed that Melpomene *did actually play the lyre*: (my italics again). Precisely.

If one does not shut out in advance the idea of Horace's own practical musicianship, surely the thing is perfectly plain? Horace the minstrel is invoking Melpomene, the singing and lyre-playing Muse, just where one would expect him to do so, *at the very end of his Epilogue*.[2]

Euterpe occurs nowhere else in Horace's writings; except for her association here with pipes, no other or special reason appears for Horace to introduce her name. In any case he does not rely very much on her for his general inspiration; nor for that matter on Polyhymnia either, who by the time of Ausonius anyhow was seemingly patroness of mimetic art rather than anything in the music line, in spite of her name.[3]

In the view of Dr. J. Gow[4] the two Muses named by Horace in I i represent respectively nothing more — by a sort of metonymy — than 'public' odes of the Pindaric kind (dithyrambs *etc.*) on the one hand, and 'private' lyrics on the other, such as Alcaeus, Sappho and Anacreon wrote.

---

[1] *ibid.* p. 306 n.2.

[2] Fraenkel, *Horace*, p. 306 n.2, rightly comments: "*Odes* IV iii refers back to III xxx (and to I i), and it is for this reason that Melpomene is there invoked."

[3] Idyll xx 9 reads: *signat cuncta manu, loquitur Polyhymnia gestu.*

[4] *Ad loc.*

The *tibiae* were used to accompany the choral odes; the *barbitos*, a large 7-string affair, the singing of the song-lyrics, as in I xxxii. And here I am reminded of Dr. J. R. Postgate's comment on this last-named reference: "When Horace says to his harp:

> .... age dic Latinum,
> barbite, carmen,

he does not mean that it is to rehearse a Latin poem, but to accompany a Latin song".[1] I need scarcely state my hearty agreement with this *dictum* from a recognised authority.

We must not overlook the fact that I i, so far from being an early work, was almost certainly one of the latest to be written. By this time Horace had quite literally resorted to *tibia* and *barbitos* for the performance of his works. He now wants to get the approval of two Muses for his *carmina non prius audita* and the musical instruments linked with them. No doubt he is thinking in figurative terms as well as real, and is not intending his words to be taken literally *simpliciter*. But the music atmosphere remains unmistakable, and the whole passage does nothing whatever to bolster up the Opposition case: indeed, if anything, the repeated appearance of the same alleged metaphor rather tends to weaken it.

Which brings us to an extract with equally troublesome problems for commentators and editors. What does Horace mean when he says that he is *princeps Aeolium carmen ad Italos deduxisse modos* (III xxx 13–14)? "The whole phrase is a metaphor — rather an odd one: we should expect him to say 'compose Italian songs to Aeolic music'". Thus Mr L. P. Wilkinson.[2]

With all due respect, I cannot see why, if the end-product is allowed to be a *musical version of the material worked upon*.

---

[1] *Prosodia Latina*, p. 4, *C.* I xxxii 3–4 quoted. However, Fraenkel disagrees, see *Horace*, p. 168 n. 7 and 283–4.

[2] *Golden Latin Artistry*, p. 104 footnote.

There is no need with Sturtevant to go to the length of translating *deduxisse* 'adapt', if only because the Latin will hardly stand it anyhow. No doubt the process involves some adaptation, as all composition does; but the spinning or drawing out of threads into a new form of garment remains the paramount idea.

Considerable help, I venture to think, comes from the *Ars Poetica*, 128–9:

tuque
rectius Iliacum carmen deducis in actus.

It looks as though one of the Pisos was about to write a play, and perhaps had asked Horace's advice about subject-matter and background. At all events, this time the end-product was not to be a musical setting, but a play consisting as usual of 'acts'. Horace is telling him that he is wise to choose *Iliacum carmen* to *deducere in actus*, familiar stuff rather than things unknown and unsung before.

But this cannot mean that Piso was being advised to lift whole chunks of Homer's Greek, as it stood, and cast them without more ado into dramatic 'acts'; any more than Horace himself was claiming to have been the first to set the Greek text of Sappho or Alcaeus, as it stood, to Italian music. In each case there was to be a new creation in the *Latin* tongue: and as a matter of history Horace of course had already achieved just that. *Aeolium carmen* and *Iliacum carmen*, then, have a strong general affinity in denoting the working material drawn out, or to be drawn out; and with the necessary changes *in actus* is not so very far apart from *ad Italos modos* as the new resulting end-product.

Mr Wilkinson, no doubt having an eye on a fit English translation, would expect Horace's claim to be stated with words in the reverse order. But even here the order of things is not really so odd. In English we commonly speak of Schubert having 'set' Schiller to music. But this is not in fact what has happened. The Schiller was there first; and strictly it is Schubert who has had to 'set' (compose) his music to the Schiller text. Is Horace then really being any more illogical than we in English? A roughly parallel sort of 'reversible' construction can be seen in his use of *mutare*: sometimes he changes A for B, sometimes B for A. (*Cf.* I xvi 25–6 and xvii 1–2 with I xxix 14–5).

There are so many passages in Horace's works that mention music either sung or played or both, that it would be idle to quote and attempt a comment on them all. Except when the context permits it no alternative, these will never be admitted by the Opposition at any price as fit to be taken at their face value. We must always be finding that metaphor somehow. When Horace says (IV iii 22–23), that he is publicly pointed out by the finger of passers-by as *Romanae fidicen lyrae* (player of the Roman lyre), no conceivable link here exists with the facts of the Ovid quotation from *Tristia* discussed earlier; or so we are asked in effect to believe! Even the possibility of Horace's having intended these three words to have both a real and a figurative meaning at once hardly seems to have crossed any one's mind, except my own unlearned one! Must plain commonsense for ever take a back seat?

Before I leave the Carmina there is one more extract that certainly deserves attention. I refer to the first stanza of IV ix. "Don't imagine my works are going to perish" — would be a rough-and-ready summation of the gist. Note again that the basic thought here is quite circumstantial (the Aufidus river ran near Horace's home town), almost prosaic, entirely realistic. Then we get the highly relevant lines:

> non ante volgatas per artis
> verba loquor socianda chordis,

"words I utter to be joined to strings by arts not hitherto made public".[1]

Let me suppose that I am wrong in my general theory: even so, that gerundive still needs a lot of explaining away, if it can be done at all. A past participle *sociata* would have opened the door more easily to the now overworked 'metaphor' line of argument. *Socianda* (with its undertone of 'fit to be' or even 'that must be') becomes a distinctly harder nut for the Opposition to crack. Page translates it as literally as I have done 'to be wedded', but leaves it at that. Dr. Gow says simply 'i.e. lyric poems'. Unfortunately Professor Fraenkel has nothing to say about it semantically at all. An unintentional omission, one hopes.

I would add that the only other places where Horace uses the word *chorda* are the three I have already mentioned.[2] In each case the context could not possibly be more matter-of-fact, more earthy if you like. And the inference to be drawn? Why surely this, that it is high time the homely principle were applied here of sauce for the goose being also sauce for the gander. Since Horace's only other *chordae* were real ones, is it not the turn of the Opposition to prove an exceptional metaphor in *verba loquor socianda chordis*?

Enough has been said, I hope, to convince the reader that Horace himself has provided a *prima facie* case for an affirmative answer to the questions posed. For good measure I would conclude with two quotations from his works which, I think, cannot easily be brushed aside by the modern scholiast of the Opposition camp. Though the evidence they

---

[1] *Cf.* Ovid, *Met.* xi 4–5:

> tumuli de vertice cernunt
> Orphea percussis sociantem carmina nervis.

Lit. "From the top of a knoll they see Orpheus joining songs to thrummed harp-strings."

[2] *Ars Poetica* 348, 356: Sermo I iii 8.

offer is not perhaps directly and immediately relevant to our main question, it has a close bearing on the very important subsidiary one — were Horace's Odes (or some of them) designed for singing and in fact sung? I use the word 'sing' of course in its largest comprehensive sense to include not only vocal rendering but string and/or pipe accompaniment.

So let the reader turn up *Epistles* II ii 84–86, and then go on to line 143 of the same. He will read:

hic ego . . . .
verba lyrae motura sonum conectere digner?

"Here (in Rome) am I to deign to put together words to awaken the sound of the lyre?" Again let us look at the surrounding context. In brief, Horace is complaining of the noises that go on in the streets of Rome: noises by day, noises by night. "How, Florus, do you expect a poet to compose melodious (*canoros*) verses amid all these distractions? How do you expect him to 'sing' (*canere*) decently and pursue the narrow path that minstrels have to tread? In the midst of all this turmoil, am I to lower myself . . . . ."?

And then comes the crucial noun *sonum*. The words of his poems, he says in effect, if they only had a chance, would not only move the lyre but the *sound* of it. That is what he says quite plainly. The contrast between the melodious verse he is expected to compose in Rome and the appalling clatter going on outside his window could hardly be made more effective. True, *fluctibus* and *tempestatibus* in line 85 belong to metaphor, but it is a metaphor that needs no apology, so hackneyed is it in all languages of the world, ancient and modern. Besides, nobody could suppose for a moment that Horace here meant us to understand that tangible sea waves and storms of bad weather were literally raging around him as he tried to write. What the Opposition must explain or explain away, if it can, is the very down-to-earth realism of the general context here and, in the middle of this, why suddenly a figurative meaning has to be assigned to the plain words *lyrae sonum*. It cannot be argued that this passage occurs in anything but *musa pedestri*; and it is simply manufacturing difficulties to pretend that the *lyrae sonum* here is any less real to Horace's ears as an objective phenomenon than the competing row going on outside in the streets of Rome, as against the quietude of sequestered Athens, referred to in line 81, *ibid*. Besides *motura* suggests purpose as well as futurity. The only sensible conclusion we can draw is that *verba lyrae motura sonum* merely amounts to another way of saying *verba socianda chordis* which we have just discussed. If one of these phrases is to be construed literally and taken to mean just what it says, so must be the other. You cannot blow hot and cold in the same matter simultaneously with any hope of keeping up a consistent case.

Line 143 (*ibid.*) is not quite so compulsive, but it calls for a mention: *ac non verba sequi fidibus modulanda Latinis*, 'and not to go after words to be tuned to the Latin lyre'. That Latin lyre yet once again! Is this just another bit of 'figurative' talk on Horace's part now so familiar? If it stood alone, perhaps. Integrated with the rest of the evidence and read along with it, it must make us wonder why the scholiasts should have had it all their own way for so long. *Modulanda* is of course the key word: its musical flavour can hardly be unintended, especially as in the very next line we have a patently indisputable metaphor in "the rhythms (*numeros*) and music (*modos*) of true living." So once more Horace speaks of tuning words to his Latin lyre, that *modulanda* reminding us forcibly of the *socianda* of IV ix 4.

That Latin lyre, if it really be but trite metaphor (which is the essence of the Opposition's case), belongs, however, to the same alleged metaphor as Horace has only just used some 60 or so lines earlier in the selfsame Epistle. By this time the number of figurative lyres Horace is made to have piled up must almost be equalling that bought up by the hypothetical ass in Sermo II iii 104 to whom I alluded earlier! But, unlike Horace himself, the ass never claimed to be *studio citharae* or *Musae deditus ulli*, as Horace is at pains to explain. Indeed, the direct coupling of these two phrases has a certain significance here all its own. To Horace's way of thinking if you were 'dedicated' (as we say to-day) to the study of lyre-playing and the art of citharoedy, that could well mean that you were also a lyric poet, like some of our own Elizabethan composers. The wider implications of the message could hardly be plainer.

II. "FOR ALL THE MUSIC COULD DO"

Horace, as I have said, probably composed the musical setting of his *Carmen Saeculare*. Most editors and commentators are against this proposition. All the same, we ought not to be in too much hurry to dismiss the words he himself puts into the mouth of one of his girl choristers in IV vi 43–4, *reddidi carmen docilis modorum vatis Horati*. This does not perhaps prove conclusively that the *modi* here were Horace's own work, as was the *Carmen*; but on the face of them his words do imply as much. The parallel with IV xi 34–35, is obvious. In both contexts *modi* and *reddere* clearly mean the same. Consistently with the same academic reluctance we have already seen to admit that a non-professional could ever compose any music, Page, Gow and other editors allow *reddere* to mean 'repeat back what has been taught', but insist upon 'measures' or 'rhythms' for *modi*. Fortunately, in the *Didascalia* to Terence's *Phormio*, for instance, we find: *modos fecit Flaccus Claudi tibiis imparibus*. Unfortunately, this cannot be the same Flaccus! But at least mention of the twin *tibiae* scotches once for all any suggestion that the *modi* in this extract from Terence could possibly be 'measures'.[1] Beyond any doubt 'music' is the correct meaning here, and this Flaccus was its composer. Why then resist the plain interpretation of *modorum* in IV vi 43? Once we accept the premiss that Horace was a perfectly competent musician (albeit a non-professional), the rest falls into place smoothly and easily.

Probabilities point to Horace as the composer for another reason besides, I think. Whoever he was, the composer of the *Carmen* chant would have to face and overcome a rather special problem connected with the Sapphic metre. Unless he were a poet as well, such a musician might fail to deal with it adequately, even if he appreciated its impact. He might even ride roughshod over it altogether, not choosing to

---

[1] *Modus* has a range of meanings appropriate to its etymological sense of "measure", and in some contexts clearly has nothing to do with music, *e.g.*, II i 2 and III vii 12: but there are several passages in Horace and in Latin written before and after his time in which the meaning of *modi* can only be "music" or "musical tones", and in some it is plainly distinguished from *numeri* ("rhythm" or "measures") *e.g.*, *AP* 211.

In IV xi 34 *modos* must have the meaning of "song": so in the first two stanzas of III xi the context with *canendo* and *testudo* clearly determines the sense of *modos* as "music" or "melody", just as in III ix 10 one who is *citharae sciens* is versed in "sweet song", since *dulcis* could hardly be used of rhythms. This evidence makes it clear that in IV vi 43 *modorum vatis Horati* means "the music of Horace the bard". It would be the musical setting not the metrical basis of the *Carmen Saeculare* that would be remembered in after-days by the performers. The fact that there is no explicit statement that Horace himself composed the chant may be a mere accident; or perhaps virtuosity in music was a skill that a *Graeculus*, but not a Roman in Horace's position, would wish to admit openly.

As for III xxx 13–4, it is true that Wilkinson, Fraenkel and many others refuse to see anything more than metaphor here. Yet can anyone see only metaphor in this brief description by Ovid of a lyre being tuned?

> ut satis inpulsas temptavit pollice chordas
> et sensit varios, quamvis diversa sonarent,
> concordare modos, hoc vocem carmine movit . . . (*Met.* x 145–7).

And if the only possible answer is "no", how can the scholiast's "metaphorical" reading of Ovid, *Fasti* ii 108 (quoted on p. 12) be validly supported?

recognize the ancient rule (reiterated by Plato) that in the partnership of music and verse it is the music that has to play the subordinate part. But as both poet and composer Horace would have in his own hands direct control of both the arts concerned.

What was this problem? For present purposes it presents in rather acute form the old question of accentual stress *vs* metrical ictus in classical Latin poetry. As we shall see, Horace's Sapphic verse — so taut and compact — was bound to throw up side-effects arising from the interplay of these two forces, side-effects of much more consequence than in, say, Virgilian hexameters. The accentual rhythms of the *Carmen Saeculare* are wonderfully rich and varied: in this formal respect Horace, I think, had never before reached so high a peak with his Sapphics. I have no doubt that the counterpoint of these accents against the metrical ictus was planned to be deliberately vigorous and invigorating in utterance.

But how was the composer (and his musical setting) to fit into the picture? That was the problem. Should he take advantage of an upward inflexion of the voice at accented syllables, and translate this into a slightly higher musical note in passing? Or would he be dealing with no more than a slight dynamic stress at such points in the cultured Latin speech then current? Quite properly, I think, he could take sides here, and (without leave from the poet) settle in favour of the 'inflexional' basis for his melody, *if*, but only if, it worked out best on all practical as well as musical grounds. (I do not think that it did or could). But his real trouble was to decide what his melody should do about the conflict between accent and pulse in the Sapphic verse, wherever this clash occurred. Would his melody have to favour one or the other? Or should it go its own way regardless and neutral after all?

Whatever contemporary philological theory might aver through Cicero or Varro, it is hard to get away from the conclusion that, in practice, dynamic stress rather than vocal inflexion was making the running, even in verse-recitation. If Horace had asked his teenagers to recite or intone the first line of his I xxxviii he would, I am afraid, have got:

Pérsicos ódi púer apparátus,

with the speech-accents well and truly stressed. Horace's Sapphic verse was particularly vulnerable to distortion in this sense that some lines, like the above, could so easily produce a secondary undercurrent rhythm with an almost regular '2-to-the-bar' beat. His youngsters no doubt would love it, as youngsters always do, but it made mincemeat of the metrical rhythm. That Horace did not intend or want this beat or lilt is amply proved, I think, by Mr L. P. Wilkinson: the theories of Verrall and Heinze to opposite effect hardly sound plausible to-day.

Meanwhile, what was Horace to do to prevent his listeners from getting confused by what Mr Wilkinson happily calls a fortuitous by-product of his Sapphic metre? At choir-practice he tries to make his youngsters 'observe the Lesbian foot' by twanging his lyre at metrical pulse-points or by beating the air with a frantic thumb (it doesn't matter which); but the habits of ordinary dynamic speech-accenting are too strong and keep breaking through. One method of wrecking this lilt was to see that some lines contained at least two iambic words (accented on the *first* syllable) preferably with an accented monosyllable falling on the ictus of the all-important third foot, as in:

iam Fídes et Páx et Hónos Pudorque . . . .

But clearly some more serviceable counteragent was needed, and Horace had already found it, it seems, in a deliberate reintroduction of the weak caesura (often called trochaic) on a generous scale. So the very first line of the *Carmen* starts the machine up in reverse gear with:

Phoebe silvarumque potens Diana.

If this does not quite amount to a throw-back to Sappho, Horace with line 70 gets about as close as he can to a 'Greek' Sapphic line:

quindecim Diana preces virorum,

where the *i* in *Diana* is at least doubtful in quantity.

So far as it went, this sort of verse must have put some check on the accentual aberrations (as Horace would regard them) of his young choristers. But it had its obvious limitations. Having normalized the strong-caesural verse for the best part of three Books of Carmina Sapphics, Horace could not now very well frame *too many* verses of the *Carmen Saeculare* to the weak-caesural pattern without making the exception seem like the norm and *vice versa*. Besides, having himself made the caesura a compulsory feature (and not merely an optional one as with Catullus), and the fourth syllable a compulsory 'long', he had in effect said good-bye to such lines as:

seu Săcas sagittiferosque Parthos,   *Catullus* xi 6;
pauca nuntiate mĕae puellae   *Ibid.* 15.

Not to mention the factor of heavy elisions present in some of Catullus's lines.

And although each of these two lines does show one point of 'conflict',[1] the feeling of a trochaic rhythm remains pretty strong. Not that 'conflict' is a bad thing in Sapphic or any other verse — far from it. All I am suggesting here is that Horace's weak-caesural lines would be more effective in killing the unwanted lilt or beat of *Pérsicos ódi* . . . than in

---

[1] Marked ˣ

promoting a more positive image of the 'Lesbian foot' in the real Sapphic metre.

Now this is just where the music of the *Carmen Saeculare* could tip the balance, as a third force ; just where a poet, who happened also to be a practical musician, would score heavily over a brother poet who was not, as I have said. Hence my text for this Section — "For all the music could do" — which is a tiny extract from Mr Wilkinson's *Golden Latin Artistry* (p. 110). I feel the suggestion implicit in it to be entirely justified. The music could certainly do something for the sort of performance Horace evidently wanted in the matter of rhythm, provided of course it were the right sort of music.

So I venture a solution of my own to the musician's problem, by way of an imaginary melody written *ad hoc*. The musical reader will of course have no difficulty in singing it at sight, the non-musical in getting a competent friend to do it for him. Nor need I underline the self-evident fact that it does not, and could not, make any claim whatever to historical authenticity. The real melody must have belonged somehow to the common Graeco-Roman tradition. In the view of the late Isobel Henderson,[1] the eminent musicologist, it would not, however, have been a tune that was more *consciously* Greek than any other music of Horace's day. I wonder.[2]

Before I set out my melody in modern form, let me say just a word about what I had in mind in writing it. First, for practical reasons of easy teaching and easy singing the

---

[1] In the letter to a friend of mine, quoted above on p. 9 n. 1.

[2] *Cf.* Fraenkel, *Horace*, p. 368 and n. 3, for an account of Mommsen's lecture on the official record of the *Ludi Saeculares* in which he pointed out that they "were performed *Achivo ritu,* and 'moved entirely within the sphere of the Hellenic gods'".

It seems reasonable to assume that this applied as much to the music as to any other part of the ceremony.

chant would have to be a very simple one. That is, it would have to avoid musical intervals likely to throw the choirs out of tune or groups of notes per syllable likely to wreck time-keeping. Amateur juveniles, however keen to give of their best, could not be expected to cope with intervals or note-groups that could give trouble even to professional adults.[1] Superficially, 'steps' rather than 'leaps' would seem to offer greater safety and stability; but in practice this is not necessarily so. What is more, a tune that moved only in seconds or merely stood still on too many repeated notes would have very little musical interest and character. Worse, it would fail to impress itself decisively and accurately on the musical memory of those who had to sing it; unless of course the 'composer' went the whole hog and 'set' the entire *Carmen* to a single intoned note throughout. On the whole, therefore, it seemed to me that fourths and fifths — as being two of the three basic consonances of all primitive musical mankind — ought to be largely in evidence in the work's musical setting. A simple diatonic tune of one note to each syllable would also have more gravity and dignity than a chromatically florid or elaborate one.

Secondly, and again in the interest of all-round simplicity, I could only suppose that one omnibus melody would have to serve all nineteen stanzas of the *Carmen*. Several other possibilities occur to mind that would offer a far more attractive musical *menu*, had we only been dealing with trained adult musicians in the twentieth century. For although musical notation in the Romanized Greece of Horace's day was not unknown, it is improbable that his *Carmen* melody would have been reduced to writing, or that

---

[1] For this reason I rejected the idea of borrowing the chants given in the *Liber Usualis* to the Sapphic hymns of the Roman Liturgy.

his teenage choristers would have learnt their parts from a
musical score. Any notion that they might have been taught
musical sight-reading would, I think, be equally fantastic
But with only one tune to be learnt — and a fairly distinctive one, capable of being hummed at home — Horace
would mostly be concerned at choir-practice with taking his
boys and girls through each of those nineteen stanzas
seriatim, with getting them to enunciate clearly and correctly,
with curing raggedness, with maintaining strict pitch and
tempo, and so forth. It would be a very different story if
every stanza had had a separate tune of its own, to be learnt
by heart and practised as well.

Thirdly, it seemed to me important for reasons I have
stated that the *rhythm* of the melody should go to the aid of
the metrical pulse rather than to the word-accentuation. So
I have provided a triple rhythm and represented it by
minims and crotchets (or their equivalent) per foot or 'bar'.
In actual performance, therefore, provided that the time-
values indicated by the musical notation were correctly
observed, the choirs would find it difficult, if not impossible,
to avoid the pulse of that 'Lesbian foot'. Indeed, the long
fourth syllable, as standardized by Horace, would in fact
be sung to an off-beat crotchet ! This, no doubt, would have
horrified the late Professor W. Beare (a contributor, by the
way, to this volume), but in practice it would work out quite
well. In practice, the 'Lesbian foot' would operate as a sort
of gentle, but regular, ground-swell upon which quite a lot
of diversified accenting (by stress) could be floated.

Fourthly, there was the problem of musical *pitch* in direct
relationship with the verbal accents to be dealt with. Nothing
could have been more tempting, as I have explained, than to
make the melody or melodies follow the voice inflexions of
educated speech, as Latin speech was inflected once upon
a time.

Musically and theoretically this would have been quite a feasible proposition. By my reckoning, it could have been done by composing some twelve or thirteen different ½-verse tunes of five or six musical notes each, as each kind of ½-verse of all nineteen stanzas of the *Carmen* required. Every verse of every stanza, whatever its accentual pattern, would thus be set to two ½-verse tunes drawn from the common pool of tunes. As Horace accents each ½-verse to left and right of the caesura, so the appropriate ½-tune (out of the dozen or so available) would be available from the pool to reflect his varied accentuations pretty faithfully in terms of pitch. But I need not discuss this business in further detail here. Delightful as it would sound musically, and surprisingly simple really for a modern adult choir (and choirmaster) to put into effect, I am satisfied that the learning of even a dozen short (5- or 6-note) ½-verse tunes, and the effort of singing them correctly in continually changing juxtaposed patterns, would prove beyond the powers of Horace's two teams and make his own task as choirmaster a veritable nightmare.

What then was to take the place of this 'inflexional' scheme? Discarding the possible, but wretchedly timid and defeatist, idea of a monotoned tune throughout the *Carmen* I turned to another line of enquiry. It occurred to me that something could be done in music with a traditional principle of oratory and oratorical delivery, whereby the rise or fall in pitch of the voice corresponded broadly with the Latin words considered as so much 'footage'. It all sounds highly artificial, to be sure, but not for Quintilian.[1] Thus an iambus or anapaest would have a rising inflexion (higher musical note); trochee and dactyl a falling one, with spondee neutral — indicating either a rise or fall, or neither.

---

[1] IX iv 136 *seqq.*

Verbal accents could still be stressed in utterance, whether
they occurred on a rising, on a falling, or on a level pitch of
musical note. In this way the words of the *Carmen* could be
made to come through as if they were metrified oratory set
to music; and the effect as such would not be lost on the
educated Roman audience at the *Ludi* performance. A single
omnibus tune framed on these lines would, naturally, be
inferior in musical interest to the variegated pattern of
melodic stanza of the 'inflexional' scheme now perforce
jettisoned; but it would be an impressive improvement on
any monotonic chanting. Above all, it would be very simple
for Horace and his choirs to handle at choir-practice and in
execution on performance day.

I shall not attempt here even to touch on the immensely
complicated question of the so-called modes in ancient
Greek and Graeco-Roman music in so far as the question
may be germane. Those interested will find a wealth of
learning and informed discussion (not to say controversy) in
the works of such experts as Curt Sachs, Isobel Henderson,
R. P. Winnington-Ingram, Donald Ferguson and others.
Nor can I be sure that the above melody really conforms to
the (pre-Alypian) Dorian idiom, as is intended. All I can say

is that it does confine itself to the Central Register of the Greater Perfect System : that is, to a compass of E – e, with its μέση hypothetically represented by the note A. As the technically minded reader will appreciate, however, this gives little or no idea of any absolute pitch in a modern sense. In fact the tune could quite properly be transposed upwards and played on the pianoforte or sung, as if its compass extended from G-flat to g-flat, let us say ; although of course this would mean inserting accidentals in the printed score so as to preserve the identical musical intervals of the tune. No one can prove for certain that this transposing would have resulted in its being any less a 'Dorian' melody than it was before. The point is that in accordance with Aristotle's directions the tune itself more or less hovers about the μέση ; whether this note in the scale can be said to foreshadow our modern concept of tonic or dominant, as some have argued, cannot be determined. It would seem legitimate criticism to urge that Horace's musical setting of the *Carmen* would more probably have echoed his beloved Pindar's melodizing than anything else, or at any rate later settings of Pindaric odes which Horace may well have heard at Athens in his younger days. But in fact Pindar's own music had been forgotten three centuries or so before Horace's time ; and in any event, it would have been quite unsuitable for transplanting to the service of the Sapphic *Carmen*, the metrical differences in the work of the two poets being enormous.

All things considered, however, I have preferred a melody that may have seemed like an archaic reconstruction even to Augustan ears of B.C. 17. One cannot suppose any complaint on this score from Ateius Capito, the learned antiquarian, who advised the *XVviri sacris faciundis* on the ceremonial details of the *Ludi* ; nor from the Princeps himself, ever anxious to give his innovations the varnish of ancient tradition. Anyhow, the last word on the choice of melody would surely have rested with Horace rather than with an imaginary professional musician coming forward with the very latest thing in 'contemporary' Roman or even Etruscan idiom, if there was such a thing. "Splendid!" we might imagine Horace replying with genial irony: "please take over at once the training of the fifty-four kids, and teach them to memorize *your* tune so as to get it note-perfect and performed without a single hitch or flaw on June 3rd next. And the best of Roman luck!"

Chapter Two

The Aeolic Odes

ʽΗ ἀκοὴ τέρπεται μὲν τοῖς μέλεσιν, ἄγεται δὲ τοῖς ῥυθμοῖς.

A. *INTRODUCTION*

THERE ARE CERTAIN characteristic features of the Odes of Horace. They consist of four-line stanzas with only two exceptions, III xii and IV viii; and the former is only apparently an exception, since the Ionic metre is not reducible to verses in this way.

The fact that enjambment does occur frequently raises the question of the reality of the stanza as an element in the structure of the Horatian ode. Since Meineke noted that, with these two exceptions, odes of Horace consist of a number of verses divisible by four, editors have varied in the manner of printing the Odes. Some print all odes in four-verse stanzas, others only those odes in metres that clearly have a four-verse structure, that is, the Alcaic, Sapphic, Fourth and Fifth Asclepiad stanzas. In the printing of odes formed from one or two verse forms, such as the first three Asclepiad metres, editors have varied still further, seeing that the structure in quatrains is obvious in III ix but not so obvious in the other odes in these metres.

Büchner was the first to ask whether the *Lex Meinekiana* was a rule consciously observed by Horace or a mere coincidence.[1] The fact that Horace's thought normally develops by balancing one element against another means that at the simplest level one idea is balanced against another, and to do this within the brief compass of the typical lyric verse almost inevitably requires a balance of two verses against two. Is divisibility by four merely an effect of this symmetrical structure?

Büchner's important study has settled this question. By examining first those odes that by their metre consist of four-verse stanzas, Büchner established the extent to which this metrical structure was exploited by Horace to develop his thought. He then sought the same features in the remaining odes. His conclusion is that Horace was conscious of a structure in four-verse stanzas and does use it, but that in odes of early composition his striving after form had not yet reached this ultimate solution : Büchner found that in Book IV all the odes require this structure to obtain their full effect.[2]

After Büchner's study there can be no doubt of the reality of four-verse stanzas in the Odes. But an unvarying succession of such stanzas, if end-stopped, especially in the longer odes would become monotonous ; hence the artistic value of Horace's use of enjambment and stopping.

The metres are Greek in origin ; frequently an ode begins with the translation in the same metre of a Greek verse, and then leads on to Roman variations on this theme.

It is regularly addressed to some god, person or thing

---

[1] K. Büchner, *Horaz*, pp. 52–101. See also L. P. Wilkinson, *Golden Latin Artistry*, pp. 204–7.

[2] It is therefore not surprising that editors resort to easy excisions to make IV viii conform to the rule. But for another approach to this ode, see *For Service to Classical Studies*. Essays in honour of Francis Letters. Ed. M. Kelly, Cheshire, Melbourne 1966, pp. 194–6.

(*pia testa*, III xxi 4) ; the exceptions are noted and explained by Heinze.[1]

The sentimental attitude of the elegiac poets is absent from the Odes: as a result, words that are diminutive in sense are avoided, while those diminutive in form only such as *particula* (I xvi 14) or *parmula* (II vii 10) are admitted.

Words are carefully selected by Horace and carefully placed in the patterned framework of sentence and stanza to maximum artistic effect.

Diction. As has been pointed out by L. P. Wilkinson,[2] both Virgil and Horace use ordinary words to a marked degree, no doubt as a deliberate reaction against the preciosity of their immediate predecessors. Even so this did not reduce their work to the level of the plain style ; for in some cases even ordinary words gained freshness and overtones in bold and novel combinations as well as from poetical or abnormal constructions.[3]

It is also clear that Horace used words that were not ordinary to adorn his odes : so Staedler[4] notes the frequency of words of six syllables throughout the works of Horace, which goes against the tendency of the Latin language to avoid long words. It is significant that 13 of the 22 examples of hexasyllabics in the Odes occur in the Alcaic metre where

---

[1] *Vom Geist des Römertums*, p. 172: III xii (the monologue of Neobule), I xxviii (the monologue of Archytas), I xv (the address of Nereus to Paris), III ix (a dialogue), II xv and I xxxiv (addressed by the poet to the aristocracy obsessed with building and to the divinity respectively, but without a specific address to an individual).

One might add III ii, which by its position in the group of 'Roman' odes is adequately covered by the opening stanza of III i.

[2] *The Language of Virgil and Horace*. *CQ* ix 1959 181–92.

[3] Cf. B. Axelson, *Unpoetische Wörter. Ein Beitrag zur Kenntnis der lateinischen Dichtersprache*, esp. c. IV, which deals with Horace.

[4] E. Staedler, *Über den Gebrauch vielsilbiger Wortbildungen bei Horaz*. *Glotta* xxvii 1938/9 199–206.

Horace uses his most carefully elaborated style. Moreover, Bellinger[1] has shown that in the Lesser and Greater Asclepiad verses words of choriambic form, or phrases scanned as such, occur with unusual frequency. Further, in conformity with the conservative Roman respect for the past, there is a group of words with an archaic flavour, such as *hosticus*, *civicus*, *adorea*, *etc*. A less skilled artist might well have produced a grotesque effect by overdoing one or more of these elements, but it is characteristic of Horace's *curiosa felicitas* that all these elements are blended into one of the supreme achievements of classical literature.

Balanced Decoration.[2] Horace has a marked liking for word-groups consisting of two nouns decoratively balanced against one adjective (sometimes, two nouns against two adjectives). The whole group is frequently conterminous with a verse. Sometimes the collocation is purely formal and adventitious ; more often it is directly self-contained in sense.

Concords. An inevitable result of the liking for Balanced Decoration is the prominence of spaced Concords, which are of course by no means peculiar to Horace. One form of this consists in an adjective at the caesura qualifying a noun at the end of the same line and very often rhyming with it.[3] With these — let us call them "Horizontal" Concords — go the "Vertical" ones, almost as numerous. The verticals are formed by the final word (adjective) of one verse in agreement with the final word (noun) of the next.

In a recent study[4] Professor O. Skutsch examines such Concords and concludes that "Horace avoids rhyme, except

---

[1] A. R. Bellinger, *The Lesser Asclepiadean Line of Horace. YCIS* xv 1957 101–9.

[2] Cf. Pasquali, *Orazio Lirico*, p. 128.

[3] Cf. Wilkinson, *Horace and his Lyric Poetry*, p. 137; and *Golden Latin Artistry*, pp. 32–4.

[4] *BICS* xi 1964 73–8.

between words syntactically related". Even if these Concords are at least in part an inevitable result of the nature of the inflected language and short lyric verses used by Horace, they are too important a feature of the Odes to be overlooked.

Euphony. Ancient literature was intended to be read aloud, sometimes intoned, and the ancients were more sensitive to the heard sound of a work of literature than is the modern reader. However, the Roman was not necessarily sensitive to what may appear blemishes to us since he was accustomed to accept without hesitation features inherent in the nature of an inflected language: for instance, repetition of the same vowel sound without any special onomatopoeic effect was tolerated even by Horace, *e.g.*,

> praesens
> Italiae dominaeque Romae,   IV xiv 43–4;

and by Cicero in his speeches, *e.g.*,

> invitissimis viris,   *Pro Planc.* 89.

Moreover, the Roman liking for alliteration survived into, and beyond, the Golden Age; assonance and onomatopoeia were cultivated. How far these effects were intended and how far merely the accidental result of the nature of the inflected language must remain a matter for each reader's personal judgment; but attention is drawn to these elements of Horace's poetic art in chapters III and IV.

For all that, careful writers did avoid certain collocations of sounds and syllables that were ambiguous in meaning, harsh in sound or difficult to enunciate clearly, such as *ars studiorum*, *sicque* and the repetition of the same syllable as in *occurri rides* (*Epp.* I i 95).[1]

---

[1] Cf. Quintilian ix 4. 37, and Kühner-Stegmann, *Lateinische Grammatik* II 595. 8.

Word Order.

Darnley Naylor has devoted a book to Horatian word order,[1] which is one of the most striking features of the poet's art. Effective use is made of the emphatic positions at the beginning and end of sentences and stanzas ; Balanced Decoration is achieved by the separated placing of nouns and adjectives in agreement ; and contrasts are pointed by the juxtaposition of contrasting terms with striking effect in such memorable cases of oxymoron as *arida nutrix* or *splendide mendax*.

SOME NOTES ON HORATIAN WORD-USAGE

Horace's preference for concise brevity and Balanced Decoration, and the restrictions imposed by the narrow compass of the short lyric verse, leave little or no room for otiose adverbs or other parts of speech. Adverbs of manner he seldom uses, but when used by him they bear a marked emphasis of meaning in the context.

The adverbs *haud, quidem* and *nimirum* are not found in the Odes, but *scilicet* appears in all four Books. *Posthac*, not *postea, simul*, not *simulac*, are Horatian. As a variant to *posthac*, we find *mox* and *postmodo* (I xxviii 31). *Semel*, especially in the sense "once for all", and *male*, are favourite adverbs. *Iam* is not found with an imperative, except in association with *age*. *Quando* (mostly with elision), *plerumque* and *usque* are found, but not the Catullan *identidem*. *Quoad* is wanting, as is *priusquam* (though *prius* is common), for which Horace prefers *antequam*. The prosaic *dein, deinceps, deinde* and *denique* are absent; but *tandem* is found to express a succession. *Ultra* and *supra* are favoured both as adverbs and prepositions; note *quod ultra est* (II xvi 25) = "the future". All four Books have *utcunque*.

Of the adverbs of comparison Horace has *quam si* (III v 53), and prefers *velut* to the Virgilian *ceu*; but he avoids *tamquam, proin(de)* and *quasi*. (*Non*) *aeque* occurs several times; as does *non secus*, but without *ac* or *atque*.

---

[1] Horace, *Odes and Epodes. A Study in Poetic Word Order*. Ed. by H. D. Naylor, CUP, 1922.

Prepositions. Occurring once each only are *apud*, *ob* and *tenus*; *infra*, *iuxta*, *pone*, *prae* and *propter* occur not at all. *Ultra* and *praeter* are favourites, the latter in all senses including the use to express the superlative degree for which Horace does not use forms in *-issimus*, *e.g.*,

> ille terrarum mihi praeter omnis
> angulus ridet,   II vi 13–14;

and in conjunction with *nihil* to express an exception,

> nihil astra praeter
> vidit et undas,   III xxvii 31–2.

Non sine (= *cum*) is characteristically Horatian.

Personification. The personification of abstract nouns is a common feature of the Horatian style, *e.g.*, *caecus Amor sui.*

Proper Nouns & Adjectives. So too in large measure Horace likes concrete references to particular persons and places, for which a less poetic and more philosophic approach would require general or abstract statements with common nouns.

Connexion of Thought. Although parataxis is common (since the explicit statement of the connexion of thought savours of prose rather than poetry), most of the common conjunctions are also found in Horace's lyrics. But note that Horace alone of the Roman poets prefers *atque* unelided.[1] The conjunctions favoured by him might be called the lightweight ones. They include *et, ac (atque), -que, vel, -ve, aut, an, nec (neque), neu (neve), ne, -ne, ut, sed, tamen, at* (not *ast*), *si, seu (sive), nisi* (rather than *ni*), and *quodsi*. *Attamen* occurs nowhere in the Odes, nor does *autem*. But Horace likes *atqui* as a forceful adversative = "and yet".

Although *et* practically never begins a stanza as its first word, it is quite frequently put as second word of a stanza or verse: *ausa et iacentem visere regiam* (said of Cleopatra in I xxxvii 25) is Horatian. So too *quin et* + Proper Name and even *adde quod* make characteristic Horatian starts to a stanza or verse.

In spite of being lightweights, the causals *quod* and *quia* occur less often in the Odes than one might perhaps expect. *Quoniam* Horace never uses in his lyrics at all; the nearest he gets to it is with a solitary *quatenus* (III xxiv 30). This is probably because lyric poets should not appear to make a habit of prosy reasoning or explanation in so many words. Perhaps, too, this is why *nam, namque*, and *enim* occur less than a dozen times apiece there. *Nam* or *namque*,

---

[1] M. Platnauer, *Elision of* atque *in Roman Poetry*. *CQ* xlii 1948 91–3.

however, can and should introduce a parenthesis (twice in III xi) and it may properly introduce a paradigm (as with Lalage, I xxii 9). Nor is there anything against a student's slipping into his own work an occasional, unobtrusive *enim*, if he wishes. But the Ovidian *quippe* is to be avoided: Horace uses it only once in the Odes, and then only ironically (I xxxi 13). The same applies to *nempe*.

¶ Of the concessives both *quamquam* and *quamvis* are found in the Odes. They have the disadvantage of bringing a faintly prosy flavour to lyrics: on the other hand, they do aid constructional continuity and help to prevent short, choppy sentences that throw up too many sense-pauses too often. And note that Horace, unlike Virgil, nowhere has *etsi*; but he does sometimes use *cum* or *licet*, or a simple concessive clause without any conjunction, in much the same sense.

Itaque, igitur, ideo, idcirco, quapropter, quare, and all their like, though strictly classifiable as adverbs, really have a conjunctional function. In the Odes Horace avoids them all; and the student in his own work should of course do likewise. The only exception appears to be *ergo*. For some reason Horace uses it twice in the Odes, twice in the Epodes. Maybe he liked the sound of it as a solemn spondee unelided, or found it metrically convenient when elided. And perhaps the prize for sheer un-Horatian prosiness might go to the student who insisted on using *quominus* in his lyric verse after a verb of preventing as he has learnt to do from his Grammar. Horace himself of course has the infinitive with such a verb as *prohibere*. *Quominus* he bans not only from the Odes, but even from the Satires and Epistles.

Horace likes repeating *nec* (*neque*), *sive* (*seu*), *neve* (*neu*), *non* and *aut*. These short words maintain the connexion of thought without obtruding it; see IV ii 9–24 for a good example of this, and from here it is an easy step to Anaphora when it is possible to repeat a word that can bear this emphasis.

B. *THE SAPPHIC ODE*

THE SAPPHIC STANZA consists of four verses, three Lesser Sapphics followed by an Adonic. The scheme is as follows:

vv. 1, 2, 3: $-\,\cup\,\mid\,-\,-\,\mid\,-\,\parallel\,\cup\,\cup\,\mid\,-\,\cup\,\mid\,-\,\underline{\cup}$

v. 4: $-\,\cup\,\cup\,\mid\,-\,\underline{\cup}$

Horace's scheme differs from that of Catullus in that (1) the fourth syllable of the verse is always long — that is, the second foot is a spondee instead of a trochee ; (2) the caesura is normally at the fifth syllable or exceptionally at the sixth, thus dividing the verse into two balanced elements consisting of 6 + 5 or 5 + 6 syllables. Polysyllabic words such as *sagittiferos, septemgeminus, praetereunte* are therefore inadmissible in Horace's scheme for the first three verses, since they would throw his metrical structure and rhythm into confusion.

The strong caesura was standardised in order to preserve the normal balance of the rhythmic line, the weak caesura being occasionally introduced in the interests of rhythmic and melodic variety, especially in the later odes. A large proportion of Horace's Sapphic stanzas consists of non-stop lines.

Subject Matter. In general the Sapphic metre has a slightly plaintive note and limited variety, better suiting it to rather brief treatment of themes in a less virile manner than is appropriate to the Alcaic, which is the medium preferred for graver matters cast in a more exalted mould. Hymns to deities, letters to friends male or female, isolated reflections on some aspect of life (grave or gay) all go well in the Sapphic metre.

FURTHER NOTES ON SAPPHICS

1 THE LESSER SAPPHIC:

(a) *Caesura.* Where a weak caesura occurs (after the sixth syllable) the word preceding it is usually[1] an antibacchic trisyllable (*e.g.*, *curvaeque* in I x 6): this may be preceded by either another trisyllable (*e.g.*, *nuntium curvaeque*) or by two words — a monosyllable followed by a dissyllable or *vice versa*:

e.g., iussa pars mutare, *CS* 39;
    iam mari terraque, *CS* 53.

---

[1] In 40 of the 48 cases.

A quadrisyllable preceded by a dissyllable is also permissible, and five examples occur in the *Carmen Saeculare* which begins with

Phoebe silvarumque potens Diana,

and two examples in IV ii.

A single instance, which is best not imitated, of a dissyllable before the weak caesura is found in IV xi 29:

semper ut te digna sequare et ultra.

The weak caesura does not usually appear more often than once in three verses, and may be completely absent from a Sapphic ode. It is generally followed by another caesura two syllables later.[1]

In only five places (II ii 21; III viii 14; III xxvii 39; CS 26 and 37) is a single monosyllable permitted before the caesura. In all of them elision occurs before the monosyllable, and in one the textual reading is doubtful. However, two monosyllables at this place are not rare, there being 26 cases, of which 5 are in III xi.

¶ A single monosyllable at this place without elision would make a trochaic rhythm based on the stress-accent inevitable. So $1 + 3 + 1$ is not a possible opening and Horace nowhere has it.

(b) *Diaeresis* must be avoided in choosing words for the first half of the verse when a strong caesura is used: that is, the opening words must not coincide with the feet. Thus, two consecutive dissyllables such as

saepe | magnam | te

are forbidden, the correct sequence being:

saepe te magnam.

Note further that Horace never begins a verse with a word of four or five syllables, and never $2 + 1 + 1 + 1$ (*saepe | te si | quis*). An occasional $1 + 4$ start is permissible, even laudable: Horace has nine instances.

(c) *The End of the Verse.* Monosyllabic endings are rare, (fewer than 20 cases) and the last syllable is nearly twice as often long as short.

¶ It is worth noting that Horace hardly ever ends a Lesser Sapphic verse with a trochaic word having a short final vowel. Exceptions are *arma* (I xxxii 6), *atque* (II x 21 and III xi 18, but the text of this stanza is itself suspect), *unde* (III xi 38), and *rura* (III xviii 2). So whereas a word like *redire* is quite permissible in this position, *ire* should not be so used by the modern composer.

2 THE ADONIC:

(a) The Adonic should consist of a dissyllable + a trisyllable or the reverse. Exceptions to this normal pattern are:

---

[1]   36 of the 48 cases.

Fabriciumque I xii 40 (cf. I xxx 8, II vi 8);
est hederae vis, IV xi 4; *Bellerophontem*, 28;
seu Genitalis, CS 16;
and 12 lines of the type *se quoque fugit*, II xvi 20.

(b) The stanza must not end with an adverb or nominative present participle. There is, however, less objection to a final trochaic word of the Adonic ending in a short vowel than to a similar trochee in the Lesser Sapphic: there are in fact 12 cases, a much greater frequency proportionately.

3 THE SAPPHIC STANZA:

(a) *Elision.* Elision is infrequently used; that is, in about one verse in nine. The easiest elision occurs with a final short vowel (43 cases); then comes a syllable ending in *-m* (38 cases), and rarely a long vowel or diphthong (12 cases). Horace has elision in the Adonic only once (II xvi 8 *ven | ale neque auro*), and even this could be eliminated by reading *nec* for *neque*. ❡ No elision is allowed at the weak caesura, and Horace allows elision at the strong caesura only four times (II iv 10, xvi 26, III xxvii 10; IV xi 27).

(b) *Interlinear Hiatus and Synaphea.* In spite of some exceptions to the rule, there should be no hiatus between the last syllable of one verse and the first syllable of the succeeding verse *in the same stanza*. This continuous scansion between verses in the stanza is known as *synaphea*. It permits the elision of a hypermetric syllable at the end of a verse, *e.g.,*

dissidens plebi numero *beatorum*
eximit Virtus,   II ii 18;

tibi tollit *hinnitum*
apta quadrigis equa,   II xvi 34;

plorat et vires animumque *moresque*
aureos educit in astra *nigroque*
invidet Orco,   IV ii 22.

(and *cf.* III xxvii 10–1, if *imminentium* be read, and *CS* 47–8); and also the division of a word between the third and fourth verses (I ii 19–20, xxv 11–2; II xvi 7–8).

When there is hiatus between one verse and the next, the final syllable is very rarely a short vowel, generally a long one or *-um* or *-em*.

(c) *Enjambment of Stanzas and Stopping.* Sapphic stanzas are most frequently self-contained and end with a full-stop or a colon. Out of a total of 179 Sapphic stanzas 119 are end-stopped (the final stanza of an ode is obviously end-stopped and is therefore excluded from these figures). This leaves 60 stanzas not ending with a full-stop, colon or question mark; 13 of which have no stop, but run on to the next stanza.

Nine of the odes have no sense-pause within the verses of the stanza, and IV ii (with 15 stanzas) has but one such pause. The *Carmen Saeculare* has none (a commendable feature in a sung ode).

The only verses (apart from the Adonic) that are normally end-stopped are the first and second; although out of a total of 615 Lesser Sapphic verses there are only 30 such examples in Horace's Sapphic odes (21 at the end of the second, 8 at the end of the first and 1 at the end of the third verse).

¶ The modern composer should therefore aim as far as possible at bringing his sentences to an end either at a point *within* one of the first three verses of a stanza or at the end of the Adonic. No Sapphic stanza should have more than one strong internal sense-pause (exceptions are II x 17–8, xvi 18–9; III xxvii 37–8; IV xi 34–5), which may come at the end of the second verse, rarely at the end of the first verse, more often at any strong caesura (especially that of the second verse); *never at a weak caesura*.[1] The strong pause at the strong caesura occurs 13 times in the second verse, 8 times in the third and 3 times in the first. The next in frequency comes after the third syllable of the second verse (6 cases).

Less commonly Horace has pauses at other points in a verse;[2] but a strong pause may occur neither after the ninth syllable, nor before the Adonic (except IV xi 3, where Anaphora carries all before it).

¶ There can be no doubt that Horace favours a Sapphic stanza *woven without seam from top to bottom*; and he avoids a too frequent use of clauses coinciding exactly with successive verses and producing what we may call a "square-cut" effect.

(d) *Parentheses*. A parenthetical clause should not be introduced without

---

[1] In his edition of the Odes Dr. J. G. Gow emends and punctuates the text of the difficult 11th verse of III xiv to read as follows:
    iam virum exspectate. male ominatis . . . . .
For two reasons this emendation cannot stand:
  (a) It would be the sole example in III of a weak caesura in a Sapphic ode.
  (b) It would be the only case of a strong pause at the weak caesura in any Horatian Sapphic ode.

[2] *Cf*. L. J. D. Richardson, *Hermathena* lix 131 n.2, "While it cannot be claimed that even a major pause is not to be found after the third syllable of the Horatian Sapphic line, such a break is very infrequent, and the tendency to treat the two "halves" of the line as metrical and phrasal units increased with time; in IV there are only two instances of the first "half" being seriously broken at this point (IV xi 14,34)."

good reason, as it tends to break up the rhythm and demands a pause in the melodic flow in order to be recognisable as such. Only three examples occur in Horace's Sapphics: III xi (two beginning with *nam*) and IV xi (one beginning with *non enim*).

(e) *Length of Ode*. The shortest odes consist of two stanzas (I xxx, xxxviii and III xxii). The longest (III xxvii and *CS*) have nineteen stanzas. A Sapphic ode is likely to gain in poetic effect by being kept short, since subject-matter weighty enough to require lengthy treatment will have the advantage of the greater metrical variety offered by the Alcaic metre.

(f) *Rhyme*. It is inevitable that in an inflected language final syllables will recur that are in grammatical agreement and in many cases even rhyme. A stylist will ensure that this feature of the language is not merely accepted but exploited to mark the structure of a literary work. This is done with telling effect in the Odes of Horace, who makes such frequent use of rhymed endings that a modern composer should also go out of his way to introduce this feature in his own work.

The rhyming syllables may occur within (horizontal Concords) or at the end of verses (vertical Concords). A few examples of each kind will suffice:

Within the verse:

displicent nex*ae* philyra coron*ae*,	I xxxviii 2;
contrahes ven*to* nimium secun*do*,	II x 23;
servit Hispan*ae* vetus hostis or*ae*,	III viii 21;
est mihi no*num* superantis an*num*,	IV xi 1;
Phylli, nectend*is* apium coron*is*,	3.

These are all spaced Concords, that is, adjectives and their nouns in agreement, a device which is frequently employed in the pentameter verse of an elegiac couplet and is indeed regarded by many scholars as an essential feature of that metre.

At the end of the verse:

nec te, metuende cer*ta*	
Phoebe sagit*ta*,	I xii 23–4;
aridas frondes hiemis *sodali*	
dedicet *Hebro*,	I xxv 19–20;
signa cum caelo gelidaque *divos*	
morte *carentis*,	II viii 11–12;
vincta verbenis avet immolat*o*	
spargier agn*o*,	IV xi 7–8.

There are 56 cases in the Sapphic odes of a noun and its epithet placed respectively at the end of verses 3 and 4 as shown in the last example; 22 of these are *rhymed* Concords, excluding such cases of mere assonance as:

> acer et Mauri peditis cruent*um*
> vultus in host*em*,   I ii 39–40.

Note that the noun is usually placed in the Adonic, the rhymed epithet ending the preceding verse (50 of the 56 cases).

C. *THE ALCAIC ODE*

THE ALCAIC STANZA or quatrain consists of four verses, two Greater Alcaics (or Alcaic Hendecasyllabics), followed by an Alcaic Enneasyllabic and a Lesser Alcaic (or Alcaic Decasyllabic). The metrical scheme[1] is as follows:

$$\text{vv. 1, 2 :} \quad \smile\,\perp \mid \smile\,\perp \mid - \parallel \perp \mid \smile\,\smile\,\perp \mid \smile\,\smile$$
$$\text{v. 3 :} \quad \smile\,\perp \mid \smile\,\perp \mid - \,\perp \mid \smile\,\perp \mid \smile$$
$$\text{v. 4 :} \quad \perp\,\smile\,\smile \mid \perp\,\smile\,\smile \mid \perp\,\smile \mid \perp\,\smile$$

In the movement of the Alcaic stanza as perfected by Horace an educated Roman of his day perhaps sensed a refined and disciplined version of the old Saturnian measure familiar to him from his school-days. This would be so both in the movement of the Greater Alcaic verses and of the stanza as a whole.

Those who explain Horace's Alcaics as a trochaic metrical scheme[2] are obliged to make the opening syllable of the first three verses an *anacrusis* so as to start the "verse proper" with a trochee. Thus:

---

[1] The arrangement of vv. 1 and 2 is due to my brother, the late W. Bonavia-Hunt, M.A.

[2] According to Dr. J. H. H. Schmidt (*Rhythmic and Metric of the Classical Languages*) the original Greek Alcaic did have a basically trochaic rhythm with anacrusis in verses 1, 2 and 3. While I myself am far from convinced that Horace's Alcaic metrical *scheme* embodied this *anacrusis*, I regard it as not at all improbable that the citharist would at this point strike a musical note on the lyre with his plectrum so as to enable the singer (or singers) to keep time or "catch on". In other words the real anacrusis was not an integral part of the metre at all, but simply a sort of conductor's baton beat in audible musical form: N.A.B.-H.

vv. 1, 2 : — | — ◡ | — — ‖ — ◡ ◡ | — ◡ | —
v. 3 : — | — ◡ | — — | — ◡ | — —

Horace adapted Alcaeus' scheme to Latin measures by (1) making the first foot of the first three verses a spondee — out of a total of 951 such verses only 28 start with a short syllable — (2) dividing the first and second verses into their two elements by introducing a regular caesura after the fifth syllable, and (3) making the fifth syllable of each of the first three verses long.

As in the case of Sapphics, the modern composer of Alcaic odes must be guided by certain canons essential to artistic results.

Subject Matter. The metre is suited by its varied and impressive rhythm to the expression of the more serious and exalted themes. Indeed the very fact that it is so preferred for such themes makes it the chosen metre for burlesque, as in III xvii and xxi ; for Horace had a taste for the mock-heroic. In Greek the parody of serious literature goes back to the *Margites* ; and Horace in his ability to lay aside Roman *gravitas* — no doubt more easily done by a *privatus* — and indulge in parody or burlesque showed himself essentially a Roman who could appreciate with intimate sympathy the Greek attitude to life.

Anaphora. Anaphora suits the Alcaic ode particularly well, and may be freely used : if the opportunity offers, it may effectively be spread over two or more stanzas, and so with advantage replace the use of prosaic connecting particles or conjunctions.

Euphony. When recited aloud the words of the ode should produce an effect of melodic euphony, with every verse moving as it were on oiled wheels in the course of a long run. Clashing sibilants and bunched consonants (especially gutturals) must be avoided, as also must be frequent pauses that only produce a fidgety effect foreign to the spirit of the

Alcaic *genre*, which sweeps forward smoothly like a rolling river.

FURTHER NOTES ON ALCAICS

1 THE GREATER ALCAIC (First and Second Verse):

(a) *Caesura*. The caesura falls after the fifth syllable. In 18 cases it is obtained by the elision of vowel + *-m*, e.g., I xvi 6; in 4 cases by elision of a long vowel, e.g., I xxxiv 10; and in 4 cases by elision of a short vowel, e.g., I xxxv 10. This rule is absolutely broken only thrice (I xxxvii 14 and IV xiv 17): but imperfect caesura occurs thrice (I xvi 21, xxxvii 5 and II xvii 21) with the caesura falling after the prefix of a compound word.

It is noteworthy that in Book IV Horace admits neither elision at the caesura nor imperfect caesura.

(b) *Diaeresis*. As in the case of Sapphics the opening words must not coincide with the feet: such a sequence as

idem | viget | flos

is forbidden. True, we find *antehac | nefas* in I xxxvii 5, but it is not to be copied even if some excuse may possibly be found for a trisyllable with synizesis as the opening word.

Initial monosyllables are far safer in that they split up the feet, so long as they are not allowed to exceed the artistic limit of harmonic proportion. A verse opening like *est ut viro vir* (III i 9) or *te, Liber, et si* (III xxi 21) is not objectionable, provided that it is realised that Horace has only twenty-one Greater Alcaics with monosyllables in the first and fifth places, and has more than one verse of this pattern in only four of the odes (II xvii 2, 5, 17; III v 13 and 33; IV iv 37, 73; xiv 33, 41, 45).

Five-syllabled words are meritorious, such as *praegestientes, oblivioso, desiderantem, fastidiosus, incontinentis*, which Horace uses to begin the first verse, and *formidolosus, tumultuosum, insanientem, sententiarum, dissentientes*, which begin the second verse. Horace only three times starts a verse with a quadrisyllable.

❡ In the selection of words to form a verse regard should be had to the variety of syllabic distribution which Horace achieves in all his Alcaic odes. The latter half or element of the Greater Alcaic should exhibit the same verbal and syllabic diversity:

Palladis aegida			3	3
mole ruit sua		2	2	2
non ego te meis	1	2	1	2

ut premerer sacra	1	3	2
dic age tibia	1	2	3
notus et integrae	2	1	3
nominis et togae	3	1	2
conveniet lyrae		4	2
lite relinqueret		2	4
dum sapientiae		1	5
condicionibus			6

5 + 1 occurs only in IV ix 1 (*interitura quae*) and 1 + 3 + 1 + 1 in II xi 13 (*vel platano vel hac*).

The student should make a point of not using too often a sequence of three consecutive dissyllables, which appear to come the most readily of all and may produce a bad sonic effect if unduly repeated in the same ode. In no circumstances should such a sequence be allowed to end two consecutive verses. The same caveat applies to two trisyllables. The best and surest safeguard against such repetition is deliberately to introduce as much syllabic variety as possible, as Horace himself does.

(c) *The First Syllable*. This is regularly long: of the 634 Greater Alcaics of Horace only 18 have an initial short syllable, and none occur in Book IV.

(d) *The Fifth Syllable*. The fifth syllable may be a monosyllable, even if this is not frequent. There are some 45 cases and it is noteworthy that in 20 of these another monosyllable precedes, *e.g.*,

Soracte, nec iam,   I ix 2;

and in 21 cases (including 7 of the 20 just mentioned) another monosyllable begins the verse, *e.g.*,

nil interest an,   II iii 22.

The composer should therefore use a monosyllable in fifth place only occasionally and should support it by another, either in fourth place or in first.

The fifth syllable is always long. In III v 17 it is long by diastole.

(e) *The Last Syllable*. The last syllable is common: in Horace 319 cases are long, 315 are short.

2 THE ALCAIC ENNEASYLLABIC (Third Verse):

(a) *The Beginning of the Verse*. Horace prefers an initial long syllable: a short syllable occurs only 10 times.

The verse should not begin with a quadrisyllable scanned as such: Horace has only three, but in each case the last syllable is elided (III xxiii 7, xxvi 7, xxix 59). The verse begins 1 + 3 only twice in Horace (I xxvi 11; II iii 27). He has no verse beginning 2 + 2, which would amount to diaeresis.

(b) *The Middle of the Verse*. The fifth syllable is always long. The favourite word with Horace for this part of the line is a trisyllable; but in fact this "cross-beam" word may be of anything from three to five syllables. It carries the main weight of the whole stanza.

(c) *The End of the Verse.* The final syllable is preferably long: in the Alcaic odes 205 are long, 112 short.

❡ Horace ends the verse with a quadrisyllable only twice (II iii 3, xix 19). No instance occurs in III or IV. Verses do end 3 + 1, but nearly always the monosyllable is proclitic, *e.g.*, I xxxv 11 (where elision and proclitic *et* lessen the quadrisyllabic effect). There are 36 instances of 1 + 3.

It is possible to have 2 + 2, but only with limitations. There are 8 instances in Horace, in 5 of which the first dissyllabic word is immediately repeated by Anaphora at the beginning of the fourth line (I xvi 3–4, xxvi 7–8; II xiii 27–8, xiv 11–2, xix 7–8): contrast I xxix 11; II i 11, xix 11. As a rule this 2 + 2 sequence is one to be avoided by the modern composer.

❡ (d) *Favourite Rhythms.* Horace prefers a third verse consisting of three words only, and ending with a bacchic trisyllable. In the interests of variety, however, other rhythms and other endings deserve to be exploited by the modern composer. Of possible endings Horace likes:

Dissyllable + enclitic, *e.g.*, II vii 19, xiii 23.
Dissyllable preceded by a monosyllable or short
syllable at the end of a longer word, *e.g.*,
I xvii 19; II xiii 19.
Thus the following rhythms are musically effective
and are particularly to be imitated:

audita Musarum sacerdos,	III i 3;
infame damnatusque longi,	II xiv 19;
fias recantatis amica,	I xvi 27;
morem verecundumque Bacchum,	I xxvii 3.

3 THE LESSER ALCAIC (Fourth Verse):

(a) *Caesura.* There is nearly always a caesura after the fourth syllable, *e.g.*, I ix 20; II i 8; III iii 44.

If there is no caesura after the fourth syllable, there is practically always one after the seventh, *e.g.*, I ix 4; II xiv 20; III i 8.

There is sometimes a quasi-caesura at the end of the third syllable, or at the end of the sixth, but neither is to be recommended *e.g.*, I xvi 16; II xiii 4; III iv 36.

There are verses with caesura missing after both the fourth and seventh syllables, *e.g.*, I xvi 20; II v 24; III i 44; IV iv 64.

In the second dactyl a weak caesura is avoided as giving too rapid a movement to the verse. Exceptions are I ix 8, xxxi 16; II i 36, xiii 8. In I xxvi 12 the emphasis in the repeated *teque tuasque* gives a weight to the verse which outbalances the weak caesura; while in I xxxv 36 the question mark after the third syllable gives the necessary pause.

(b) *Diaeresis.* The fourth verse should never consist of feet each consisting of a single word. In fact, there is only one case in the Odes of breaks occurring at both the third and sixth syllables, namely in III iii 64:

> coniuge me Iovis et sorore.

The caesura is usually at the fourth syllable, and Horace was especially fond of a quadrisyllabic opening, *e.g.*,

> impavidum ferient ruinae, III iii 8;

but better still sounds a rhyming Concord such as the following:

> virgine*a* domitus sagitt*a*, III iv 72;
> Hesperi*ae* mala luctuos*ae*, vi 8;
> composit*is* venerantur arm*is*, IV xiv 52.

Needless to say, a word of six syllables such as *deterioribus* is never used to start this verse. One of five syllables occurs in II iii 8, *interiore nota Falerni*, and in IV ix 8, *Stesichorive graves Camenae*: in I ix 8 and xxxi 16 we find 1 + 4, *O Thaliarche, merum diota* and *me cichorea levesque malvae*.

A break at the sixth syllable sometimes occurs after one at the fourth, as in IV iv 12, *egit amor dapis atque pugnae*; ix 28, *nocte, carent quia vate sacro*; and xv 4, *vela darem. tua, Caesar, aetas.* More usually the verse opens with a quadrisyllable or 1 + 3:

> explicuit sua victor arma, IV ix 44;
> dum rediens fugat astra Phoebus, III xxi 24.

A 1 + 3 at the end of this verse occurs only once:

> sperne puer neque tu choreas, I ix 16.

This excludes an enclitic or proclitic monosyllable before a final trisyllable, *e.g.*, I xxxvii 20, III iii 64; IV iv 52. The most frequently occurring fourth verse sequence is:

$$\overline{}\ \smallsmile\ \smallsmile\ \overline{}\ \|\ \smallsmile\ \smallsmile\ \overline{}\ \smallsmile\ |\ \overline{}\ \overline{}$$

that is, a break at the fourth syllable followed by 4 + 2. Out of a total of 317 stanzas there are no fewer than 122 examples of this sequence in the Odes, 36 of which begin with a quadrisyllable, *e.g.*, *composita repetantur hora* (I ix 20).

The sequence $\overline{}\ \smallsmile\ \smallsmile\ \overline{}\ \|\ \smallsmile\ \smallsmile\ \overline{}\ |\ \smallsmile\ \overline{}\ \overline{}$ occurs 59 times, 29 of which begin with a quadrisyllable, *e.g.*, *Sardiniae segetes feraces* (I xxxi 4). There are 110 examples consisting of three words only, showing Horace's predilection for long words. The opening quadrisyllable occurs 88 times.

The sequence $\overline{}\ \smallsmile\ \smallsmile\ |\ \overline{}\ \smallsmile\ \smallsmile\ \overline{}\ \|\ \smallsmile\ \overline{}\ \overline{}$ occurs 43 times, *e.g.*, *vertere funeribus triumphos* (I xxxv 4). There are 48 cases of a break at the sixth syllable, *e.g.*, *post equitem sedet atra Cura* (III i 40).

The sequence — ∪ ∪ | — ∪ ∪ — ∪ | — — occurs only 4 times, *e.g.*, *levia personuere saxa* (I xvii 12), *cf.* II xi 20, xv 16, and III xxi 8. There are also 11 of the same metrical form with enclitic *-que*, e.g., *funditus imprimeretque muris* (I xvi 20), and two cases of — ∪ ∪ —‖ ∪ ∪ — ∪ — —, *divitias operosiores* (III i 48) and *progeniem vitiosiorem* (III vi 48), both of which occur in the last verse of the ode.

Three cases of — ∪ | ∪ — ∪ ∪ — ∪ | — — are found, *i.e.*,

ales Hyperboreosque campos,	II xx 16;
vitis Achaemeniumque costum,	III i 44;
maius Echioniaeve Thebae,	IV iv 64.

A variant occurs in II xx 24: *mitte supervacuos honores* and in III i 8: *cuncta supercilio moventis*. A further variant is found in III v 56: *aut Lacedaemonium Tarentum*.

⁋ To sum up: all sequences are permissible here to the modern composer except those which introduce a diaeresis with the first two feet; but we have seen that Horace showed a distinct preference for certain sequences, and *these it is desirable to employ with due regard to the need for variety*. It should also be noted that Horace frequently introduced an enclitic (*-que*, *-ve*) at the eighth syllable, *e.g.*, *per titulos memoresque fastos* (IV xiv 4). There are no fewer than 63 examples in the Odes, and for some reason their aesthetic effect is peculiarly satisfying.

(c) *The Fourth Syllable*. The fourth syllable may be a monosyllable, but is not often so, *e.g.*, I xvi 24 (*in*).

(d) *The Last Syllable*. The last syllable is long twice as often as it is short.

4 THE ALCAIC STANZA:

(a) *Elision*. Elision occurs in roughly one Greater Alcaic verse in five;[1] in one Enneasyllabic in eight;[2] and in one Lesser Alcaic in ten.[3]

---

[1] In the 634 verses there are 122 cases of elision (68 times of *-am*, *-em*, *-um*, 32 of a short vowel, 21 of a long vowel, and once of a diphthong.) There is only one example of elision before the tenth syllable, namely in II iii 10, where elision is intentionally expressive.

[2] In the 317 verses there are 42 cases (20 times of a short vowel; 17 times of *-am*, *-em*, *-um*; and 5 times of a long vowel). These include both certain cases of the elision of a hypermetric syllable at the end of the verse; see below under *Interlinear Hiatus and Synaphea*.

[3] In the 317 verses there are 33 cases (15 times of a short vowel; 15 times of *-am*, *-em*, *-um*; and 3 times of a long vowel).

Only 13 Greater Alcaics have two elisions; only one Enneasyllabic; and only three Lesser Alcaics.

(b) *Interlinear Hiatus and Synaphea.*

Elision between the verses is much rarer than in the Sapphic stanza. There are only two certain cases (II iii 27; III xxix 35); to which may be added II xiii 8, if the reading of the inferior group of MSS be preferred.

Hiatus on the other hand does occur; but a verse ending in -*m* or a vowel is rarely (if a short vowel, very rarely) followed by a verse beginning with a vowel.[1]

(c) *Enjambment of Stanzas and Stopping.*

❡ Enjambment of stanzas occurs more frequently in the Alcaic than in the Sapphic metre. Excluding the 37 final stanzas, we have 280 Alcaic stanzas, of which 158 are end-stopped, 63 have no stop, and 59 have only a light stop. In fact the modern composer as a working rule should study to make his Alcaic verses and stanzas "overflow" rather than otherwise.

Only one Alcaic ode (II xiv) has no sense-pause within the verses of the stanzas, and five have but one case (I ix, xvii; II ix; III xxiii; IV xv). I xxvi, xxix and xxxiv are examples of short odes with all stanzas enjambed.

In 33 cases the *first* line of the stanza has an internal sense-pause: of these 30 occur at the caesura, and one each after the seventh, eighth, and ninth syllable.

In the *second* line there are 60 cases of internal sense-pause: 39 at the caesura, 10 after the third syllable, 6 after the eighth, 4 after the second, and 1 after the ninth.

In the *third* line there are 19 cases: 6 after the second and fifth syllables, 4 after the third, and 3 after the sixth.

There are only 7 cases in the *fourth* line, 4 after the third and 3 after the fourth syllable.

Apart from end-stopped stanzas, there are 39 cases of end-stopped verses in the stanzas: 20 at the end of the second verse, 14 at the end of the first, and 5 at the end of the third.

❡ The third verse of a modern composer's Alcaic ode should, therefore, run on to the fourth as often as possible. A sense-pause within the third verse should not be introduced, unless the sentence following it can be carried on to

---

1 Hiatus occurs 27 times after a long vowel; 12 times after a diphthong; 6 times after a vowel + -*m*; and 3 times (4 times, if *Colcha* be read at II xiii 8) after a short vowel.

the end of the stanza or over into the next stanza: Horace has only one exception to this rule (I xxxv 35–6). The most suitable place for a sense-pause within the third verse is after the second or fifth syllable; the least suitable place is at the end of the verse itself.

¶ In the first verse sense-pauses at the caesura or at the end of the verse are the only ones permissible for the modern composer; in the second verse only those at the caesura and at the end of the verse (both these pauses being more frequent than those in the corresponding places in the first verse), with an occasional pause after the third syllable. Sense-pauses in the last verse are rare, and permissible only after the third and fourth syllables.

The series of indignant questions in I xxxv 34–8, forms a most unusual pattern in the stopping, with internal pauses in five successive verses. There is a similar succession of five questions in six verses at II vii 22–7, expressing impatient haste. No other passage shows such a concentrated use of internal stopping.

(d) *Parentheses*. In the 37 Alcaic odes only four cases of parenthesis occur: the excited *credite posteri* in II xix 2; the indignant *pro curia inversique mores!* in III v 7; the lengthy digression in III xvii 2–9, which in this short ode by its very length and pomposity adds to the burlesque effect; and the shorter digression in IV iv 18–22 with its suggestion of Pindaric aetiology.

As in Sapphics, parenthetical clauses should only be used very sparingly by the composer.

(e) *Length of Ode*. The shortest odes consist of three stanzas (I xxvi, III xxvi). The longest (III iv) has twenty.

(f) *Rhyme and Concords*. As in Sapphics, the inevitable recurrence of suffixes produces horizontal and vertical Concords in Alcaics, and some of these go as far as to constitute internal and external rhymes.

The following selected examples illustrate the point:

(i) *Horizontal Concord*:
   Bacchum in *remotis* carmina *rupibus*,   II xix 1;

(ii) *Vertical Concord*:
   silvae laborantes *gelu*que
       flumina constiterint *acuto*,   I ix 3–4;

(iii) *Internal Rhyme*:
   compos*ita* repetantur h*ora*,   I ix 20;

(iv) *External Rhyme*:
   privata deduci super*bo*
       non humilis mulier triump*ho*,   I xxxvii 31–2.

⁋ The skilled artist will always turn to the resources of his language to obtain artistic effect, for the tessellation of the structure of the Horatian Ode by these Concords cannot be mere accident. There are no fewer than 35 examples of rhyming Concords between third and fourth verses, to say nothing of unrhymed Concords. So it is never amiss for a modern composer of Alcaics to introduce at least one rhyming verse or couplet in any ode of his own.

D. *THE ASCLEPIAD ODES*

THE FIVE ASCLEPIAD METRES consist of various combinations of the following verses : the Lesser Asclepiad, the Greater Asclepiad, the Glyconic and the Pherecratean.

FURTHER NOTES ON ASCLEPIADS

1 THE LESSER ASCLEPIAD :

$$ - - \mid - \smile \smile - \parallel - \smile \smile \mid - \smile \smile $$

(a) *Caesura.* The caesura is carefully kept after the choriamb. The only exception is IV viii 17; in II xii 25 the prefix *de-* gives a quasi-caesura.

The caesura falls after a monosyllable in I vi 14, xxiii 9; III xvi 35; IV v 26, 33; viii 4, 14, 26; xiii 17. It falls after a monosyllable before which elision occurs in I i 2, vi 5. Elision occurs at the caesura in I xv 18, xxi 13; II xii 6; IV i 22; v 13, 22; viii 16.

(b) *Diaeresis.* Whatever the theories of ancient and modern metricians, Bellinger has shown that Horace thought of the Lesser and Greater Asclepiad verses as choriambic, and that he favoured in them words and phrases of choriambic form.[1] ⁋ As a result the Asclepiad verses differ sharply from Sapphics and Alcaics in not avoiding diaeresis, indeed in featuring it on a considerable scale.

In a total of 509 Lesser Asclepiad verses, there are 143 varieties of syllabic division, of which only 24 occur 6 or more times. Of these the favourite is of the form

$$ - - - \mid \smile \smile - \parallel - \smile \smile \mid - \smile \smile $$

e.g., Maecenas atavis edite regibus, I i 1. This type occurs 44 times:

---

[1] A. R. Bellinger. *The Lesser Asclepiadean Line of Horace. YClS* xv 1957 101–9, where the favoured varieties of these are listed. This section is indebted to his article, but our counts of frequency differ slightly — partly no doubt through the use of different editions.

the next in frequency is

(2) — — | — | ˘ ˘ — ‖ — ˘ ˘ | — ˘ ⌣̱

illum si proprio condidit horreo, I i 9, which occurs 23 times.

The others which occur 10 times or more are:

(3) — — | — ˘ ˘ — ‖ — ˘ ˘ | — ˘ ⌣̱   21 times

debes Vergilium finibus Atticis, I iii 6;

(4) — | — — | ˘ ˘ — ‖ — ˘ ˘ | — ˘ ⌣̱   17 times

sic fratres Helenae lucida sidera, I iii 2;

(5) — — — | ˘ ˘ — ‖ — ˘ | ˘ — ˘ ⌣̱   17 times

obstrictis aliis praeter Iapyga, I iii 4;

(6) — — | — ˘ | ˘ — ‖ — ˘ ˘ | — ˘ ⌣̱   16 times

ignem fraude mala gentibus intulit, I iii 28;

(7) — — — ˘ | ˘ — ‖ — ˘ ˘ | — ˘ ⌣̱   16 times

collegisse iuvat metaque fervidis, I i 4;

(8) — — — | ˘ ˘ — ‖ — | ˘ ˘ | — ˘ ⌣̱   14 times

secernunt populo si neque tibias, I i 32;

(9) — | — — | ˘ ˘ — ‖ — ˘ | ˘ — ˘ ⌣̱   12 times

hic saxo liquidis ille coloribus, IV viii 7;

(10) — — | — ˘ ˘ — ‖ — | ˘ ˘ | — ˘ ⌣̱   12 times

nunquam dimoveas ut trabe Cypria, I i 13;

(11) — | — — | ˘ ˘ — ‖ — | ˘ ˘ — | ˘ ⌣̱   10 times

dis miscent superis me gelidum nemus, I i 30;

(12) — — — | ˘ ˘ — ‖ — ˘ ˘ — | ˘ ⌣̱   10 times

turparunt umeros immodicae mero, I xiii 10.

❡ The observance of the caesura and frequency of diaeresis in both halves of the verse are obvious.

Choriambic words can occur in two places, and in fact do occur more frequently than in Horatian hexameters where five places are available. There are 133 choriambic words, 81 in the first, 52 in the second place. Ten verses have choriambic words in both places.

(c) *The Final Syllable*. The final syllable is common: a long final syllable is however slightly more frequent, occurring 287 times as against 222 shorts.

The final syllable is rarely a monosyllable. There are only five cases (I xxi 14; III xxv 18; IV iii 24, xiii 1 and 6); and two of these are cases of *est* with prodelision.

2 THE GREATER ASCLEPIAD:

$$- - \mid - \smile \smile - \parallel - \smile \smile - \parallel - \smile \smile \mid - \smile \underline{\smile}$$

(a) *Caesura.* The caesura is carefully kept after the second choriamb. In I xviii 16 there is a quasi-caesura after the prefix *per-*. There is a caesura after the first choriamb also, except in IV x 5, where elision gives a quasi-caesura.

(b) *Diaeresis.* As Bellinger has shown[1] the proportion of choriambic words is even higher in the Greater than in the Lesser Asclepiad. Choriambic words are found in 14 of the 32 verses, of which one has two (IV x 3) and one three (I xi 5).

One must take into account also word groups that scan as choriambs, such as *scire nefas.* In only one Greater Asclepiad (I xviii 16) is there no such choriambic combination, as against the 183 such verses out of the total of 509 Lesser Asclepiads.

There are three possible positions for a choriambic word: of these the second has 10 such words, the third 5, and the first 2. If the combinations be included the second position is always so filled, except in I xviii 16, which verse has no choriambs at all. There are almost as many variations of syllabic division (29) as there are verses, and only one occurs more than twice (I xi 4, 7; xviii 15).

In 17 verses there is diaeresis after the first spondee; and in 12 verses diaeresis after the first dactyl. ⟨ But for the composer the important points to be observed are the regular caesuras after each choriamb, and the choriambic word or word group in second place.

(c) *The Final Syllable.* The final syllable is common: Horace has 18 long and 14 short.

3 THE GLYCONIC:

$$- - \mid - \parallel \smile \smile \mid - \smile \mid \underline{\smile}$$

(a) *The Caesura.* The caesura generally falls after the third syllable, but occasionally after the fourth, *e.g.,* I iii 1, 3. Of the 262 Glyconic verses 99 have the caesura after the third syllable, 59 after the fourth, and 104 have no regular caesura.

(b) *Diaeresis.* In a total of 262 Glyconic verses there are 42 varieties of syllabic division, of which only 16 occur six or more times. Of these the favourite is of the form

$$- - - \parallel \smile \smile - \mid \smile \underline{\smile}$$

---

[1] *Loc. cit.*

e.g., *commisit pelago ratem*, I iii 11,
which type occurs 27 times.

The others which occur nine times or more are:

(2) — — | — ‖ ⏑ ⏑ — | ⏑ ⏒   24 times
pennis non homini datis, I iii 35;

(3) — — | — ⏑ ⏑ | — ⏑ ⏒   24 times
audax omnia perpeti, I iii 25;

(4) — — | — ⏑ ⏑ — | ⏑ ⏒   20 times
reddas incolumem precor, I iii 7;

(5) — | — — ‖ ⏑ ⏑ — | ⏑ ⏒   18 times
quem mortis timuit gradum, I iii 17;

(6) — — | — ⏑ ‖ ⏑ — ⏑ ⏒   13 times
mater saeva Cupidinum, I xix 1;

(7) — | — — ‖ ⏑ ⏑ | — ⏑ ⏒   11 times
neu promptae modus amphorae, I xxxvi 11;

(8) — | — | — ⏑ ⏑ — | ⏑ ⏒   9 times
nec flos purpureus rosae, III xv 15;

(9) — — | — ⏑ ‖ ⏑ — | ⏑ ⏒   9 times
rixae sive puer furens, I xiii 11;

(10) — — — ⏑ ‖ ⏑ — | ⏑ ⏒   9 times
ventorumque regat pater, I iii 3.

There are two places in the Glyconic at which diaeresis may occur: in the 262 Glyconics there are 149 verses with diaeresis after the second syllable, of which 56 have diaeresis also after the fifth syllable; and 35 others have diaeresis after the fifth syllable.

Thus it is again clear that the frequency of diaeresis in Asclepiads is much greater than in Alcaics and Sapphics.

(c) *The Basis*. The first foot is always a spondee except at I xv 24 and 36; at the former place the better supported reading *te* removes the irregularity, while Postgate[1] has suggested that in the latter Horace may have been imitating Homer's treatment of Ἴλιον, Ἴλος, whereby these words may

---

[1] *CQ* xvi 1922 33. However, many critics will prefer emendation. The most plausible is Jones' *barbaricas* which accounts for the corruption by haplography (see Wilkinson, *Golden Latin Artistry*, p. 104 n†). But it should be noted that *barbaricus* does not occur elsewhere in Horace, while *Iliacus* does, at *Epp.* I ii 16 (with interlinear hiatus) and *AP* 129.

or may not cause elision of a preceding vowel. For the avoidance of elision, cf. *Iliad* iv 164 and vi 448, which may have led Horace to treat the foreign word as equivalent to one with an initial consonant.

(d) *The Final Syllable.* The final syllable is more often long than short: there are 153 longs and 109 shorts. In five cases it is a monosyllable (I iii 19, 37, xix 13; IV i 33, iii 21).

(e) *Elision.* Elision of long syllables is very rare in Horatian Glyconics: there are only four cases, I iii 37 (*est* with prodelision); xxiv 8; III xvi 8; IV iii 21 (*est* with prodelision).

Elision of a vowel followed by -*m* occurs 16 times, and of a short vowel 14 times.

4 THE PHERECRATEAN:

$$— \ — \ | \ — \ \smile \ \smile \ | \ — \ \underset{\smile}{—}$$

(a) *Caesura.* There is no regular caesura.

(b) *Diaeresis.* In a total of 35 Pherecratean verses there are 12 varieties of syllabic division, of which only 5 occur more than once. Of these the favourite is of the form

$$— \ — \ | \ — \ \smile \ \smile \ | \ — \ \underset{\smile}{—}$$

e.g., nigris aequora ventis, I v 7. This type occurs 9 times.

The others are:

(2) $— \ | \ — \ — \ \smile \ | \ \smile \ — \ \underset{\smile}{—}$ 5 times
 vix durare carinae, I xiv 7;

(3) $— \ — \ | \ — \ | \ \smile \ \smile \ | \ — \ \underset{\smile}{—}$ 5 times
 fidit tu nisi ventis, I xiv 15;

(4) $— \ — \ — \ \smile \ | \ \smile \ — \ \underset{\smile}{—}$ 5 times
 interfusa nitentis, I xiv 19;

(5) $— \ — \ | \ — \ \smile \ | \ \smile \ — \ \underset{\smile}{—}$ 4 times
 Persas atque Britannos, I xxi 15.

There are two places in the Pherecratean at which diaeresis may occur: in the 35 Pherecrateans there are 23 verses with diaeresis after the second syllable, of which 15 have diaeresis also after the fifth syllable, and 2 others have diaeresis after the fifth syllable.

It was only to be expected that this verse, which is merely a variant of the Glyconic, would, like it, show a high frequency of diaeresis.

(c) *The Final Syllable.* The final syllable is normally long: there are 31 longs and 4 shorts. It is a monosyllable at I xiv 3 only.

(d) *Elision.* Horace allows no elision in this verse at all.

1. *The First Asclepiad Metre.*

This consists of the Lesser Asclepiad verse κατὰ στίχον.
Horace uses it in only three odes, I i, III xxx and IV viii,
the last of which is the only exception to the *Lex Meinekiana*.
The authenticity of IV viii has consequently been impugned,
or at least some verses of the ode; but there is no sufficient
reason to doubt that it is genuine, and it is simpler to
suppose that Horace thought of this metre as composed in
couplets.

(a) *Elision*. Elision is rare in the Lesser Asclepiad verse, but occurs more
often in this metre than in the other Asclepiad metres. The average frequency
is one elision in five verses, though it varies from 1 in 2 (in III xxx) to 1 in 10
(in IV viii). Only one verse (III xxx 7) has two elisions.

(b) *Interlinear Hiatus and Synaphea*. Elision between the verses does not
occur, but there are four cases of hiatus, all involving a final long vowel or
diphthong (I i 11, 18; IV viii 17, 24).

(c) *Enjambment and Stopping*. The most frequent strong sense-pause in
this metre is at the end of the verse. It occurs 16 times (excluding the three
final verses of the three odes). The next in frequency is the stop at the caesura,
which occurs 6 times, and there are single instances of a pause after the fourth
and tenth syllable.

Normally there is a continuous run of more than a verse after a strong pause.
The only exceptions occur in IV viii 10–1 and 27–9, where pauses occur at
briefer intervals.

(d) *Length of Ode*. Horace ranges from 16 verses in III xxx to 36 verses
in I i.

(e) *Rhyme and Concords*. Horizontal and vertical Concords are found,
although of course only on a very restricted scale, and III xxx 1–2 barely
qualifies as a vertical:

    (i) *Horizontal Concord and Internal Rhyme:*
        non incisa *notis* marmora *publicis,*   IV viii 13;
        hunc si *mobilium* turba *Quiritium,*   I i 7;

    (ii) *Vertical Concord and External Rhyme:*
        exegi *monumentum* aere *perennius*
        regalique situ pyramidum *altius,*   III xxx 1–2.

In the 86 verses of this metre it is not possible to find so many instances as here are in Alcaics and Sapphics; but the Horatian pattern of stopping does produce a new type of Concord in this metre whereby a final syllable may form a Concord and even rhyme with the syllable before the caesura in the *next* verse, *e.g.*,

> princeps Aeolium carmen ad Ital*os*
> deduxisse mod*os*,   III xxx 1 3–4.

(f) *Subject Matter.* Horace uses this metre for special purposes, as the introduction and epilogue to the original scheme of the Odes, and as the keystone in the structure of Book IV, where its central position is intended to recall I i and III xxx.

The modern composer may wish to experiment with this metre, even if he will hardly have Horace's special occasions for using it.

2. *The Second[1] Asclepiad Metre.*

This consists of the Greater Asclepiad verse κατὰ στίχον and does conform to the *Lex Meinekiana*. Horace uses it only three times, I xi, xviii and IV x.

(a) *Elision.* In the 32 Greater Asclepiad verses there are only two cases of elision (I xviii 5; IV x 5).

(b) *Interlinear Hiatus and Synaphea.* Elision between the verses does not occur; but there are five cases of hiatus, three of which involve a final long vowel or diphthong.

(c) *Enjambment and Stopping.* In this metre also Horace prefers a continuous flow for his verse. A notable instance of this is IV x which has no strong pause at all between its first and last words. On the other hand, I xviii has three successive end-stopped verses (4–6). If the three final verses are excluded, the favoured places for pauses are at the end of the verse (4 instances) and at the caesura after the sixth syllable (4 instances). Single instances of pauses after the second and third syllable are found.

(d) *Length of Ode.* Horace has two of eight verses and one of sixteen.

(e) *Rhyme and Concords.* These features appear in this metre also, as the following examples show:

---

[1]   The fifth according to another system of numbering the Asclepiad metres, which takes first all the metres including the Lesser Asclepiad verse.

    (i)   *Horizontal Concord:*
        et tollens *vacuum* plus nimio Gloria *verticem,*   I xviii 15;

    (ii) *Internal Rhyme:*
        nunc et qui color est punice*ae* flore prior ros*ae,*   IV x 4.

The few verses in this metre afford no instance of vertical Concord or external rhyme; but the feature noted in the First Asclepiad whereby the final syllable of a verse is in concord and rhymes with the syllable before the caesura in the next following verse does occur, *e.g.,*

        finem di dederint, Leuconoe, nec Babylonio*s*
        temptaris numero*s,*   I xi 2–3.

    (f) *Subject Matter.* Horace displays his virtuosity in this metre, and his example will attract the more adventurous modern composer.

3.   *The Third Asclepiad Metre.*

    This consists of the Glyconic and Lesser Asclepiad Verses alternating. Horace uses it in twelve odes (I iii, xiii, xix, xxxvi; III ix, xv, xix, xxiv, xxv, xxviii; IV i, iii).

    (a) *Elision.* In this metre there is on the average one elision in 6 verses, the extremes being none in III xv and one in the 28 verses of III xix and one in 3 in III xxv. Six verses have 2 elisions.

    (b) *Interlinear Hiatus and Synaphea.* Elision between the verses occurs once (IV i 35). There are 13 cases of interlinear hiatus, 10 involving a long vowel or diphthong, 2 a vowel followed by -*m*, and one a short vowel.

    (c) *Enjambment and Stopping.* Horace writes sequences of eight (*e.g.,* I iii 1–16), and even twelve verses (III xxiv 33–44), without a major sense-pause. It is unusual to find strong sense-pauses in successive lines, but cases do occur, *e.g.,* I iii 36–7. The most remarkable passage for its frequency of pauses is III xix 17–22. Three verses have 2 sense-pauses (III xix 22, xxiv 30; IV i 2).

    Of the 96 strong sense-pauses counted, 64 come at the end of the Lesser Asclepiad, 13 at the end of the Glyconic, 11 at the caesura of the Asclepiad, 3 after the sixth syllable of the Glyconic, 2 after the second syllable of the Asclepiad, and one each at the caesura of the Glyconic, after the fifth syllable of the Asclepiad and the second of the Glyconic.

❡ The modern composer should aim at unbroken series of verses, a series of four being the most common. It is noteworthy how often a strong pause falls at the end of every fourth verse without a pause within the stanza; *e.g.*, I xiii, III ix, which are wholly constructed in this way. In fact it is definitely in the Horatian manner to write without a major pause for up to eight or twelve verses on end. The comparative rarity of internal sense-pauses is also remarkable.

As a rule the composer should carry on the sense to the end of a verse, avoid pauses in successive lines (unless he aims at a special effect such as the excitement of the preparations in III xix 18–22, or the inspiration of III xxv 1–3), and occasionally pause at the caesura of the Lesser Asclepiad.

(d) *Length of Ode.* The shortest odes in this metre have four stanzas (I xix, III xv and xxviii), the longest has sixteen (III xxiv).

(e) *Rhyme and Concords.* These characteristics of Horatian style are found in this metre also, as the following examples show:

(i) *Horizontal Concord:*
    nec vincire *novis* tempora *floribus,*   IV i 32;

(ii) *Vertical Concord:*
    quos irrupta tenet copula nec *malis*
        divulsus *querimoniis,*   I xiii 18–9;

(iii) *Internal Rhyme:*
    et serves anim*ae* dimidium me*ae,*   I iii 8;

(iv) *External Rhyme:*
      nec Damalis nov*o*
    divelletur adulter*o,*   I xxxvi 18–9.

There are also examples of the concording of the last word of one verse with the word before the caesura of the next, *e.g.*,

    navis, quae tibi credit*um*
        debes Vergili*um,*   I iii 5–6;

and *cf.* I xiii 9–10, xxxvi 17–8.

❡ (f) *Subject Matter.* This is Horace's favourite Asclepiad metre. The alternation of short and long verses recalls the atmosphere of the epodic metres and so makes the metre suitable for the excitement of III xxv or the indignation of III xxiv. It is not so grave as the Alcaic nor so light as the Lesser Sapphic; so it becomes a proper medium for a graceful tribute to Virgil (I iii), or for one of Horace's most finished works of art, III ix, where the characteristic end-stopped stanzas (which are not peculiar to this ode) contribute to the success of this masterpiece of symmetry.

The modern composer should find in this metre a mean between the grandeur associated with the Alcaic and the lighter nature of Sapphics.

(g) *The Final Syllable*. In the notes on the verses it has already been stated that a final long syllable in the Lesser Asclepiad is only slightly more frequent than a short[1], and that in the Glyconic the ratio of long to short is roughly as 3 : 2[2]. But Postgate[3] has drawn attention to an interesting variation in Horace's practice in the Third Asclepiad Metre. If I iii be excluded, the final syllable is always at least as frequently long as short, and in most odes is more frequent in the ratio 4 : 3. In I iii the ratio is 2 : 3, which is reversed in I xiii (the next ode in this metre) with the ratio 3 : 2. Horace has chosen to place odes at the beginning of Book I so demonstrating his versatility in the use of lyric metre, and in the case of the first two in the Third Asclepiad Metre a marked divergence even in the same metre.

So too in the first two Sapphic odes there is a metrical variety: I ii has no weak caesura, but I x has several.

4. *The Fourth Asclepiad Metre.*

This consists of stanzas formed by three Lesser Asclepiad verses followed by a Glyconic. Horace has nine odes in this metre (I vi, xv, xxiv, xxxiii; II xii; III x, xvi; IV v, xii).

(a) *Elision*. In this metre there is on the average one elision in seven verses, the extremes being one in twenty verses in IV v and one in four verses in III xvi. Seven verses have two elisions.

(b) *Interlinear Hiatus and Synaphea*. There are ten cases of interlinear hiatus, nine involving a long vowel or diphthong and one a vowel followed by *-m*.

(c) *Enjambment and Stopping*. In this metre no major sense-pause occurs within the Glyconic. Of the 63 stanzas, only 20 are enjambed, and 43 (including the nine final stanzas) are end-stopped. This stop at the end of the stanza is easily the most frequent; next in frequency comes the pause at the end of the Lesser Asclepiad (15 times), at the caesura (12), after the second syllable (5), after the third or fourth syllable (2 cases of each), and after the ninth syllable (once).

In I vi all five stanzas (except one) are end-stopped and no other major pause occurs. In IV xii all stanzas are end-stopped, but other pauses occur

---

within all except three of the stanzas. As in the Third Asclepiad, unbroken runs of four verses are common, and runs of up to eight are found (II xii 1–9, 13–20, 21–8; IV v 17–24).

After a strong pause there is seldom another within the compass of a verse, and generally the interval amounts to several verses. In this respect I xv 10–2 is noteworthy; but an exclamatory passage frequently varies normal Horatian practice in stopping. A similar influence is at work in verses 26–7 of the same ode. So in I xxiv 19 the abrupt dissyllable with strong pauses before and after it may be compared with the Virgilian use of a spondee followed by a pause at the beginning of a hexameter, *e.g.*, *G.* i 477; iv 164, 196; *A.* vi 172,590. In both poets the unusual rhythm gives very strong emphasis to the dissyllable.

The only other passage in which a second major pause follows within the compass of a verse is at III xvi 42–3, where the pithy gnome, *multa petentibus desunt multa*, etc., rounds off the stanza impressively.

¶ Horace's practice stresses the stanza as a metrical unit. The modern composer should accordingly construct stanzas that are more often than not end-stopped, aim at sequences of four or more verses without strong sense-pauses, allow pauses within the stanza only at the end of the Lesser Asclepiad, or within it at the caesura or (very occasionally) after the second or third or fourth syllable, and avoid pauses within the Glyconic.

(d) *Length of Ode*. The shortest ode in this metre has four stanzas (I xxxiii), the longest eleven (III xvi).

(e) *Rhyme and Concords*. The following examples illustrate the characteristic Horatian use of rhyme and Concord:

(i) *Horizontal Concord:*
nec *Laestrygonia* Bacchus in *amphora*,   III xvi 34;

(ii) *Vertical Concord:*
fulgentes oculos et bene *mutuis*
     fidum pectus *amoribus*,   II xii 15–6;

(iii) *Internal Rhyme:*
quis Martem tunic*a* tectum adamantin*a*,   I vi 13;

(iv) *External Rhyme:*
declinat Pholoen; sed prius Apul*is*
     iungentur capreae lup*is*,   I xxxiii 7–8;

(v) *Concord and Rhyme of Final Syllable and Syllable before the Caesura:*
immitis Glycerae neu *miserabilis*
     decantes *elegos*,   I xxxiii 2–3;
dicunt in tenero gramine pingu*ium*
     custodes ov*ium*,   IV xii 9–10.

(f) *Subject Matter*: Horace uses this metre almost as frequently as the Third Asclepiad and for a variety of themes: for a deprecating statement to the great on the limitations of lyric verse (I vi, II xii), for myth (I xv), for the lament for Quintilius (I xxiv), for love poetry (I xxxiii, III x), for a characteristic eulogy of moderation (III xvi), for praise of the emperor (IV v), and to invite a friend (IV xii).

⁋ The modern composer can obviously use the metre for a similarly wide variety of themes; and if he is translating, the frequency of end-stopping in this metre makes it especially suitable for originals that have a strongly marked structure in stanzas.

L. P. Wilkinson[1] comments on the propriety of this metre for the theme of IV v and on Horace's skill in exploiting the possibilities of the metre itself.

5. *The Fifth Asclepiad Metre.*

This consists of stanzas formed by two Lesser Asclepiad verses, followed by a Pherecratean and a Glyconic. Horace has seven odes in this metre (I v, xiv, xxi, xxiii; III vii, xiii; IV xiii).

(a) *Elision*. Elision is rare in this metre. It occurs on the average once in nine verses, the extremes being none in I v and xiv, and more than once in three verses in I xxi, which is also remarkable in having three elisions in one verse (I xxi 14). The elisions are of the easiest kind as befits the lightness of this metre. Of the 16 instances, 9 involve a short vowel, 6 a syllable ending in *-m*, and only one a long vowel in the remarkable verse (I xxi 14), almost Catullan in its excess of elision.

(b) *Interlinear Hiatus and Synaphea*. There are only six cases of interlinear hiatus, all of which involve a final long vowel or diphthong. Moreover, Pasquali[2] points out that hiatus between the Pherecratean and Glyconic occurs only in I xxiii (verses 3–4 and 7–8), and is avoided altogether in later odes.

(c) *Enjambment and Stopping*. Of the 35 stanzas only 11 are enjambed, 24 (including the 7 final stanzas) are end-stopped. This stop at the end of the stanza is easily the most frequent. Next in frequency come the pause at the caesura of the Lesser Asclepiad (6 cases), after its second syllable (5 cases), at its end (4 cases); after the second syllable of the Pherecratean (2 cases); and

---

[1] *Horace and his Lyric Poetry*, ed. 2, p. 144.

[2] *Orazio Lirico*, p. 711.

single instances after the third, ninth and tenth syllable of the Asclepiad, at the end of the Pherecratean and after the third syllable of the Glyconic respectively.

In I xxi and xxiii, all stanzas are end-stopped; in III vii and xiii all but one are end-stopped. On the other hand only the final stanza is end-stopped in I v.

As in the Third and Fourth Asclepiad Metres unbroken runs of four verses are common, and the longest unbroken sequence is I v 5–12. The eight-verse sequences of the Third and Fourth Asclepiad are not found in this metre.

After a strong pause there is seldom another within the compass of a verse, and generally the interval amounts to two or more verses. In this respect the Ship Ode is quite exceptional, with three pauses within two lines (I xiv 2–3). (But strong agitation is always apt to change the normal pattern of Horatian stopping). In III vii 21 and xiii 6, the emphatic isolated dissyllable may be compared with *durum* in I xxiv 19 and the Virgilian examples cited on p.71. The stopping in IV xiii 17–8 with its animated questions may be compared with the similar stopping in I xxxv 34–8.

¶ In this metre (as in the Fourth Asclepiad) Horace's pattern of stopping stresses the stanza as a metrical unit; so that the modern composer should in this metre also construct stanzas that are more often than not end-stopped, aim at sequences of four verses without a major pause and allow pauses within the stanza only occasionally, at the caesura of the Lesser Asclepiad or at other points mentioned above.

(d) *Length of Ode.* The shortest ode in this metre in Horace has three stanzas (I xxiii); the longest eight (III vii).

(e) *Rhyme and Concords.* These characteristic features may be illustrated as follows:

(i) *Horizontal Concord:*
perfusus *liquidis* urget *odoribus*,   I v 2;

(ii) *Vertical Concord:*
interfusa *nitentes*
    vites aequora *Cycladas*,   I xiv 20;

(iii) *Internal Rhyme:*
cui flav*am* religas com*am*,   I v 4;

(iv) *External Rhyme:*
Quid fles, Asterie, quem tibi candid*i*
primo restituent vere Favoni*i*,   III vii 1–2;

(v) *Concord of the Final Syllable*
     and Syllable before the Caesura:
     intemptata nites me tabula *sacer*
     votiva *paries,*   I v 13–4.

(f) *Subject Matter.* Of the seven odes in this metre, four are love poems
(I v, xxiii; III vii; IV xiii), two are quiet prayers (I xxi and III xiii), and the
seventh is the Ship Ode (I xiv). The Ship Ode is one of Horace's earliest
poems and clearly was written before he had decided on the proper themes
for this metre. In his later practice he makes it predominantly a metre for love
poetry, including one of his most polished masterpieces, the Ode to Pyrrha
(I v). In this ode the absence of elision, the interlinear hiatus and end-stopped
stanzas, and the skilful use of Balanced Decoration and Concords contribute
much to the formal artistry that has made this a favourite for so many.

The modern composer should also reserve this metre for highly polished
treatment of lighter themes, especially love poetry.

Chapter Three

Composing in Horatian Metres

« Y lo que sería peor, hazerse Poeta, que, segun dizen, es enfermedad incurable, y pegadiza. »

IN THE LAST CHAPTER an attempt was made to formulate the rules of Horatian metrical practice. It goes without saying that even a faithful observance of these rules would produce no more than a skeleton for a modern Horatian ode. In this chapter more arbitrary suggestions will be made how this skeleton may be clothed in appropriate flesh.

The composition of Latin verse in Horatian metres may of course be approached in more than one way, varying with the ethos and atmosphere of the original material to be rendered, if any, and with a number of other factors not strictly classifiable and sometimes hardly definable.

One Method of composition aims primarily at a close and faithful translation into classical Latin and little else. No attempt is made to add colour to the original, or to imitate consciously any characteristic features of Horatian diction or style. The version correctly scans : in other respects it is not characteristically Horatian, and it follows the structure of the original rather than the structure of a Horatian ode with its typical varieties of enjambment and stopping. The version might just as well have been done in Elegiacs : in fact, there seems no particular reason why Horatian metres should be used at all for it. Still, this Method does win admirers and verse competitions, and it has regularly been practised by outstanding classical scholars of the past, such as the great H. A. J. Munro.

The other Method aims at a real replica of the Horatian Ode in spirit as well as letter, thus aiming at an ideal that is almost certainly incapable of realisation. Insofar as it succeeds it may produce a version that has some claim to some literary merit. Naturally, there are risks for the composer who adopts this Method. He will not be tied to a close rendering of the original, he will paint with a broad brush in Horatian pigments, he will deliberately use Horatian diction, idiom and formal features, such as enjambment and stopping, in designing the structure of his ode; he will paraphrase in Horatian terms rather than attempt a close literal translation; he may add touches of imaginative fancy not corresponding directly to anything in the original; and he will not hesitate temperately to heighten the colours of a flat or unpoetic passage in the original. Even so, will he not merely fail to translate, fail to convey the message of the original? Will he not merely travesty Horace at the same time? No doubt he will often fail in this way; but καλὸς ὁ κίνδυνος and the one who takes the risk might well adopt as his motto *nil desperandum Flacco duce et auspice Flacco*.

Both these Methods are extremes, and the composer's own experience and taste will determine where between these extremes he will direct his own efforts. In this chapter there will be a definite leaning towards the Second Method, if only because any modern Latin verse written in Alcaic, Sapphic or Asclepiad metres inevitably attracts comparison with Horace, both as to form and to content. Only religious verse and deliberately comic or slapstick versions are patently exempt from this comparison.

Whichever Method the composer prefers on the basis of his skill and sense of literary propriety, there are risks as we have said. The risks of the Second Method have been mentioned above, and the composer who follows it may often hope for nothing better than a splendid failure. On the other hand, will the First Method produce something good *sui generis*, or in a different way from the Second will it merely give the impression of being "bad Horace"? Αἰτία ἑλομένου. In any case the crucial test for every version will always be *how does it stand up without the crib?*

Individual preferences are also involved. H. A. J. Munro once said of William Johnson Cory (1823–92), Fellow of King's College, Cambridge, that he considered him the writer of "the best and most Horatian Sapphics and Alcaics that have been written since Horace ceased to write" — a judgment that many of us familiar with both Cory and Horace would certainly challenge to-day, now that Mgr. R. A. Knox and A. B. Ramsay have come and gone from our midst. Even in Munro's own day, this judgment may not have been well founded, and the Horatian verse of some of Munro's contemporaries, say, Sir Richard Jebb, H. J. Hodgson, or Edward Balston, suggests that his eulogy was too sweeping.

Munro's version[1] of Tennyson's *Vision of Sin* is so typical of the First Method of approach to the composing of verse in Horatian metre that it deserves some discussion. It may be of course that this distinguished classic really supposed that he was writing an ode in genuine Horatian style, in other words that his approach was by the Second Method. If so, he must have been singularly optimistic about it after dispensing with so many Horatian features that would at least have given "artistic verisimilitude to an otherwise bald" set of verses. Thus, like the original itself, stanza 1 has no addressee, and begins at once without more ado :

---

[1] Taken from *Arundines Cami* (6th Edition 1865), pp. 76–7. Deighton, Bell & Co., and Longman Green, London.

Fill the cup and fill the can,
  Have a rouse before the morn:
Every minute dies a man,
  Every minute one is born.

Pone crateram cyathisque sumptis
liber indulge genio ante lucem:
quodque momentum videt hos perire,
  nascier illos.

Whether or not an abstraction like *momentum* can properly do any "seeing" in Latin we need not stop to query: within its narrow limits the stanza translates Tennyson adequately, but no more. The second stanza continues:

Drink, and let the parties rave:
  They are filled with idle spleen,
Rising, falling like a wave,
  For they know not what they mean.

tu bibe et caeco sine factiones
splene delirent; sibi nescientes
quid velint, crescuntque caduntque rursum
  ceu maris aestus.

Still no vocative, whereas by now Horace would certainly have slipped in a *comes* or *amice*.[1] As for its sound effects, verse 3 is perhaps the worst Sapphic verse ever written: bumpity-bump-bump, and what a mouthful of bunched consonants! But of course for composers by the First Method this unmusical sort of thing does not matter at all. Or perhaps is it Munro's playful way of suggesting the rising and falling of the waves?

---

[1] See L. Moritz, *Some 'Central' Thoughts on Horace's Odes. CQ* xviii 1968 116–31, and especially his summary on p. 122: "It seems, therefore, that any addressee's name could stand in the first stanza or at the beginning of the second stanza . . . Any later position seems to have implied some kind of distinction . . . But the striking point is that, as far as vocatives are concerned, Maecenas and Virgil alone appear to have been allowed the exact centre, while the end was wholly reserved for Caesar".

And with his stanza 3 we have what must be the quint-essence of academic non-Horace, although Flaccus himself would certainly have underwritten the substance of this Tennysonian thought :

> He that roars for liberty
>> Faster binds the tyrant's power:
> And the tyrant's cruel glee
>> Forces on the freer hour.

> artius contendit eri ferocis
> vincla libertatis ineptus auctor:
> huius adventum properat maligno
>> ille triumpho.

A literal construe would apparently give us : "The clumsy promoter of liberty stretches the chains of the fierce overlord more tightly : with spiteful triumph that one (*erus ferox*) accelerates the arrival of this one (*ineptus auctor*)". Or does *huius* refer to *libertatis* in the preceding verse? One can only conclude that it does *by peeping at the crib*; which is the very thing that the composer ought not to compel his reader to do. In any case the stanza never catches the subtler nuances of Tennyson's sense properly, and illustrates only too clearly the perils of the First Method of Horatian verse-writing.

Libertas, having appeared in the third person, now suddenly becomes the ode's principal addressee from the fourth stanza to the end. Looking at all seven stanzas of Munro's version one notes the presence of expected things and the absence of Horatian ones. He has no compunction about using a non-Horatian, insensitively prosy vocabulary at times — *e.g.*, *factiones*, *splene*, *gratulamur*, *pervetustum*, *deinde*, *maxima natu*. Nor do the rules of Horatian periodizing and planning trouble his Muse overmuch. Concords are few and far between, and Anaphora appears not at all;

although, sure enough, faithful to his Tennyson Munro repeats word for word the first verse of his stanza 1 as the first verse of his stanza 4.[1]

To sum up: criticism of this sort of writing in Horatian metres as such is really misconceived, once we accept the First Method of composing as a perfectly legitimate form of exercise. It is not so much that its practitioners are to be regarded as inferior composers to those who attempt to follow the Second Method: rather it is that the two schools at times hardly speak the same language. The one sees its products in terms of the literal original at the expense (if necessary) of Horace; the other in terms of Horace at the expense (if necessary) of the literal original.

How then would an exponent of the Second Method set about rendering this same Tennyson? For one thing, he would certainly choose the Alcaic metre. This would give him more elbow-room in his stanzas while keeping them more or less in step with Tennyson's. Moreover, Alcaics would bring in overtones from I xxxv, the atmosphere of barricade and tumbril (*ad arma, cessantis ad arma*) and the *arbitrium popularis aurae* of III ii 20, so clearly demanded by the spirit of the original. Further, an addressee in the vocative would be supplied, and there would be plenty of Concords and Balanced Decoration. The diction would be more concrete and graphic than Munro's, with some attempt made to dispense with the prosier words. For instance, instead of *factiones* one might have *aemulae partes*, and there is really no need to make the "firstborn" *proles* so laboriously *maxima natu* rather than simply *prima*. Again, our composer, unlike Munro, would try to work in a Proper Name or two: the "sea-wave" might be Carpathian or any other name of metrical convenience, the "dust" might be Olympian or

---

[1] This never happens in Horace, unless the repetition of *audivere, Lyce*, in IV xiii 1 and 2, can be regarded as a faint equivalent.

belong to the crowded Circus. As for the idea of Liberty devouring her children, the author has used Horace's *Lamia* (*AP* 340) in his own Alcaic version of this piece to cover this thought in Tennyson's closing couplet. In short, our composer would keep his eye on the parade of ideas in the original material rather than on Tennyson's actual words. Finally, the version would have to justify itself as a self-sufficient ode without the support of the English crib.

Munro's composition in Horatian metres often so aptly illustrates what we have called the First Method that another short example[1] of his work is worth quotation and comment.

Sweet Western Wind

Sweet Western Wind, whose luck it is,
    Made rival with the air,
To give Perenna's lips a kiss
    And fan her wanton hair,

Bring me but one: I'll promise thee,
    Instead of common showers,
Thy wings shall be embalmed by me,
    And all beset with flowers.

                ROBERT HERRICK.

Libare nostrae quatenus osculum,
suavis Favoni, contigit, aeris
    rivalis, et lenam Perennae
        caesariem tibi ventilare,

huc o vel unum fer mihi basium:
sudes odoris sic opobalsamis,
    non imbre plebeio, vagasque
        floribus impediare pinnas.

---

[1] *Arundines Cami*, 6th ed., pp. 174–5.

First note the choice of metre — was this the child of mere caprice on Munro's part? Certainly it is typical of the First Method to ignore the fact that Horace himself has no Alcaic ode of less than three stanzas. We are evidently not to expect anything in the way of a formal imitation except for metre and prosody : and this impression is confirmed when we come to examine the style and diction. For instance, Herrick's "wanton hair" becomes *lenam caesariem*. How foreign to the spirit of this little poem (though not to the lexical *word* "wanton") is the undertone of loose morals suggested by Munro's appositional *lenam*, we must leave the reader to judge. But *lena* does literally mean "a wanton", and that is good enough for an exponent of the First Method : the Second Method might suggest the Horatian epithets *lascivus* and *protervus* at most.[1]

Again, Herrick says that he, the lover, promises a sort of beauty treatment for the wings of Favonius as a reward for bringing him one of his girl friend's kisses. The only hint in Munro's Latin of such a promise is presumably intended by that unobtrusive *sic* : there is no other clue. Taken at its face value that *sic* could imply not a promise but something quite different, unless the crib were consulted. It could easily mean to the reader that *Perenna's kiss* would itself moisten the West Wind's wings with fragrant *opobalsama*[2] and would itself encumber them with (figurative) flowers. A not unpleasing conceit in English lyric, and no more artificial for Latin versifying purposes than the one Herrick actually uses. Unfortunately, this is not what Herrick says.

---

[1]   And even these adjectives may be a trifle too strong. Surely Herrick means little more than a mixture of "luxuriant" and "untidy", and *cf. lascivis hederis* (I xxxvi 20).

[2]   Not an unmusical word, and for that reason potentially good Horace, although not in fact used by him. Unfortunately, it has special association with the embalming of corpses — the very last thing wanted in a context like this! The Second Method might suggest the Horatian *malobathrum*.

Munro, however, makes no attempt to represent the lover as giving his promise on the condition stated. In the long run does this omission matter very much? To an exponent of the First Method it certainly ought to matter a lot, because the missing element is really the whole basis of the poem's message.

One cannot help suspecting that by now Munro had come to realize that by taking on this job in the first place he had bitten off rather more than he could chew, and that if he had to pursue the thing consistently his Latin was likely to suffer from indigestion. So the general sense of his Latin (unassisted by the crib) remains discreetly dark. It may be magnificent "tutorial" stuff, but it is not Horace. "And not unequivocally Herrick, either" — the reader might feel inclined to add *sotto voce*. Which is odd, seeing that the one claim to superiority of the First over the Second Method is supposed to lie in its more faithful rendering of the original.

Of course there is a distinct object-lesson here for any composer of Latin verse in Horatian metres. An extremist of the Second Method would probably contend that this Herrick is the sort of thing that should never be attempted at all. His objection would be on literary grounds. True, like Virgil, Horace would have no more difficulty in fitting wings to a Wind than to *Mars*, *Fatum* or *Fama*,[1] but when it comes to the poet's embalming and beflowering these wings as a reward for services rendered, all this would probably be too much for Horace's cool, unromantic fancy, however congenial to the luxuriant imagination of Kalidasa![2] On the

---

[1] *Cf.* II ii 7–8.
[2] *Cf. Meghadūta* 32

जालोद्गीर्णैरुपचितवपुः केशसंस्कारधूपैर्बन्धुप्रीत्या भवनशिखिभिर्दन्तनृत्तोपहारः ।
हर्म्येष्वस्याः कुसुमसुरभिष्वध्वखिन्नान्तरात्मा नीत्वा रात्रिं ललितवनितापादरागाङ्कितेषु ॥

other hand, if a Second Method composer did decide to take the risk after all, he would certainly have to hedge at the critical spot, as Munro does; but at least he must hint somehow at that vital promissory element so as to make it perfectly clear where his Latin stood in relation to the general sense of Herrick's theme. To achieve this as Horace might have done it of course calls for a high and delicate art: dodging the issue altogether merely runs counter to the professed aims of the First Method.

In practice probably no modern composer will want to attach himself unreservedly to either camp. However much he may be in sympathy with the aims and ideals of the Second Method, he soon comes to realize that he can seldom fully get his own way in applying them. Originals vary so much in literary character, style and mood, that his hands are going to be tied anyhow. He cannot be guaranteed material that is "100% Horatian" in spirit every time; nor would it be desirable for him to refuse to touch anything but what conduced to a thoroughgoing application of the Second Method. He ought in fact to be prepared to tackle anything that can reasonably be turned into classical Latin somehow: it does not follow that he must always accept the challenge. But when he has made his decision upon material with little or no real Horace in its content (a Christian hymn, for example), he can at least, like Prudentius, make his verse as Horatian in style and manner as he knows how. It will not

---

"Your body will grow fat with the smoke of incense from open windows
where women dress their hair.
You will be greeted by palace peacocks, dancing to welcome you, their
friend.
If your heart is weary from travel you may pass the night above mansions
fragrant with flowers,
Whose pavements are marked with red dye from the feet of lovely
women".
(translated A. L. Basham).
(Addressed to the Cloud Messenger).

be his fault then, if everybody is perfectly well aware that
Horace himself would hardly have owned it as a legitimate
offspring of his own Carmina.

¶ Here suggestion may be made of some suitable sources
for material to be rendered into Horatian verse: namely,
Cowper, Drayton, Herrick, Ben Jonson, Lamb, Landor,
Marlowe, Marvell, Milton (sonnets), R. L. Stevenson,
Tennyson, Goethe, Heine, Arthur Waley, Pushkin, Betje-
man. The list might be extended indefinitely; for even when
there is a marked difference stylistically the philosophy of a
modern poet may resemble Horace's enough to enable the
follower of the Second Method to attempt an expression of
it in the Horatian manner.[1] Themes that go well into
Horatian Aeolic verse include the simple joys of life; green
thoughts in green shades; Chloe and her lyre close at hand;
wine in Chestertonian plenty; the banishing of care; plain
living and high thinking; moderation as a rule; scorn of
luxury and wealth; light love affairs; advice in the Epicurean
manner to friends; mockery of vulgar shams in the Evelyn
Waugh spirit; prayers to gods or heroes; praise of sturdy
yeomen and rural life; detestation of civil war but ready
acceptance of foreign wars against barbarians; *carpe diem*
and the common end for kings and beggars alike in death.

Although followers of both Methods must agree on the
metrical facts stated in chapter II, the rest of this chapter is
directed primarily to those who adopt the Second Method
and aim at the closest possible following of the Horatian
model.

Structure.

Of the 104 odes of Horace, 79 are composed in four-line
stanzas, 18 are in couplets or pairs of couplets and 7 only are
monostichic. The *Lex Meinekiana* applies in all except two

---

[1] See also L. M. Kaiser, *Modern Alcaics and Sapphics and the Reading of
Horace. CJ l* 1954 120–2.

of these, but the exact significance of Horace's preference in the Odes for the quatrain as a metrical unit has been variously interpreted. The quatrain supported by regular caesuras and determined quantity for each syllable would clearly make the Odes more suitable for singing and lyre accompaniment. Even those who do not accept the views advanced in chapter I cannot deny the existence of the quatrain as a basic element in the Horatian Ode. And there is a rich variety in Horace's treatment of this unit, as the detailed analysis of the metres in chapter II has shown. Whether end-stopping or enjambed stanzas be characteristic the quatrain clearly had impressed itself on the poet's mind as an important working unit.

Neither the presence of this metrical unit nor the periodic structure discussed by Wilkinson[1] reveals the whole secret of the structure of the Horatian Ode, however. For the Ode has a unity of theme and a symmetrical structure based on a balanced treatment of the various aspects of the theme. The symmetrical structure is obvious in an ode such as III ix, not only in the alternating of stanzas but also in the careful set-off of thought and even of word in each reply. When Horace needs greater space to develop his ideas — and frequently he does — we find pairs of stanzas (*e.g.*, IV v), triads (*e.g.*, I xii[2], II iv), and even more complex groupings

---

[1] *Golden Latin Artistry*, pp. 207–12; and *cf.* E. K. Rand, *Horace by Heart. Hermathena* lxii 1943 15–7, who draws attention to the variety in Horace's sentence construction from the simplest possible expression of an idea as in *nunc est bibendum* to the "flowing style" in which the sentence runs on for many verses or even stanzas (as in I xxxvii 12–32 or IV ii 5–24, where his description of Pindar as a mighty river itself flows on for five stanzas without a break), and to the "interwoven style" in which Horace makes full use of the nature of an inflected language to suggest at once all the strands in a scene or story (as in I x 9–12, where Mercury confronts Apollo).

[2] *Cf.* Fraenkel, *JRS* xxxvi 1946 193.

of stanzas *e.g.*, $\overbrace{3 + 2 + 2 + 3}$ (II xiii),[1] or $4 + 8 + 4$ (III xxix).[2]

This architecturally-conscious development of his ideas produces two consequences. It causes the enjambment of stanzas to occur especially in the Alcaic metre, where Horace gives a more expansive treatment to his more important themes. It is also responsible for the few passages where Horace may be suspected of resorting to padding.[3]

❡ Ideally, therefore, though in practice it is seldom realizable, the modern composer should first plan a symmetrical structure for his ode based on a proportioned distribution of the material. This will help him to determine his choice of metre and remind him that continuous treatment of an idea over two or three stanzas is most common in the Alcaic or Third Asclepiad metres for themes requiring lengthy handling. And even if Horace himself has to resort to padding on occasions to fill out a stanza or group of stanzas in the development-pattern of his theme, it is as well to reflect that he is not on that account reduced to banal words or phrases as a lesser artist might be. Every word still adds something to his subject, as is shown by a study of his use of Epithets, Geographical and Proper Names.

Epithets, Geographical and Proper Names

Geographical names had a fascination for both Greeks and Romans, and sometimes a passage gains in effect from a geographical reference.

Related to this is the Roman liking for concrete examples rather than abstract theorizing — we are reminded here of the kind of instruction in morals that Horace received from

---

1 *Cf.* P. J. Enk, *De Symmetria Horatiana. Mn* iv 1936/7 164–72, for a study of this aspect of Horace's art.

2 *Cf.* Viktor Pöschl reviewed by Wilkinson in *CR* xii 1962 95.

3 *Cf.* Wilkinson, *Golden Latin Artistry*, p. 212.

his father. So the Horatian adjective may suggest an *exemplum*; not "generous conditions" but *Attalicis condicionibus* ("terms such as an Attalus might offer"): or name a place outstanding for its connexion with the activity described (*pulverem Olympicum*): or give a vividly realistic description of a prominent feature in the scene (*teretes plagas*, "the curve[1] of the net").

The modern composer must be equally discriminating in his choice of adjectives. Sir William Watson somewhere calls the Adjective "poor bondslave to a haughty noun", but adds — "Oft in his wallet he hath carried all his master's wealth." Horace would certainly have subscribed to that sentiment. For, as T. E. Page reminds us, no author is more careful in his choice of epithets. With him they are seldom idle, but are expressly designed to animate the picture of the noun they qualify within the context for the time being. As we have seen, they are essential to the Horatian features of Concord and Balanced Decoration. They are also very much a part of the "frightening realism" (*furchtbare Realität*)[2] noted by Goethe, especially in the Odes.

At all events, from Horace's own practice in this respect the student composer will of course not be slow to profit. Frequent resort to the Concordance will remind him of what Horace does with a given catalogue of epithets and adjectival participles, but he need not limit his enquiries to the Odes and Epodes: the Satires and Epistles also make an invaluable thesaurus. Nor need he, nor should he, restrict his own Muse to actual Horatian usages. His own poetic sensibility and invention will readily suggest other cunning combinations of adjective and noun: a sixth sense will soon

---

[1] *Cf. CR* xiii 1963 17.

[2] For the meaning of this phrase see W. Kranz, *SPHRAGIS. RM* civ 1961 118. Frightening, that is, against the conventions and artificiality of 18th-century literature and life.

tell whether it is the sort of combination Horace himself would have liked. For, as we know, the master himself was all for enterprise in the devising of a *callida iunctura* (*AP* 47), and the student can do no less than take his cue from this hint.

A version containing an epithet or two that can really be said to bite at once gains something in distinctive overall force and finish. *Canities* MOROSA ("crabbed age"), INVIDA *aetas* ("envious time"), INSOLENS *laetitia* ("extravagant joy"), PUTRES *oculi* ("languishing, melting eyes"),[1] PLACENS *uxor* ("congenial wife"), BRUTA *tellus* ("torpid earth") — to expect the average student to match this sort of thing in his own work would be too much; but at least it shows that he ought not to be too timid in experiments on similar lines.

¶ And so in revising a provisionally completed version it is a good practice to see what can be done to tone up the quality of one's own epithets throughout. Does an alternative here sound more musical? Does a substitute there limn the sense more sharply? Will the replacing of this or that one by a Proper Name add a pleasing touch of *décor* to an otherwise bare surface? Or will it localise the noun it qualifies more aptly in the Horatian manner? For instance, where nothing in the context turns specially on the temper or colour of the animals, *lions* do not invariably have to be *feri* (wild) or *feroces* (fierce) or *fulvi* (tawny): as with both Horace and Virgil, they should sometimes be *Gaetuli*. But note how Horace in I xxiii 10 has a *Gaetulus leo* and a *tigris aspera* so suggesting both the ferocity of wild beasts which underlines the contrast with *ego* and the fascination of a remote district overseas. So, in similar circumstances of context, *marble* (let us say) might often be better described as *Parium* or

---

[1] *Cf.* Virg. *G.* i 44 *putris glaeba* of the clod breaking up under the influence of the weather; Solinus 27.38 *putris soli faciem aura mutat* of the changing shape of the dunes on the North African coast.

Hymettium rather than by some lame and obvious adjective such as *album* (white) or *planum* (flat).

Personification (Prosopopoeia)

His predilection for vivid realism, local colour in geographical names, and the concrete reference in Proper Names, naturally disposed Horace to make good use of the personification of abstract nouns. In this he was typically Roman as is shown by the common cult of abstractions in Roman religion and the later cult of the virtues of the emperor. An impressive use of personification occurs in the *Carmen Saeculare* 57–60, where the religious context makes it especially appropriate; and it is by no means confined to such contexts in Horace, *e.g., Iocus* (I ii 34),[1] *Amor sui* (I xviii 14), *Gloria* (*ibid.* 15), *Fides* (*ibid.* 16), *etc.* So there is nothing to prevent the modern composer from doing a little personification on his own account, as indeed the author himself does in his own tribute to Horace on p. ix.

Sound Effects

However, conversation with the master should not be restricted merely to turning his pages over by night and day. It cannot be stressed too strongly that the literature of Greece and Rome was written to be heard. This point has been admirably made in L. P. Wilkinson's *Golden Latin Artistry*; and the importance of sound effects has been more than once mentioned in this book. Plainly it is a factor essential to the success of an ode intended to be sung, as is made clear in chapter I; but even if it is to be merely read aloud an ode aiming at the Horatian model must aim at a melodious distribution of vowels and consonants, avoid harsh combinations of sibilants and gutturals, undue

---

[1] *Cf.* Milton's "And Laughter holding both his sides."

congestions of consonants and repetitions of syllables not authorised by Horatian precedent.

Such points are also made by the ancient rhetoricians and are of course based on their experience of the languages as living tongues heard as a constant part of their environment; indeed to such an extent that a satirist could well protest: *semper ego auditor tantum?*

But how is the modern composer to get anything like this experience? Even those who have heard the Public Orators of Oxford and Cambridge are comparatively few, and those who have this experience regularly still fewer. And there are perhaps none at all to-day who subscribe to the ancient medical belief in reading aloud as a beneficial and gentle exercise.[1] Certainly there is no better way of acquiring a familiarity with the sounds of Latin, and no better trainer in this form of exercise than Horace himself. Once again the old-fashioned school has its justification. In requiring pupils to commit passages of the best authors to memory the traditional classical training not only gave its pupils a lasting treasure for storing in their conscious minds but also an influence that even subconsciously led them to write prose and verse that really sounded like Latin.

With the resources of twentieth century technology so readily to hand we can go further than this old traditional method took us, since the aspiring composer can now tape-record himself as he recites the Odes, and learn much from an inevitable self-criticism when he plays back his recording. Such a practice may do little for the general health of the community, in spite of Oribasius; but it is bound to put the composer on a sounder footing in his quest for the

---

[1] *Cf.* Oribasius, *Synopsis ad Eustathium.* i 5.1, ἐν ταῖς ἀναφωνήσεσιν ἡ μὲν εὐμέλεια καὶ χρηστοφωνία οὐδὲν ἂν συμβάλλοιτο πρὸς ὑγείαν, ὁ δὲ τῶν βαρυτέρων φθόγγων ἦχος χρήσιμος, ὥστε τοῦτον ἀσκητέον, and see the rest of the chapter for some curious, but quite irrelevant, lore.

acoustics of the Horatian model : also perhaps it will produce classical students less abashed and less tongue-tied in the presence of eloquent modern linguists with their overt scorn for the 'dead languages.'

Besides, such reading aloud will demonstrate in a vivid way Horace's art in periodizing, stopping, enjambing, placing and patterning of words and combinations of sounds, as discussed in this book ; and combined with the study of any ode it will bring home to the student the reality of these elements in the poet's art, with beneficial consequences for his own composing.

By way of example there follows an analysis of three odes of three different metres : they are among the poet's finest, though his own high standards have ensured that almost any ode submitted to such an analysis would yield results of equal value. To get the full "3-dimensional" effect intended by Horace the student should also of course recite them aloud, and tape-record his recitations too, if possible.

The Alcaic ode chosen for examination is the Cleopatra Ode (I xxxvii) :

Nunc est bibendum, nunc pede libero
pulsanda tellus, nunc Saliaribus
    ornare pulvinar deorum
        tempus erat dapibus, sodales.

antehac nefas depromere Caecubum
cellis avitis, dum Capitolio
    regina dementis ruinas
        funus et imperio parabat

contaminato cum grege turpium
morbo virorum, quidlibet impotens
    sperare fortunaque dulci
        ebria. sed minuit furorem

Now is the time for drinking, now is the time to beat the earth in dancing with foot free from restraint, now is the time, as we thought, to honour with Salian feast the couches of the gods, my comrades!

Before this day it had been a sin to bring forth the Caecuban from our grand-fathers' store-rooms, while the Queen was preparing mad ruin for the Capitol and destruction for our power along with her polluted band of creatures shamed by vice, wild

vix una sospes navis ab ignibus,
mentemque lymphatam Mareotico
    redegit in veros timores
        Caesar ab Italia volantem

remis adurgens, accipiter velut
mollis columbas aut leporem citus
    venator in campis nivalis
        Haemoniae, daret ut catenis

fatale monstrum: quae generosius
perire quaerens nec muliebriter
    expavit ensem nec latentis
        classe cita reparavit oras;

ausa et iacentem visere regiam
vultu sereno, fortis et asperas
    tractare serpentis, ut atrum
        corpore combiberet venenum,

deliberata morte ferocior,
saevis Liburnis scilicet invidens
    privata deduci superbo
        non humilis mulier triumpho.

enough to hope for anything and drunk with Fortune's favour.

But the escape of scarcely a single ship from the flames lessened her fury, and Caesar brought her mind deluded by Mareotic wine back to real fears as he rowed close behind her in her flight from Italy, just as a hawk pursues gentle doves, as a swift hunter a hare on the plains of snow-clad Thessaly, in order to put in chains the monster sent by Fate. Yet she seeking to die a nobler death neither shrank from the sword with womanish fear nor sought to gain hidden shores with her swift fleet; she even dared to go and see with face serene her fallen palace, with courage too to handle fierce asps in order to draw into her body the full draught of dark venom, fiercer from her resolve to die, begrudging to be sure the heartless Liburnians her being led as a queen no longer in an insulting triumph, no lowly woman she!

Commentary. The ode has the appearance of a spontaneous expression of the Roman's exultation at the news of the death of the foreign queen they feared; and metrical irregularities (absence of caesura in 14, quasi-caesura in 5) show that this is an early work. However, it is far from artless in its simplicity. The first words are a translation of Alcaeus' expression of joy at the death of Myrsilus:

νῦν χρὴ μεθύσθην καί τινα πρὸς βίαν
πώην ἐπειδὴ κάτθανε Μύρσιλος·

At once the reader's thoughts are turned to the politics of early Greece, to the lyric verse of Lesbos and the Alcaic metre. But in Horace's characteristic manner the Greek motto leads at once to Roman variations with the reference to a Roman priesthood and religious practice in verse 2.

Stanza 2 shows that this is not merely an academic exercise on an Aeolic theme : the relief is real from a real fear of the Romans for their power, such as they had not experienced since Hannibal was at large in Italy.

In his eagerness to stress the overwhelming victory of Octavian Horace overstates his case by representing the opposing force as contemptible and the victory as inevitable. In his excitement, too, he does some violence to historical fact, since it was Antony's fleet that was burned, while Cleopatra's fled ; and Octavian did not follow Cleopatra until 30, a year after Actium — so much for *adurgens*. However, Horace moves on to a rare (for a Roman) appreciation of the nobility of the defeated foe, for it is Cleopatra who really steals the limelight.

Many elements of Horatian art appear already in this early ode dating probably from the last quarter of the year 30. Apart from the exceptions noted above, the strict observance of the caesura and the long quantity of the fifth syllable in the Greater Alcaic are already established. But a sign of early work is the diaeresis in 5, *antehac | nefas |*.

Horace's predilection for polysyllables appears in *Saliaribus, Capitolio, contaminato, Mareotico, generosius, muliebriter, deliberata* — indeed the very frequency of these five-syllabled words suggests an excessive indulgence of a newly found power, but there is still much variety in syllabic distribution in the Greater Alcaic Verse. Only verse 22 has an initial short syllable: we note the early establishment of another Horatian metrical practice.

Horace had clearly succeeded already in determining the pattern of the Enneasyllabic, which shows no irregularity in this ode. So too the Lesser Alcaic is quite regular.

Fortunately, he decided that the metrical irregularities noted above did not disqualify the ode for publication; one may only wonder how many experiments were discarded before he reached this degree of skill in handling the metre.

The ode shows Horace's skilful periodizing ranging from the terse statement *nunc est bibendum* to the long period of more than five stanzas (vv. 12–32) with which the ode ends. This structure inevitably produces plenty of enjambed stanzas and characteristic Horatian stopping.

Vertical Concord (*latentis . . .oras*) appears in 23–4; horizontal in 25; vertical Concord and external rhyme in 27–8 and 31–2.

Anaphora (*nunc . . . nunc . . . nunc*) is seen in stanza 1.

Haemoniae illustrates the liking for a concrete reference in a simile and for a poetical alternative to the ordinary geographical name. Something of the same taste is shown in *Mareotico*; while a Roman character is expressed by *Saliaribus*, *Caecubum* and *Capitolio*.

For an example of his Sapphics let us turn to II ii:

Nullus argento color est avaris
abdito terris, inimice lamnae
Crispe Sallusti, nisi temperato
    splendeat usu.

There is no brightness in silver when hidden away in the miserly earth, Sallustius Crispus, who hate worked metal unless it shine with moderate use.

vivet extento Proculeius aevo,
notus in fratres animi paterni;
illum aget penna metuente solvi
    Fama superstes.

Proculeius will live with lifetime prolonged, known for his fatherly feeling for his brothers; him will enduring Fame bear on with undrooping wing.

latius regnes avidum domando
spiritum, quam si Libyam remotis
Gadibus iungas et uterque Poenus
    serviat uni.

You would rule a wider realm by subduing a greedy heart than if you should join Libya to distant Gades and if Carthaginians on both sides should be slaves to you alone.

crescit indulgens sibi dirus hydrops,
nec sitim pellit, nisi causa morbi
fugerit venis et aquosus albo
    corpore languor.

By self-indulgence the dreadful dropsy grows, nor does the sufferer banish thirst, unless the cause of the illness has fled from his veins and the watery languor from his pale body.

redditum Cyri solio Phraaten
dissidens plebi numero beatorum
eximit Virtus, populumque falsis
    dedocet uti

Though Phraates has been restored to the throne of Cyrus, Virtue disagreeing with the rabble removes him from the number of the fortunate, and unteaches the people to use false names, conferring a kingdom and diadem unassailable and a laurel all his own on him alone, whosoever he is who looks on huge piles of treasure with an eye that turns not back.

vocibus, regnum et diadema tutum
deferens uni propriamque laurum,
quisquis ingentis oculo irretorto
    spectat acervos.

One sees at once some striking differences from the Alcaic Cleopatra Ode. Just as that was addressed to unnamed *sodales*, so this is addressed to a prominent citizen, Sallustius Crispus. As that was remarkable for its sequence of enjambed stanzas, so this shows the Sapphic preference for end-stopped stanzas, there being only one case of enjambment. The ode (composed about 25 B.C.) shows a favourite structure in pairs of stanzas, in one case with enjambment. Each pair consists of stanzas that balance one another. So Sallust in 1 balances Proculeius in 2, insatiable greed in 3 balances incurable disease in 4 ; and the emptiness of Phraates' accession in 5 is balanced by the real kingdom conquered by Virtue in 6. This is characteristic Horatian ymmetry. Superficially the Cleopatra Ode gives the impression of a free and spontaneous outburst; technically it has the form of an enlarged *tricolon* construction, with stanza 1 as the first member, stanzas 2–3 the second, and 4–8 the long third member. In short, 1 + 2 + 5 there is contrasted with (1 + 1) + (1 + 1) + (1 + 1) here.

This Sapphic ode is quite regular metrically. The strong caesura used throughout is only varied by the rare use before it of the monosyllable with elision in 21, and of two monosyllables in 10. Elision is used very little (7, 21, 23), but one of the rare cases of elision of a hypermetric syllable in Horace is found at 18.

Horizontal Concords occur in 5, 13; vertical in 3–4, internal rhyme in 5. Balanced Decoration occurs in 1, 2, 5, 6, 10, 19, 21.

Andrewes[1] has drawn attention to the allusive nature of the language of the first stanza obtained by using *avaris*, *lamnae*, *splendeat*, and *usu* with double effect so as to give with remarkable conciseness what in prose might become an elaborate comparison: "Metal, in the form of silver, loses its lustre buried in the miserly earth, but becomes bright with handling: metal, in the form of wealth, is without value when hoarded by the miser, but is made illustrious by well-directed expenditure".

Horace's boldness in the use of language is shown in the same stanza by the construction of the *nisi*-clause which depends on the vocative *inimice*, as pointed out by Bentley. Other features of Horatian diction appear in the "Greek" genitive *animi paterni* in 6 and in *metuente* = "shrinking from" in 7.[2]

M. Andrewes, *An Aspect of Horatian Imagery*. *CR* lxii 1949 111–2. See the whole article for this Horatian practice of using words with primary and secondary meanings, and the longer article by the same author, *Horace's Use of Imagery in the Odes and Epodes*. *G & R* xix 1950 106–15.

Cf. Wickham *ad loc.*, for this usage, first found in Virgil.

The unusual frequency of sibilants in stanza 4 suggests to Wilkinson[1] that Horace intended the sound to be as ugly as the subject.

Let III ix represent the Asclepiad odes:

Donec gratus eram tibi
nec quisquam potior bracchia candidae
   cervici iuvenis dabat,
Persarum vigui rege beatior.

As long as I was pleasing to you
and no more favoured youth threw
his arms about your fair white neck
I flourished more blessed than the
king of the Persians.

"donec non alia magis
arsisti neque erat Lydia post Chloen,
   multi Lydia nominis
Romana vigui clarior Ilia."

"As long as you were not more in
love with another and Lydia ranked
not after Chloe, a Lydia of high
renown, I flourished more glorious
than Roman Ilia."

me nunc Thraessa Chloe regit,
dulcis docta modos et citharae sciens,
   pro qua non metuam mori,
si parcent animae fata superstiti.

Thracian Chloe sways me now
versed in sweet tunes and mistress of
the lyre, for whom I shall not fear to
die, if the Fates will spare her life
still left.

"me torret face mutua
Thurini Calais filius Ornyti,
   pro quo bis patiar mori,
si parcent puero fata superstiti."

"Calais, son of Ornytus of
Thurii, fires me with a mutual
passion, for whom I shall twice
endure to die, if the Fates will
spare the lad still left."

quid si prisca redit Venus
diductosque iugo cogit aeneo,
   si flava excutitur Chloe
reiectaeque patet ianua Lydiae?

What if the old love returns and
brings together with a yoke of brass
those now estranged, if fair-haired
Chloe be dismissed and the door
stands open for rejected Lydia?

"quamquam sidere pulchrior
ille est, tu levior cortice et improbo
   iracundior Hadria,
tecum vivere amem, tecum obeam
          libens."

"Although he is fairer than a star
and you lighter than cork and more
passionate than the restless Adriatic
with you I would love to live and
with you I would gladly die."

---

[1] *Horace and his Lyric Poetry*, p. 138, and see pp. 137–43 for the music of the sounds in Horace.

Readers of Horace are generally in agreement that this
ode, like the Pyrrha Ode (I v), is one of the most finished
works of art in Latin Literature, and yet Nisbet dismisses it
"as a particular favourite of those who like Horace for the
he wrong reasons."[1] If the elements that make this a
most polished work of Horatian art are the wrong reasons,
we may well be sorry for Nisbet rather than Horace : he might
as well dismiss the Taj Mahal because it is not a British
railway station.

In the long tradition of song taking the form of a dialogue
between lovers, that stretches at least from the Song of
Marisa[2] to Brahms' *Vergebliches Ständchen*, this ode deserves
a place of honour as a model of artistic perfection. It may
well have been set to music by Horace.

The symmetrical structure is obvious, and it is worked out
in some detail. Each stanza uttered by the man is answered
by the girl with a stanza that not only has verbal echoes of
the preceding stanza but caps its thought with one that
improves on it. So Roman Ilia replaces the oriental king,
and the rather negative approach of stanza 5 is answered by
the generous affection of 6. This results in the exaggeration
of *bis patiar mori*, which is, however, not out of character.

The metre is quite regular. Elision is again very little
used — in verses 6, 19, 22 (*bis*), 24 (*bis*) — and is of the
lightest kind, involving a short final syllable in all cases
except one (-*um* in 24). There is one case of interlinear
hiatus (22–3).

There is horizontal Concord in 12, 16, 18, 19 ; vertical
in 22–3 ; and Balanced Decoration in 2, 4, 7, 10, 12, 14, 16,
18, 20, 22.

---

[1] *Critical Essays in Roman Literature*: *Elegy and Lyric*. Ed. J. P. Sullivan,
p. 185. Reviewed in *CR* xiii 1963, 299.

[2] See R. Wünsch and W. Crönert, *Das Lied von Marisa*. *RM* lxiv 1909
433–48, for a discussion of this song.

In diction we may note the genitive of description depending on a proper noun in 7, and the "Greek" genitive after *sciens*. The elaboration of the name of Calais deserves note: it not only contrasts with the Thracian slave or freedwoman Chloe, the freeborn youth having father and *patria*, but may well be meant to suggest καλὰ ἵς and Θούριος ὄρνις[1] just as *Liparaei nitor Hebri* may suggest λιπαρός.[2]

For the possible significance of such unknown names in the Odes, see Appendix I in Wickham's edition.[3]

---

[1] Cf. I. Düring, Thurini Calais filius Ornyti. *A Note on Horace* Carm. *III ix.* *Eranos* l 1952 91–7.

[2] W. E. Gosling, *CR* xlvii 1933 220.

[3] A friend writes: "Prof. D. R. Dudley of the University of Birmingham once criticized this ode as making the lovers' tiff mended much too soon. I think he has missed the whole point. The lovers are only pretending to have a row; they chaff one another (as lovers do) before 'making it up' or rather pretending to do so. To my mind the whole ode is masterly in the beauty of its diction as well as in its accurate psychological insight into the minds and ways of lovers. *Horace knows!*".

Chapter Four

A Demonstration

Βουλεύονταί τ' ἄριστα περὶ τῶν μελλόντων οἱ παραδείγματα ποιούμενοι
τὰ γεγονότα τῶν ἐσομένων.

WHEN WE EXAMINE the form and structure of the lyrics of Horace we find there a neatness and finish that induce in us a feeling of near-despair if we are thinking of imitating him. At any time it is hard enough to render an English or other original into Latin verse in such a way that these qualities are preserved. Indeed the student cannot hope to tread in the shoes of one whose verse is almost inimitable, even if a bare, slavish imitation for its own sake were true art. And then there is the verbal music of Horace to be considered : how many modern composers have been able to make anything significant of that important element? Are we therefore to infer that nobody today ought to attempt Latin lyrics in Horace's style and manner? Surely not. Let the inner magic elude him, there is still nothing to prevent the student from seeking to capture Horace's characteristic modes of thought and literary approach to what is often quite a simple proposition when it is boiled down. He can also try to import into his own work the personification of abstract ideas, the concrete imagery, the geographical similes and tropes, the occasional philosophical flash, the tinctures of Greek or Roman history or mythology, all of which pervade the Odes and re-create for the reader a definite image of Horace the man and artist.

Our student might also do worse than look at the other side of the coin. Thus, as a deliberate exercise in un-Horatian versifying, the ninth stanza of II xvi, for example, could be rendered as follows, without upsetting the basic sense:

> Multa sunt armenta tibi pecusque
> plurimum; nec deest equa iam quadrigis
> apta, vestiri neque sumptuoso
> dives amictu,
> Grosphe, tu parcis.

But how vastly superior with its allusive, specific, almost "3-D" kind of concrete detail is Horace's own:

> te greges centum Siculaeque circum
> mugiunt vaccae, tibi tollit hinnitum
> apta quadrigis equa, te bis Afro
> murice tinctae
> vestiunt lanae.

The same wilful transformation of Horatian gold into lead is shown in the following version of III x, which preserves only the broad sense and indicates little or nothing of the master's characteristic finger-printing:

> Si longe coleres in Scythia domum
> saevo nupta viro, vix lacrimis carens
> velles ante fores linquere me, Lyce,
> tempestatibus obditum.
>
> quam nunc adsidue murmurat ostium
> ventis et resonat tecta nemus tua
> circum! nonne vides ut glaciet nivem
> aether iam sine nubibus?
>
> ut places Venerem, pone superbiam,
> ne coepti nimium nos onus opprimat:
> non iactare potes Penelopes genus,
> recte quae fugiit procos.

> a quamquam neque te munera, nec preces
> flectant, nec miserorum angor amantium,
> nec coniunx alia victus ab aemula
> furtim, supplicibus tuis
>
> parcas! nam nisi mox cor rigidissimum
> molliri poterit, spe sine denique
> desistam ante tuas esse diutius
> aedes in pluviis iacens.

So for Horace's concrete imagery is substituted a general paraphrase couched in colourless diction: in particular, adverbs tend to oust Balanced Decoration, which is accordingly reduced to minimal proportions. The alert student will also notice the feeble present participle singular as the final word of stanza 5 and the superlative in -*issimus*, a form avoided by Horace in the Odes apparently for reasons of euphony.[1]

Even a noble Alcaic stanza may be thus sacrificed to the cause of showing what is not Horatian, albeit still in correct Horatian metre, as the following grotesque version of II iii 25–8 shows:

> omnes eodem mors premit, et dies
> funesta tandem quemque sua inferis
> addit, neque in terras regressum
> di fieri patientur unquam.

Now let us suppose a student to be confronted with the task of putting Robert Herrick's familiar lyric "To Maidens" into Horatian verse. The English text is:

> Gather ye rosebuds while ye may,
> Old Time is still a-flying;
> And this same flower that smiles to-day
> To-morrow will be dying.

---

[1] *Pessima* in IV viii 4 seems to be the only exception.

The glorious lamp of heaven, the sun,
    The higher he's a-getting,
The sooner will his race be run,
    And nearer he's to setting.

That age is best which is the first,
    When youth and blood are warmer;
But being spent, the worse, and worst
    Times still succeed the former.

Then be not coy, but use your time,
    And while ye may, go marry;
For having lost but once your prime
    You may for ever tarry.

The poem's message of course is not only simple and direct, but for present purposes it has the advantage of echoing Horace of the Carmina here and there in its general thought. We will further assume that our student chooses or has prescribed for him the Sapphic quatrain as the medium for his Muse. So he sets to work, and in due course after much sweat (and perhaps secret tears) he produces something like the following:

Dum licet, gemmas lege nunc rosarum;
nam vetus tempus volat usque pennis:
ecce ridet flos hodie, sed idem
    cras morietur.

sol, poli magni speciosa lampas,
quo magis se tollet in aethera altum,
hoc suam metam citius tenebit
    ipse relabens.

optima est aetas ea prima quae fit,
cum magis sanguis calet et iuventus:
peior hanc actam tamen insequetur,
    pessima tandem.

nube iam sponso posito pudore
sic diem carpens, mora neu sit ulla;
heu carens forsan sedeas decore
innuba in aevum.

Schoolmaster critics would probably be inclined to call this quite a creditable effort for any Sixth Former; indeed, some might be able to find little wrong with it as an adult product. Perhaps it takes a Horatian connoisseur, as distinct from a Horatian pedant, to explain why this version hardly begins to measure up to Horatian standards. Here we must be content with criticism on a lower level; and certainly there are points, both of matter and form, that justly invite it.

As a whole, it is not unfair to say, the rendering sticks too closely and literally to the English text, and so misses too much of the Horatian idiom and style to make a passable ode. In particular, stanza 3 has a dismal prosiness about it, admittedly not absent from the corresponding Herrick stanza itself: but this is where a modern composer (not a versifier merely) would surely try to impart a little poetic lift to a pedestrian original.

Coming down to formal, technical and aesthetic detail, we may note the following points:

Verse 1. No addressee in the vocative.

Verse 2. *Nam* belongs rather to prose and is usually out of place in Horatian lyric. (Of the 71 occurrences in Horace, only 9 are found in the Odes). *Vetus tempus* borders surely on the canine as a translation of "Old Time" in a 17th-century literary sense. *Pennis* is, alas, padding here.

Verse 3. *Ecce | ridet | flos* offends the diaeretic rule, but could be corrected to *ecce flos ridens* . . . with a modified sequel.

Verse 4. The Adonic sequence 1 + 4 occurs only once in Horace (*CS* 16).

Verse 5. Prosodically correct. The euphony would be

improved by interchanging the positions of *magni* and *lampas*, though the poverty of invention apparent in the adjective remains.

Verse 6.   Prosodically weak. The sole specimen of a trochaic word immediately before a weak caesura occurs at IV xi 29, and the student is advised to follow Horace's regular practice by using a trisyllable or quadrisyllable at this point. A further fault is the elision before the tenth syllable, *aether(a)   altum* — never in a weak-caesural line.

Verses 7 *and* 8.   *Ipse* is again another bit of padding, and might better perhaps give way to *nocte*, for instance. The present participle *relabens* has no place in an Adonic, though *relapsus* would be unobjectionable here. Or *relabens* and *tenebit* could merely change places. The lack of enterprise shown by the threefold 1 + 2 start to the verse is a poor formal feature of this stanza, especially after another two of the same sequence in the preceding stanza.

Verse 9.   Prosodically correct, but hopelessly prosy. Forms of the pronoun *is* are not found in the Odes, except *eius* which is found twice (III xi 18, IV viii 18).

Verse 12.   An adverb as final word of an Adonic is unprecedented.

Verses 13 *and* 14.   Horace never uses *iam* with an imperative, unless supported by *age*. The two unrelated *-o's* in the same verse jingle meaninglessly, and *sponso* implies a betrothed couple — not surely Herrick's meaning here. *Sic* is almost indefensible as Latin in this context; and a short-vowel trochee (*ulla*) is best avoided as the last word of a verse.

Verses 15 *and* 16.   Hiatus twice in one stanza is too much, and so are three short vowels to end three successive verses. The elision in the Adonic cannot stand.

To complete a general criticism, we may feel that too many stanzas have a "square-cut" look as compared with

Horatian models. Nor is the look of the ode as a whole improved by an entire absence of Concords both horizontal and vertical, especially when coupled with a mediocre handling of Balanced Decoration.

The version which follows attempts no more than to illustrate some of the main requirements of Sapphic verse-writing as set out in these pages. If it seems to depart too far from the English sense occasionally, this is mostly for the purpose of illustrating some Horatian feature or other for the student's benefit. It certainly makes no claim to academic impeccability.

> Nunc rosae primos legitote flores
> antequam tempus vetet usque currens,
> virgines, et flos hodie renidens
> 		cras cadat idem.
>
> Sol rotam quanto levat altiorem,
> lucidum caeli decus, occupabit
> ocius tanto breviore calcem
> 		tramite pronus.
>
> dote si summa calidoque suco
> ver Iuventatem beat, hoc sequentur
> res minus faustae, neque tardat atram
> 		bruma ruinam.
>
> occupare aude, Pholoe, maritum,
> dum licet: lapso semel heu nitore
> nuptiarum expers sedeas anile
> 		forsan in aevum.

Comment:

Note how the problem of an addressee is treated: first, the poet addresses maidens in general; then one in particular, known by Horace to be man-shy (*fugax*, II v 17).[1] We have

---

[1] Not a strictly Horatian solution, however, because final stanzas in the Odes are reserved for Caesar exclusively as addressee in the vocative.

three horizontal Concords (unrhymed), three verticals (one rhymed). Observe how a good flow is maintained throughout with no heavy stops at verse-ends to interrupt, and only one heavy internal stop anywhere, apart from the Adonic ones. Nor does any stanza have an excessively "square-cut" look. Notice too the double end-rhyming in the final stanza (*cf.* I xii 13–6).

Variety in the choice and distribution of syllabic sequences shows up fairly well. Verses 5 and 6 each end with a quadrisyllable, and verse 10 begins with a useful 1 + 4. The student's weak string of 1 + 2's is avoided.

As for substance, note how an attempt is made to infuse a little poetry into Herrick's prosy third stanza by drawing upon the Seasons to express the gist of it ; but this of course is only to take a leaf out of Horace's own book. *Dote* in the same stanza has the advantage of a possible figurative meaning, as has *suco* also : indeed, the whole of verse 9 might pass for a hendiadys — a very Horatian device. *Calcem* (winning-post) and *rotam* (disc-wheel) in the preceding stanza are meant to hint at Herrick's race-course trope : and the emphatic sense of *pronus* (setting) is shown by its prominent position at the very end of the stanza.

Not least, in the important matter of Balanced Decoration is there a considerable improvement on the student's version. Further, note the indirect link provided by *occupabit* and *occupare* (*cf.* IV xi 21).

The light simplicity of Herrick's lyric is no fatal bar to an Alcaic rendering — II xi, for example, is no weightier — but for other reasons the poem does not take at all kindly to Alcaics. The trouble is that at least one Alcaic stanza ought to run on, without a heavy sense-pause, into the next, if Horatian models are to be followed correctly. This tends to disturb the stopping scheme, and makes continuity a much more difficult proposition than in Sapphics, where English and Latin stanzas can comfortably march in phase. However, for the sake of illustrating prosodical as well as other faults a student's Alcaic version is appended :

> Gemmas rosarum carpite, dum licet;
> nam tempus antiquum adsidue volat.
> flos ecce nunc laete renidet,
> cras iacet heu moribundus idem.

> sol, illa caeli fax nitidissima,
> quanto levarit se magis in polum,
> tanto suum cursum minorem
> finiet ocius occidendo.

> primum illud aevum quod venit, optimum est,
> cum sanguis ardet, cum iuvenis calet:
> acto sed huic mox peius instat;
> denique pessimum adest vicissim.

> ergo pudorem ponite, nec mora;
> et nunc maritos quaerite, dum datur:
> nam forsan amisso colore
> permaneatis et usque solae.

Criticism :

The complete absence of enjambment of stanzas is a bad formal feature, as is also the jejune amount of internal enjambment of verses. The whole version in fact suffers from the same "square-cut" look as the student's Sapphic just discussed, with the sense of too many lines corresponding exactly with the metrical span. Not a single spaced Concord graces the diction anywhere, and the feeling for Balanced Decoration seems but poorly realised.

Diaeretic flaws mar verses 7, 8 and 11 : verse 16 could perhaps just pass muster on the precedent of *interiore nota Falerni* (II iii 8), but the student's syllabic sequence is not good. And the presence of so many short words in verse 11 only makes the line sound bitty.

From the literary aspect the version of course displays the student's usual fault of hugging too closely the very words of the English, with but scant regard for Horatian idiom or liveliness of Latin expression.

It is better sometimes to risk the charge of departing too far from the literal words of original material, if one can wind up a version with a real touch of imagination like this :

> . . . . desit honor genis,
> vos forsan innuptas Cupido
> spernat anus fugiente penna.

Without being too pernickety about it or indulging over-much in too many subjective fads and fancies, one can still find several un-Horatian details in the student's rendering just quoted. The elision at the caesura in verse 2 is quite in order, but *tempus antiquum* is "dog" rather than Horatian Latin. *Nitidissima* as a hissing superlative cannot stand in verse 5, and *illud* in verse 9 must be taken as equally repugnant to Horace's ear, as he nowhere uses it in the Odes. For Anaphora in verse 10 the student deserves a good mark, but a bad one for omitting to provide his ode with any sort of addressee. Two explanatory *nam's* in one ode are usually two too many, although there is no special cast-iron rule about it (*cf.* III xiii 6). But it is in his use of adverbs that the student's diction perhaps shows up at its worst. Not only are there too many of them all told (a natural consequence of too little Balanced Decoration), but the presence of two in verse 12, one of which is a final word, is quite indefensible. It is only fair to say that *ergo* has a perfectly respectable Alcaic precedent in *ergo obligatam* . . . . (II vii 17).

The following poem by William Blake (1757–1827) lends itself much more naturally than the Herrick to an Alcaic rendering. No doubt its musico-poetic strain would have appealed to Horace himself; but there is more to it than that. For the English conveniently furnishes the modern composer with a ready-made set of *sive . . . . seu's* and a non-stop sentence chain. Thanks to these things, the problem of periodizing and stopping almost settle themselves; and (with slight compression) the Latin stanzas can be made to tally with the English ones in such a way that a fair amount of enjambment of stanzas is still possible.

> Whether on Ida's shady brow
>   Or in the chambers of the East,
> The chambers of the Sun, that now
>   From ancient melody have ceased;
>
> Whether in heaven ye wander fair,
>   Or the green corners of the earth,
> Or the blue regions of the air
>   Where the melodious winds have birth;
>
> Whether on crystal rocks ye rove,
>   Beneath the bosom of the sea,
> Wandering in many a coral grove;
>   Fair Nine, forsaking Poetry,
>
> How have you left the ancient love
>   That bards of old enjoy'd in you!
> The languid strings do scarcely move,
>   The sound is forced, the notes are few.

We attempt an Alcaic version as follows :

> Ides opacae seu iuga visitis,
> Eoa Phoebi sive palatia
>   iam muta, quae pridem solebant
>   Aeolio resonare cantu;
>
> sive in reducta valle vagamini;
> seu templa, Musae, caerulei placet
>   tentare caeli, seu canoros
>   aeriis domibus Favoni

urgere flatus; seu vitreas maris
rupes in imo, Pieriae, sinu
    centumque lustratis, venustae,
      coralii nemorosa tecta,

priscam quid artem spernitis et lyram?
iam chorda parcis languet iners modis,
    nec reddit amissos poetae
      vix docili numeros Apollo.

Comment:

(*Reducta valle*, *cf.* I xvii 17). The student should note how the composer has managed to vary the syllabic sequences of most of the verses: in fact, no two successive sequences in the first two verses of any stanza are exactly identical. Verse 14, it is hoped, sounds as laborious as the thought it expresses. Again, although the last couplet hardly translates the literal words of the English, it is offered without apology as another picturesque turn to bring the version to a satisfactory conclusion.

Good Horatian ode composing aims at something better than a mere prose translation correctly metrified.

Provided that the original itself reasonably reflects something of the Horatian spirit, a Latin ode based on it must do nothing to kill that spirit as it can so easily be killed by wooden and unenterprising treatment. *Ingenium* as well as *ars* has its part to play in preserving it.

This raises the question how far the composer is justified in departing from the literal text of his original when the chance offers of an imaginative stroke that is not explicitly present in the text of his working material. Much of course depends on the mood of the material in hand at any time and on personal taste. It is also a question of degree. On the whole it is probably better to lean towards a liberal view in a Latin rendering and not to stifle an impulse towards a brief poetic flight that helps to express the basic sense more vividly. For there can be a prosiness of thought to be avoided as well as prosiness of diction. Not that ordinary words are always unfit for poetry: both Horace and Virgil use them freely, as we have seen. The test, rather, is this: provided they are not too unmusical in sound, does the effect of their use by the composer go towards conjuring up a lively picture or image that would otherwise have been absent?

Whatever the composer's approach to the problem of working to a given material, one thing is certain: any highlights conspicuous in the original must on no account be extinguished, but should somehow be reproduced in the Latin version. These highlights can often be compassed by a single Latin word. To give a very simple illustration from the Herrick lyric "To Maidens" we have just considered: the line, "the sooner will his race be run", plainly calls for some Latin hint or suggestion of the race-course itself. *Meta* would do this, but the more technical *calx* would be better still.[1] A word like *cursus* is rather too neutral and colourless to be given house-room in such a context, where every word should contribute to the picture.

By the same token a little ingenuity can sometimes make Proper Names, especially adjectives, represent general or abstract propositions in the original. Several examples will be found in the home-made odes or portions of the ode here discussed, and also of course in chapter V. The reason why this device can be very effective is that the Proper Name itself would have its own special associations for the Augustan reader or listener. Anyhow, these names in Horatian verse always add pleasing ornament to the diction. They give "a local habitation and a name" to indefinite things, as Page

---

[1] The goal or winning-post of a Roman race-course was marked out by chalk or limestone; so in a figurative sense *calx* = goal or limit in general, (*Cf. ad calcem pervenire* — Cicero, *Laelius*, 27. 101.)

well says, which is all very much in line with Horace's own practice, and therefore to be imitated by the modern composer.

Imagination and enterprise should be at work in other ways too. What might be called Horace's specialities are not to be neglected, and some of them should be given an occasional airing — for example, "Greek" genitives; infinitives (prolative or epexegetic); sentences constructed ἀπὸ κοινοῦ; neuter singular adjectives used adverbially; and of course the rhetorical figures, hypallage, hendiadys, metonymy and so on.

Walter Savage Landor's *Resignation* provides suitable material for a Sapphic setting:

> Why, why repine, my pensive friend,
>   At pleasures slipp'd away?
> Some the stern Fates will never lend,
>   And all refuse to stay.
>
> I see the rainbow in the sky,
>   The dew upon the grass;
> I see them, and I ask not why
>   They glimmer or they pass;
>
> With folded arms I linger not
>   To call them back; 'twere vain:
> In this or in some other spot
>   I know they'll shine again.

The following version again attempts (mainly) unbroken weaving of sentences within its Latin stanzas. The principal feature here illustrated is the Anaphora, too often neglected by modern Horatian composers in favour of the conjunctions which come so easily to mind.

> Quid gemis sublapsa tibi quod absint
> gaudia, Antoni? dare certa nobis
> denegant, mox et revocant iniquae
>   cetera Parcae.

intuens arcus pluvii colores,
intuens rores liquidos in herba
luceant cur aut abeant rogare
non ego curo.

non meum tristi residere voltu,
non meum vanis revocare votis
illa, quae certe Pater huc vel illuc
clara rependet.

Sublapsa (Virgil's *sublapsa spes*, *A.* ii 169) is exactly
"slipped away". For *dare denegant, cf.* III xvi 38. Note the
rhymed vertical Concord in 3–4, and the horizontal Concords in vv. 9 and 10. The metrical correspondence of
verses 9 and 10 is deliberate so as to obtain emphasis : *illa,*
sc. *gaudia.*

In the poets *cur* may follow the first word or two of a
clause or sentence *metri gratia.* Of this licence *Sat.* II vii 104
offers perhaps an extreme example. Here *cur micent* might
be read for *luceant cur,* but the meaning of *micare* in relation
to the static colours of the rainbow is distinctly unhappy. For
non meum ("it is not my way") plus infinitive, *cf.* III xxix 57.

The art of the Horatian composer, and we cannot remind
ourselves often enough of it, should constantly be directed
towards making little concrete pictures. In aid of this aim
the accommodation of sound to sense should not be overlooked, whether by direct onomatopoeia or otherwise. Here
Wilkinson's *Golden Latin Artistry* provides an invaluable
guide, and may be consulted by the student composer with
advantage.[1]

Something on these lines might be made of the opening
of Cardinal J. H. Newman's best-known hymn, "Lead,
Kindly Light", which is not unsuitable for rendering into

[1] For onomatopoeia, alliteration, and assonance, see also his *Horace and his
Lyric Poetry*, pp. 137 ff.; Kiessling/Heinze on I ii 1 f. and *Einl.* to I xxxvi.

Latin Sapphic verse, although it does not so readily admit
of the introduction of pagan names.

> Lead, Kindly Light, amid the encircling gloom,
>> Lead thou me on;
> The night is dark and I am far from home,
>> Lead thou me on.

No doubt the gloom of a very dark night would best be
suggested by a plethora of *u*-sounds; but unless these
could be worked in on a noticeable scale the effect would not
be worth any distortion of the English that might be
involved. The next best thing (and certainly easier to handle
here) would be the use of sibilants. With Horace, as indeed
with most Greek and Latin poets, the letter *s* is of course
traditionally associated with strong emotions of horror or
sometimes hatred. So perhaps it would not be too much to
begin our ode with something like:

> Noctis, heu, spissis ego cinctus umbris
> iam domo longe vagor.

What sort of picture does the rest of the English in the
first four verses conjure up? If it were not for the wanderer's
prayer for light to guide his open but unseeing eyes, one
might be tempted towards the picture of a permanently
blind man tapping his way along an unfamiliar road. But
the artist does not always have to state an idea fully and in
so many words. A deft hint is often enough, especially
where (as here) an explicit statement might lead on to a
rational inconsistency. We could therefore conclude the
stanza with:

> o Supreme,
> tu pedes tentantis iter benigna
> dirige luce,

and leave it to the reader to find in the repeated dentals (and
weak caesura) a hint of the tap-tap of the groper's stick.
Notice the apt contrast between *ego* and *tu* as well.

Just as sibilants and dentals contributed to this version, so the letter *o* can sometimes be exploited to help out a context of grief and woe. A useful illustration of this is seen in the author's Fifth Asclepiad version of the Swinyard lament on the death of the Irish musician, Moeran.

Ad Moeranum	*In Memoriam E. J. Moeran*
Heu, Moerane, iacet fracta fides tua et	Though thy harp-strings be severed
haesit perpetuo lingua silentio,	And muted thy tongue,
Neptunoque sepultum	Though the roar of the waters
cessit raucisono melos.	Has silenced thy song,
atqui vivit idem, vivit imagine	Yet its echo still lingers
dilectae resona per iuga Hiberniae,	Upon the sweet air,
saltus per recreatos	Blowing soft o'er the valleys
aurae lenibus osculis.	And hills of Kenmare.
dum stellarum hilari rite sonant chori	When the stars sing together
carmen dulce suum, mystica dum Chelys	The sweet song of joy,
exauditur ab alto,	And the sound of the Clarsach
regnorum incola caelitum,	Is heard in the sky,
connectet numeros Melpomene tuos	Thy music shall blend
Euterpeque comes grandius in melos,	In the mystic refrain,
vates quod tibi reddent	And the minstrels of Erin
terrena patrii lyra.	Shall echo the strain.

LAURENCE SWINYARD
(By kind permission of Novello & Co. Ltd.)

Notice the appearance of *o* in the Concord of verse 2 — the most effective position possible:

    haesit perpetu*o* lingua silenti*o*.

And the funeral bell goes on tolling:

    Neptun*o*que sepultum
      cessit raucison*o* melos.

The ode also shows Anaphora (*vivit . . . . vivit . . . ., dum . . . dum . . .*); Balanced Decoration on a large scale; and Horatian stopping.

The presence of moving water is often represented in Greek and Latin poets (Horace included) by repeated use of the letter *l*. Suppose then we had reached the final stanza of a Sapphic version of Lear's *The Owl and the Pussy-Cat*:

> And hand in hand, on the edge of the sand,
> They danced by the light of the moon . . . . . .

The breaking waves would be only a few yards away from the dancing couple, and so we could appropriately suggest as much by the following:

> . . . . . . ubi *l*itus aestus
> a*ll*uit, sa*l*tant hi*l*ari sub a*l*mae
> *l*umine *l*unae.[1]

These illustrate only a few of the "varieties of expressive technique", as Wilkinson calls them, that are open to the composer anxious to improve the formal qualities of his verse in the Horatian manner. For others, the composer should consult *Golden Latin Artistry*, chapter 3 *passim*.

Now let the composer imagine himself rendering the famous passage from Sir Walter Scott's *Lay of the Last Minstrel* beginning: "Breathes there a man with soul so dead . . .". This is eminently Horatian, and for the rendering of it any metre but the Alcaic would be almost unthinkable. A Latin version should therefore exhibit plenty of enjambment, both of verses and stanzas; and the "rolling river" effect to be aimed at would gain if a touch of Anaphora could be worked in as well.

At the words:

> High though his titles, proud his name,
> Boundless his wealth as wish can claim,

the opportunity offers of a stanza that illustrates one or two Horatian features in a very compact form:

---

[1] For the complete version see *G & R* xi 1964 82–3. In the same way, in verse 3 of the third stanza the composer tries to suggest the strumming of the Owl's guitar by a string of *-m's*: du*m* *m*ovet plectru*m* *m*ihi . . .

> illi sit alti purpura consulis,
> illi supersit maior Achaemene
> thesaurus, illi stirps Etrusca
> signet avos atavosque reges.

Besides concrete nouns for abstractions and Proper Names representing general types, we have here the double repetition of *illi* as first word in each clause, a *comparatio compendiaria* (as in II vi 14 and III vi 46), and an example of Horace's *tricolon* construction with the last limb slightly greater in length than the other two. The order in which Scott names the worldly advantages of the "man with soul so dead" is not followed strictly, and on this account the version is perhaps open to some criticism. But we are more concerned here with displaying the features just mentioned than in attempting any model version of this passage for its own sake.

Finally we might wind up with a rhetorical flourish :

> secum ipse vivens, frigidus in suos
> fratres, honorem scilicet aureum
> nomenque deperdit Quiritis
> nobile mox geminam daturus
>
> poenam sepulchri, cum cadet improbus
> in pulverem ex quo duxit originem,
> cum laus omittentur memorque
> nenia funereique luctus.
>
> The wretch, concentred all in self,
> Living shall forfeit fair renown,
> And, doubly dying, shall go down
> To the vile dust, from whence he sprung,
> Unwept, unhonoured and unsung.

In his own special field the modern composer of Latin verse in Horatian metres must often ask and answer for himself the question : "Am I content for my ode to play second

fiddle to the original in a more or less literal rendering?"
(This of course is the essence of the First Method.) If in
some extreme cases the answer is "no", then one of two
courses is open to him. Either the thing should be rejected
wholly or in part as working material for an ode, as Sir
Robert Tate's critics in this sort of situation suggest,[1] or
else the "impossible" passages should be drastically recast
so as to make the general setting one that the ancient
Greeks or Romans *could have* recognised as familiar. A
third possibility might be to prepare one's ode on an
awkward theme by an introductory stanza (not in the original) to explain that what followed was sheer fantasy or
fooling, as the case might be, and that the Augustan reader
was not expected to take it too seriously. This was done by
the compiler of chapter V (The Anthology) in his Sapphic
version, mentioned above, of Lear's *The Owl and the Pussy-
Cat*:

> Poscitis carmen, pueri et puellae,
> non grave et simplex? memoret iocose
> nostra portentum * lyra fabulamque
> non sine nugis.   *="tall story"

---

[1] *Cf.* p. xviii of the Introduction to Tate's *Carmina Dublinensia* (1945):
"My own rendering of (Newbolt's) 'There's a breathless hush in the
Close to-night' has been criticized . . . as an effort to translate into Latin
a passage which no one should ever have attempted. But is it beyond the
bounds of possibility that, had the Romans been familiar with cricket,
Gatling-guns, and the idea of 'playing the game', they would have ex-
pressed themselves in terms bearing some resemblance to those I suggest?"
   Another example of simple English that, nevertheless, must be aban-
doned in a Latin version is the last stanza of Samuel Rogers' "A Wish" in
The Golden Treasury:
     The village church among the trees,
     Where first our marriage vows were given,
     With merry peal shall swell the breeze
     And point with taper spire to heaven.
In substance this is quite as "impossible" as Newbolt's cricket crisis,
Gatling jammed *etc.* It could only be perpetrated by the First Method,
and would be utterly meaningless to a Roman of Horace's day.

Under cover of such a perfectly Horatian opening the author was able (without serious literary impropriety) to make his "Horace" say things that lay far outside the normal Augustan range.

But whatever course be adopted in these cases on no account may the crib be relied on to help out a Latin version that is deficient or not self-sufficient in sense without its aid.

As we have already noted, good Horatian ode writing should exhibit something of Horace's own continuity and flow of diction. An excessive amount of strong stopping in the wrong places is a sure sign that the composer has allowed his working material to dictate the cast of his Latin sentences too rigorously and exactly. We have examined some of the tools Horace himself uses to secure this continuity; and so even when we have the additional burden of composing to a fixed text, we ought to borrow from the master's workshop whatever tools we find serviceable to the same end. For instance, imagine we were tackling (in Sapphics) the first stanza of William Cowper's well known church hymn, "God moves in a mysterious way", which is not unsuitable for Sapphic or Alcaic rendering provided we address it, as Horace would have done, to a friend with the object of dispelling doubts about the purpose behind the Universe. It is more a philosophical ode than a hymn in the true sense, indeed rather like I xxxiv.

> God moves in a mysterious way
>   His wonders to perform;
> He plants His footsteps in the sea,
>   And rides upon the storm.
>
> Deep in unfathomable mines
>   Of never-failing skill
> He treasures up His bright designs
>   And works His sovereign will.

> Ye fearful saints, fresh courage take;
> The clouds ye so much dread
> Are big with mercy, and shall break
> In blessings on your head.
>
> Judge not the Lord by feeble sense,
> But trust Him for His grace;
> Behind a frowning providence
> He hides a smiling face.
>
> Blind unbelief is sure to err
> And scan His work in vain;
> God is His own interpreter
> And He will make it plain.

There would be nothing basically wrong about a literal Latin rendering here, with the first stanza divided into two main parts and a stop at the end of verse 2 as in the English. But as likely as not our stanza would get what we have called a "square-cut" look; and that look Horace himself in large measure goes out of his way to avoid. By telescoping everything into one sentence helped out by Horace's favourite *sive . . . sive . . .* (or *seu . . . . -ve* as in IV ii 21) we hit the centre of Cowper's sense nearly enough for all practical purposes, while bringing the stanza more closely into line with Horace's typical "continuous" Sapphic formation:

> Abditis miranda Pater laborat
> motibus, Delli, mare seu quietum
> calcat insanove Notos refrenat
> turbine vectus.

This version has no special merit otherwise. But notice the prominent position of *abditis*; the weak caesuras; the naming of a definite wind known for its turbulence; and — not least — the "equestrian" touch of *refrenat* and *vectus* taking up the hint thrown out by Cowper's splendid verse 4 "And rides upon the storm".

A complete version follows, with slight changes in the first two verses for variety's sake, both in diction and stopping:

Ad Torquatum

Abditis, Torquate, viis patravit
res Pater miras: mare seu quietum
calcat insanove Notos refrenat
    turbine vectus,

daedalisve alte sub humo cavernis
consili formas animique condit,
sic sibi morem gerit ipse nutu
    cuncta movente.

cornua ignavo, comes, addat idem,
si tremis: nubes tibi nunc minaces
mille te donis gravidae beabunt
    imbre sereno.

iudicare audes animo minore
numen aeternum? bene providenti
fide, sub frontis specie benigno
    fide severae.

impia quisquis Ratione caecus
spectat immensum reputatque mundum,
fallitur: iam se Deus explicabit
    et sua solus.

Note the attempt to make abstractions in the English concrete by drawing on Latin figures in verses 9, 10, 12 and 11 (where *gravidae* hints at the pregnancy trope, itself hinted at in Cowper's "big with mercy"). In verse 12 *imbre* is implied by Cowper's "break ... on your head". *Iam* in 19 has Horace's special sense of "presently", "soon".

Sometimes, despite all his ingenuity, a composer will find that a small but important element in his working material persists in sticking out and refusing to be accommodated *at the right place* in his Latin version. It is useful to remember that the problem can often be got round by bringing this refractory element into his ode at a later, or even earlier, stage than that strictly indicated by the English (or other) material.

As we have seen, original material will often have to be kneaded by paraphrase into a suitable paste, as it were, before a Horatian-type ode can be recognisably made of it. Yet the composer, if he is an artist, will take care not to overdo this paraphrasing either in depth or extent beyond the minimum necessary. Too much of a good thing can be as inept as too little. In fact, he will always try to preserve the force and flavour of any dominant figure of speech or metaphor in the original,[1] so long as a literal transfer to Latin does no violence either to Latin (especially Horatian) idiom, or (what is no less important) to essential Latin or Greek modes of thought.[2] This carry-over can sometimes be done very neatly and effectively in Horatian composing by dint of *a single Latin word fraught with the right associations*; just as the same principle *in reverse* can be seen at work by imagining an enlightened vernacular version of the Odes to be one's working material. Thus, for example, suppose we had to deal in Sapphics with an English extract that ran:

> Why do we aim so high when time must foil our
> Brave archery?

No artist-Latinist would want to pulp the toxophilite here out of existence by excessive paraphrase. In fact this English is part of James Michie's[3] admirable rendering of

---

[1] *Cf.* the perverse "lead-from-gold" alchemizing on pp. 102-3.

[2] *Cf.* Tate's elegiac rendering of the Newbolt poem referred to on p. 120 n.1.

[3] The Odes of Horace, trans. by James Michie (1964), Rupert Hart-Davis, London.

the fifth stanza of II xvi, and the Latin is of course Horace's own :

> quid brevi fortes iaculamur aevo
> multa?

Notice how the single word *iaculamur* throws up all that is needed for Michie to carry over and develop a little further the missile metaphor Horace himself clearly has in mind.

So in the last stanza of his Alcaic version of Tennyson's *Vision of Sin*, the author makes picturesque use of Horace's own word *Lamia* (vampire) in apposition :

> Let her go! her thirst she slakes
> Where the bloody conduit runs:
> Then her sweetest meal she makes
> Of the first-born of her sons.

> i quo rubentes arida per vias
> sedes cruentis fluminibus sitim!
> mox pascet[1] oblectante suco
>   te Lamiam tua prima proles.

⁋ More than once in this book the modern composer of Horatian lyric verse has been urged to make the diction of his stanzas *follow through* as continuously as possible, with a minimum of stopping to interrupt the flow. Care in this respect is particularly necessary where it is proposed to couple two or more sentences by *et*, *-que* or *ac* (*atque*). When this has been done, the composer should try to *retain one and the same subject for the verbs of all the coupled* sentences, if possible. Two examples from the many available will be enough to illustrate Horace's own general practice :

> doceri gaudet . . . virgo *et* fingitur . . . iam
> nunc *et* . . . meditatur,   III vi 21–4;
> Telephum . . . occupavit . . . puella . . . tenet*que*
> . . . . vinctum,   IV xi 21–4.

---

[1] *Cf.* III xxvii 56.

This is not to say that Horace invariably sticks to this rule himself. Sometimes he does switch to a second subject for the second coupled sentence. But in such cases there is a more or less close sense-affinity between the first and second subject as in:

> Nox erat *et* caelo fulgebat luna sereno,
>
> Epode xv 1;

or in:

> tum meae . . . vocis accedet bona pars *et* . . . .
>
> canam,   IV ii 45–7;

where the two subjects are so aptly welded together that we are hardly conscious of the join in the permanent way. What is not so good in the student's Latin verse is the equivalent of something like Samuel Foote's (1720–77) familiar :[1]

> So he died, *and* she very imprudently married the barber,

where there is not only a violent change of subject but an inconsequent switching of the sense. Could an *et* or *-que* properly perform the function of this English "and"? It is impossible to say that such a usage would be entirely foreign to the Horace of the Odes, where, for instance, we find:

> nec tibi somnos adimunt, amat*que*
>
> ianua limen,   I xxv 3–4.

Sometimes, too, *et* with Horace almost means "and so" or "and then", as at IV iii 16, with an adverbial rather than conjunctional sense. In such cases most editors mark off the first clause by inserting a comma at the word preceding *et* or *-que*. However, when all is said, when all allowances are made for exceptions or variations, continuity in his diction still remains the right thing for the student composer to aim at.

¶ In aid of such continuity what may be called the "double negative turn" is a useful device, and it will often help the

---

[1] *Nonsense written as a Memory Test.*

modern composer out of a metrical fix as well : it also has the advantage of being part of the master's idiomatic stock-in-trade. It commonly takes the form of *nec* or *non* followed by a verb expressing the converse of the wanted affirmative sense. Thus, for example, *nec parcis obiurgare amicos* would be good Horace for "And you are pretty free with your scolding of friends". Sometimes in the Odes this hardens into a regular litotes, *e.g.*, at I xxviii 14, where *non sordidus auctor* conveys exactly the force of St. Paul's "no mean (city)". Horace indeed is characteristically fond of these understatements, even when he waxes enthusiastic : no warmer tribute in three words could he pay to Cleopatra than by calling her *non humilis mulier*. Also, quite simply, *non* can be tacked on to an adjective to reverse its meaning without necessarily hinting at any meiosis : *non gravis* can mean just "light". More subtly, Horace uses *male* at times for a some-what similar purpose. But the student composer must take care to distinguish here. *Male* + adjective having a "bad" sense intensifies that bad sense : with adjective having a "good" sense, *male* weakens it. *Non sine* + ablative is another very common Horatian turn, as is also *nihil* (*nil*) *praeter* + accusative to express "only". Hissing superlative adjectives of the *-issimus* kind must not be used by the student composer ; but he can often avoid these by *non* + a comparative adjective. Thus, *non gratiori advenae* would properly be translated "to the most welcome of visitors".

One particular caveat may also be noted here. The composer should not resort to the un-Horatian expedient of "dashes" to help out his meaning, except within the very narrow limits already indicated for Horatian parentheses. The habit of suddenly foisting in clauses with "dashes" often disfigures the "Horatian" verses of our Victorian elders. Occasionally permissible, parentheses should be introduced by *nam* or *enim* and should be properly developed so as really to say something. Otherwise, "dashes" should be confined to short interjections, *e.g.*, *credite posteri*, or *heu nefas, heu*, that hardly interfere with the general flow at all. ¶Anaphora of *non*, *nec*, *sive*, *seu* is, as we have said, a favourite device of Horace: in I xvi, for example, we find *sive . . . sive*, *non . . . non . . . non . . . non . . .*, *neque . . . nec . . .nec . . . nec*; in I xxxi *non* is repeated four times, and in IV ii *seu . . . seu . . . sive*. Repeated pronouns, especially *tu* and *te*, are frequently found, as in I x. A good example of repeated *non* is found in I xvi 5–8 :

> non Dindymene, non adytis quatit
> mentem sacerdotum incola Pythius,
> non Liber aeque, non acuta
> sic geminant Corybantes aera.

He uses it freely in all his Aeolic metrical forms. Sometimes in Alcaics he develops it quite elaborately, *e.g.*, in III iii 9–15, we find *hac (arte) . . . hac . . . hac* spread over two stanzas. In III iii 65–7 *ter* occurs three times, as does *dura* in II xiii 27–8. Normally he makes one repetition of the key word. For his own part, the student-composer will of course not be slow to follow suit when he gets the chance, whether in Alcaics, Sapphics, Asclepiads or any other metre. It is not vital that the word or words concerned should be repeated in exactly the same form every time; but it is better that it, or they, should stand first in the succeeding clause or clauses. The great advantage of Anaphora is that it can often be made to do the work of a coupling conjunction, while improving the flow and polish of the diction and at the same time increasing the emotional tension.

Gemination occurs in eight cases, and is worthy of occasional imitation by the modern composer in suitable contexts. For example, an Alcaic version of the Herrick quoted earlier might begin not inelegantly :

Rosas recentes carpite carpite,
donec, puellae, vos patitur dies
festina, donec flos renidet
cras hodie moriturus idem.

Postume, Postume	II	xiv	1,
ibimus, ibimus		xvii	10,
iam iam		xx	9,
Ilion, Ilion	III	iii	18,
hic, hic		xxvi	6,
precor, precor	IV	i	2,
occidit, occidit		iv	70,
illius, illius		xiii	18.

How to make specific Proper Names do duty for general
types is well illustrated by C. S. Calverley's Third Asclepiad
version of a little exchange between the poet Herrick and
Amaryllis.[1] Herrick ("Horace") has the final word :

> Let country wenches make 'em fine
>   With posies; since 'tis fitter
> For thee with richest jemmes to shine
>   And like the stars to glitter.

> Certet rustica Phidyle
> se iactare rosis: te decorarier
> gemmis rectius Indiae
> et lucere parem sideris aurei.

Rustica Phidyle of course hits off "country wenches"
admirably; and Calverley rightly, too, localises those
"richest jemmes" as oriental. Otherwise the stanza has no
unusual significance for the student composer's observation.
Balanced Decoration would perhaps have been better served
by reading *Indicis* for *Indiae* ; and in verse 4 a repeated *te* by
Anaphora would have got rid of the interlinear hiatus,
besides emphasising again the contrast with *rustica Phidyle*.

---

[1] *Arundines Cami*, 6th ed., pp. 28–9.

An alternative rendering of verse 4, if slightly more pedestrian, might be:

> te lucere velut sidereum iubar.

Herrick says nothing about gold in relation to the lady's starry brilliance; and so even a figurative *aurei* is probably better left out of the picture altogether.

Bad stopping in Sapphics is illustrated by the Rev. H. E. D. Blakiston's version of Sir Philip Sidney's 31st sonnet, where the composer has:

> acer intendat puer ille: *namque* . . . (fresh sentence).[1]

So too William Johnson in his rendering of Wordsworth's *Restoration of Clifford* has:

> i, feri Parthos, sonat hasta: *Gallos* . . . (fresh sentence).[2]

In each case the colon is the composer's own punctuation.

In Alcaics it is the third verse of the stanza that from time to time seems to trouble modern composers; and various deviations from normal Horatian usage in the matter of prosody, syllabic quantities or distribution quite commonly occur, *e.g.*,

> per aetheris longos meatus,
> fundens humo de nigricanti,
> tot comparet caeca misellis,
> queis cuncta sternuntur, tenacis,
> fractaeque spirantes ad auras.[3]

And a fourth verse of which the first two feet exhibit diaeresis is also not to be imitated. In fact there is only one

---

1   *Nova Anthologia Oxoniensis*. Oxford Clarendon Press 1899, pp. 86–7.

2   *Arundines Cami*, 6th ed., pp. 200–1.

3   All selected from a new *Aetna* published in *Latinitas*, iii. ap. 1956. Note further that a short final vowel may not remain short before initial *sc-*, *sp-*, *squ-*, or *st-*, nor may it be lengthened. The position is avoided by the Augustan poets with two exceptions in the *Satires* and one in the *Aeneid*.
    Further, the form *queis* is not found in the Odes, with the possible exception of I xxvi 3, where it is better taken as a Nominative.

such in the whole of the Odes (III iii 64) ; which means that a verse such as the following :

vivite, cui velit ipsa, credo,[1]

from E. R. Wharton's Alcaic version of Milton's "O'er the smooth enamelled green" is, strictly, without prosodical parallel in Horace.

In preparing this revised edition we have been greatly helped by the generosity of Messrs. J. T. Christie[2] and A. G. Lee,[3] who have been willing to join in this Demonstration.

Mr Christie tackles a version of the following :

> May the ambitious ever find
>> Reward in crowds and noise,
> Whilst gentle love does fill my mind
>> With silent real joys.

> May fools and knaves grow rich and great,
>> And the world think 'em wise,
> Whilst I lie dying at her feet,
>> And all that world despise.

> Let conquering kings new trophies raise
>> And melt in court delights:
> Her eyes shall give me brighter days,
>> Her arms much softer nights.

He writes as follows :

'The brevity of the lines suggests Sapphics which Horace uses mostly for odes of personal friendship or advice but occasionally for a light love lyric (I xx and xxx). If more elbow-room is needed, one might try the Fourth Asclepiad which Horace employs for a *recusatio*, on the theme of "give

---

1 *Nova Anthologia Oxoniensis*. Oxford Clarendon Press 1899, pp. 182–3.

2 Formerly Principal of Jesus College, Oxford.

3 Fellow of St. John's College, Cambridge.

to me the life I love; I leave it to others to be great public figures (I vi, II xii)." But let us try it in Sapphics. *Stanza* 1. Suppose we address a friend:

> Praemium, Lolli, studiose famae
> sit tibi turbae favor obstrepentis.

Better *adstrepentis*, since the crowd is presumably appreciative. But we are over-translating. No suggestion that our poet is writing to an ambitious man. Keep it impersonal. Ambitious — *cupidi honoris* (or, politically, *honorum*).

> Praemium . . . . . . cupidis honorum
> turba plaudentum strepitusque vulgi.

We need a verb, and writing *praemia accedant* we get a possible opening; and the personal name is not essential.

"Whilst gentle love" etc.: *dum* is quite possible, but better a separate sentence with asyndeton. *Sed* or *tamen* would only weaken it. I write first

> me Venus mulcet tacitique vera
> gaudia amoris.

Better separate *vera* from *gaudia*, and how about the elision in the short line? Only once in the whole of the Odes (II xvi 8). We must think again. End with *gaudia mulcent*.

> me . . . . . veri taciturna amoris
> gaudia mulcent,

and we can begin *cor meum*.

Stanza 2. "Fools and knaves", *stulti* is the obvious word, and *vafri* is perhaps the nearest to "knaves". Could we address them, in singular or plural? Latin is more rhetorical than English, "Pile up your riches, you fool and you knave."

> stulte congestis opibus vaferque.

(But *vaferque* is not happy, suggesting the same man is both a fool and a knave). "Go on, be a V.I.P.: *i, potens esto, vafer*". Vigorous, and may be better in the first line. "Rich" — Horace's favourite word (sometimes ironical if rich and prosperous) is *beatus*: *et beatus*, but better repeat *i*.

Suppose we begin :

> i potens esto vafer, i beatum,
> stulte, te iacta.

But we shall need at least the last two lines in Latin for the last two of the English. Can we manage in half a line "and the world think 'em wise?" Forget "the world". It only means "be thought wise". *Sapiens vocare* or *voceris*. Possibly, but much better *sapiens et audi* — "be called a wise man" : *et* is often found second word in the sentence.

"Whilst I lie dying" etc. "All that" suggests the contemptuous *ista* : *? ista dum sperno*. "Her" : we shall need *puellae* or a proper name. "At her feet" : *ad pedes* ; not helpful. Give the sense : "to me while I faint at her feet all that world and its regards are as nothing". We may end *praemia sordent. Ista dum languens iaceo*? Too long. Let us save space with *languenti. Ista, languenti . . . . . . puellas.* If *pedes* is unmanageable and *pedibus* impossible, why not *genua ad puellae*?

Always keep an eye open for any Sapphic beginning with a vowel unless it is the first in the stanza. If it begins with a vowel, the preceding line must not end with a short open vowel. But Horace in more than a dozen places allows a hiatus if the preceding line ends with a long open vowel, so the hiatus between *audi* and *ista* is legitimate.

Stanza 3. Bracchia noctes seems an obvious ending, preceded by *mihi molliores*. But then *clariores* would be impossibly ugly, and we must say *magis claros* (beginners, beware of *plus claros* !). Suppose we write :

> dant dies claros mihi molliores

and write in the line before, *magis ora Pyrrhae*. So far, so good, but can we get the sense of the first half of the stanza into 1½ lines? We shall have to abridge : *Rex ovet victis* no ; better *victor*, in his hour of triumph and let it be his pleasure to melt etc., perhaps *libeatque luxu regio mergi*, or possibly

Persico solvi. Possible, but neither verb is quite right. I remember a phrase from Terence, on whom I lecture, *lascivia diffluo,* and the verb is used several times by Cicero; so let us write *diffluat luxu,* and we can render "court" more literally with an epithet to show the kind of court you have in mind:

> Rex ovet victor nitidave in aula
> diffluat luxu.

No doubt this version could be improved, but on the way one has learnt some good Latin, unlearnt some bad Latin, and perhaps re-read some Horace with a careful eye. Now if we wished, we should find it easier to produce a version in another metre, *e.g.,* Fourth Asclepiad.

I append the complete version in Sapphics, and another in the Asclepiad metre'.

> Praemia accedant cupidis honorum
> turba plaudentum strepitusque vulgi:
> cor meum veri taciturna amoris
> gaudia mulcent.

> i potens esto, vafer; i beatum,
> stulte, te iacta, sapiens et audi.
> ista, languenti genua ad puellae,
> praemia sordent.

> rex ovet victor nitidave in aula
> diffluat luxu; magis ora Pyrrhae
> dant dies claros mihi, molliores
> bracchia noctes.

*   *   *   *   *

> Sit merces cupidis laudis et imperi
> turbarum strepitus rauca frementium,
> me mansueta Venus sollicitat tacens,
> veri nuntia gaudii.

> auge divitias, stulte; potentiam
> nactus cresce, vafer, scitus ut audias;
> sordent ista mihi praemia, dum Lyces
> languens ad genua occido.
>
> i rex victor ova, clarus adorea;[1]
> aulae luxurie difflue. clarior
> lux ridente Lyce, mollior est mihi
> nox amplexibus in Lyces.

* * * * *

Mr A. G. Lee writes: "Instead of talking about the method of translation etc. it seemed to me best to show the gradual growth of the thing through a series of draft versions. These draft versions can conveniently be represented by a composite collection of them", and he contributes the following:

"OCCLUDED.

> Chilled is the air with fallen rain,
> Flood-deep the river flows;
> A sullen gloom daunts heart and brain,
> And no light shows.

> Yet, in a mind as dark, a hint may steal
> Of what lies hidden from an earth bound eye,
> Beyond the clouds the stars in splendour wheel,
> The Virgin huntress horns the silent sky.[2]

> Vix ripae fluvium premunt,
> suffriget pluviis aura recentibus,
> lux occluditur omnis et
> nigror pectoribus tristitiam incutit.
> at mentem subit augurem
> visum terrigenam quae species latet —
> stellarum ordo nitentium
> venatrixque regens cornibus aethera.

---

1 *Cf.* IV iv 41.
2 From Walter de la Mare, *Inward Companion*, Faber, London 1950.

The above version emerged from a series of drafts, represented by the variants below. In the stage before this it was sent to friends and benefited from their criticisms. At this stage the translator would have preferred to put it aside in order to reconsider it when he had forgotten all about it.

Ripas flumina subruunt
aequant flumina margines
iam ripas fluvio labant
vix amnem capit alveus

friget de pluviis aura recentibus
iam friget pluviis aura recentibus

lux occluditur omnis et

mortales animos umbra supervenit
mortales animos tristis obit nigror
caligant animi tristitia mei
caligant animi sollicitudine
infert pectoribus tristitiam nigror

praesagit tamen anxius
sentit caeca tamen polum

quod terrenam aciem delituit iubar
quod caeleste aciem terrigenam latet
mens qui visum oculi terrigenae latet

nubes astra rotant super
qua stellae quatiunt faces
stellarum agmina prodeunt
splendentum agmina siderum

venatorque agitat signa silentia
venatrixque gerit Cynthia cornua
venatrixque regit cornibus aethera
venatrixque regens nubila cornibus."

This is as far as most modern composers go, but Horace went further and could provide a musical setting and accompaniment. This musical aspect was one of the principal themes of the original edition of this book. In the interval between these editions the author's lead has been followed notably by A. Bonnafé of Tananarive, who has trained a choir to sing odes of Horace to tunes which he himself composed[1] and finally has recorded his reconstructions of Horatian odes with a musical accompaniment.[2]

We conclude this chapter with a set of exercises for the student's benefit. These consist of Sapphic, Alcaic and Asclepiad stanzas, or portions of stanzas, which the student is invited to scrutinise for possible defects or errors in form or prosody. The keys will be found on pp. 140-143.

Sapphic Exercises.

1 Caecubum nunc promere, Agrippa, prodest.

2 Nam fides multum est pretiosior quam
    dona quae nobis tribuunt iniquae
        optima Parcae.

3 Cur tuo me laedis, amice, questu
    quod relinquat te miserum Neaera?

4 Arte mira dux aciem in feroces
    dirigit Parthos, et acuta spernit
        pila cohortum.

5 Sol premit metam Hesperiam, sed inde
    mane resurget.

6 Me movet desiderium Megillae
    dulce canentis.

---

[1] *Cf. REL* xxxiii 1955 60-1.
[2] *L'Encyclopédie sonore, Poètes Latins — Horace (Odes)*, 190 E 829, Librairie Hachette.

7   .... iocosis
cantibus curae minuentur atrae:
     mox perituris
gaudiis faustam capiamus horam,
dum licet.

8 Fit labor noctuque dieque: nullum
barbarus servis dabit aes onustis.

9 Non minas Caesar tumidas timebit,
nec parabit consilia improbanda,
nec sinet quaesita suis libenter
     munera amicis.

10 Fusce, nunc discede; venit Chloe; usque
     sollicitas me.

11 Non nihil pravum sedet ac malignum
rebus humanis penitus, quod ultra
dignior grata vice solvet aevi
     vita futuri.

Alcaic Exercises.

1 Te iudicem voltus severi
     dulce loquens Lalage movebit.

2 Clamoribus mox candidatum et
     ictibus expulit illa turba.

3 Innupta cur sponsum retardas?
     pone moras posito pudore.

4 Quis non anhelantem senectam
     praetereuntibus horret annis?

5 Pater, mihi nunc gaudia Caecubum
     praebet: querellas infidelis
         Lesbia fundat: amor manebit.

6   Illumque non centum pericla
         impavidum quatient; nec unquam
cedet tyranno.

7 Et cerva formidans sua semper it
  ad tecta.

8 Formidolosos non metuit greges
  boum minaci fronte ruentium
     de colle; sed viso dracone
        tecta petit citiore cursu.

9 Voces amoenas iam videor meo
  audire somno et carmina, quae tibi
     emi, Chloe dulcis, canenda:
        o eadem caneret Cupido!

10 Iam sunt petendi — ne tibi sit pudor —
   desiderantes te facilem proci:
      taedae parentur nuptiales:
         non aliter capies maritum.

11 Famosus eheu tempus in omne eris,
   nec mille delebunt preces nec
      iussa notam minuent iniquam.

12 Dum te trementem dira Proserpina
   ridet cachinnis, pro patria virum
      se dedere illustri volentem
         plaudit, amansque parat coronam.

Asclepiad Exercises.

1 Laudabunt alii rura virentia:
     flumen nos iuvat atque
        pontus fluctibus horridus.

2 Quis mutabilibus virginibus credere, amice, vult?

3 Si quis legibus est cultor et improbos
  condemnat, studio funditus atque vi
     processit sapientiae.

4   Hic post militiam gravem
  consul vulneribus fessus adest, viri,
       quaerens auxilium modo
  indigno patria.

5 Si quis Manibus est sensus, in otio
    versatur: sapientibus
non magnas animas corporis exitu
extingui placitum est.

6 Cur semper careat, Iuppiter, imbribus
gens haec scire cupit, te prece multa adit
    et vult exitialem
        sortem defugere artibus.

7 Prodit Lydia cum tergeminis iuncta sororibus.

8 Caeli per labyrinthos meat astrum, adest
vesper.

9 Cantu te, numerose et citharae sciens,
dulci, Musa beat non sine tibia.

10 Depromenda Falerna, accipe pocula.

Key to Prosodical and other Errors and Defects.

Sapphic Exercises

1 (*a*) If a Lesser Sapphic opens with a cretic word, and is to be followed by a monosyllable, the third word should also be a monosyllable, see p. 48.
  (*b*) No elision permitted at the weak caesura, see p. 49.

2 (*a*) No Lesser Sapphic in the Odes ends 5 + 1, see p. 48.
  (*b*) Hiatus between the last two verses is best avoided, see p. 49.

3 (*a*) The sole example of a trochaic word before the weak caesura is at IV xi 29, and should be avoided, see p. 48.
  (*b*) The Odes show no instance of a Lesser Sapphic starting 1 + 3, see p. 48.

4 (*a*) The wholly diaeretic opening of the first verse is forbidden, see p. 48.
  (*b*) Horace does not have a short final vowel before *sc-*, *sp-*, *squ-*, or *st-*, see p. 130 n.3 and *CR* vi 1956 5 n.1.

5 (*a*) The first verse has no caesura, see p. 6 *(infra)*.
  (*b*) Horace hardly ever ends Lesser Sapphics with a dissyllable ending in a short vowel, see p. 48.

6   Again no caesura: only permissible if imitating Catullus, see pp. 31, 47-8.

7 (*a*) The heavy pause between the third verse and the Adonic is almost unknown in Horace's Sapphics, see p. 50.

(*b*) The syllabic sequence, 1 + 4, in the Adonic is found once only in Horace (*CS* 16), and that with a Proper Name, see p. 49.

8 A heavy pause after the ninth syllable is not permitted, see p. 50.

9 (*a*) The second verse lacks a caesura, see pp. 31, 47-8.

(*b*) Elision is not permissible in the Adonic, see p. 49.

10 (*a*) No sense-pause permissible at weak caesura, see p. 50. In any case two heavy pauses in one verse are intolerable in Sapphics, see p. 50.

(*b*) No long elision between ninth and tenth syllables permissible.

(*c*) A final trochaic word ending the Lesser Sapphic with a short vowel is not too good, see p. 48.

(*d*) The syllabic sequence in the Adonic is unprecedented, see pp. 48-9.

11 Prosodically correct.

Alcaic Exercises

1 The break after the fourth syllable of the Enneasyllabic should be avoided, see pp. 59-60.

2 (*a*) Enneasyllabics may not start with a quadrisyllable, see p. 55.

(*b*) Lesser Alcaic diaeretic owing to the start with two dactyls. The only similar example is at III iii 64. The student should avoid it, see p. 57.

3 The heavy pause at the end of the Enneasyllabic is rarely found in Horace, see pp. 55, 59.

4 (*a*) The big "cross-beam" word in Enneasyllabic is good, see p. 56.

(*b*) The Lesser Alcaic starting with a six-syllabled word produces diaeresis and is without precedent, see p. 57.

5 (*a*) The initial short syllable is permissible as an occasional variation in the Greater Alcaic, see p. 55. But the syllabic sequence of this verse is faulty, see pp. 54-5.

(*b*) In the Enneasyllabic a break after the second syllable should normally be followed by 1 + 3, see p. 55.

(*c*) The heavy pause after the fifth syllable of the Lesser Alcaic is not permissible, see pp. 57-9.

6 (*a*) Interlinear hiatus is better avoided by the student, see p. 59.

(*b*) Heavy stop after the seventh syllable of the Lesser Alcaic is not good, see pp. 57-9.

7 (*a*) If the verse starts a stanza and a new sentence, it should not begin with *et*, see p. 45.

  (*b*) The verse has no caesura, see p. 54.

  (*c*) The verse should not end 2 + 1, see p. 55.

8 (*a*) The first verse starts well with a five-syllabled word, see p. 54.

  (*b*) The initial short syllable in the second verse is permissible, *cf*. 5 (*a*).

  (*c*) The stop in the Enneasyllabic is possible, but rare; see p. 59.

9 (*a*) The amount of interlinear hiatus goes beyond permissible limits, see p. 59.

  (*b*) The sequence 2 + 2 + 2 in the Enneasyllabic is not permissible, see p. 55.

  (*c*) The pause at the end of the Enneasyllabic is very rare in Horace, see p. 59.

10 (*a*) The parenthesis in the first verse lacks authority, see p. 60.

  (*b*) On the Enneasyllabic, see 5 (*b*) and 9 (*c*).

  (*c*) As a result of excessive stopping, the wholes tanza is choppy and too "square-cut", see pp. 59-60, 109.

11 (*a*) Normally elision is not permissible just before the tenth syllable of the Greater Alcaic, see p. 58 n.1. But for an intentionally expressive effect Horace has *consociare amant* (II iii 10).

  (*b*) Only once in Horace does the Enneasyllabic end with a 2 + 1, *viz.*, II vii 19.

12   The syllabic sequence in the Lesser Alcaic occurs once only in Horace (I xxvi 12), and *amansque* is unmusical as a word.

Asclepiad Exercises

1 (*a*) The final syllable of the Pherecratean is normally long (see p. 65), in the Glyconic is more often long than short (see p. 65); and in the Lesser Asclepiad a long final syllable is slightly more frequent (see p. 62). A sequence of three verses with final shorts is therefore faulty.

  (*b*) The strong pause at the end of the Lesser Asclepiad is permissible but rare in the Fifth Asclepiad metre, see pp. 72-3.

2   Horace has only two cases of elision in the Greater Asclepiad neither of which occurs after the second caesura, see p. 67.

3 (*a*) The monosyllable before the caesura in the Lesser Asclepiad is permissible, but rare; see p. 61.

  (*b*) The adverb *funditus* is weak and would be well replaced by an adjective qualifying *sapientiae*, see p. 44.

  (*c*) The final syllable of the Lesser Asclepiad is rarely a monosyllable, see p. 62.

4   The strong pause at the caesura of the Lesser Asclepiad is permissible in the Third Asclepiad Metre, but not common; see p. 68.

5   In the Fourth Asclepiad Metre no major pause is permitted within the Glyconic, and the pause at the caesura of the Lesser Asclepiad is not common; see p. 70.

6   Elision is rare in the Fifth Asclepiad Metre, and is one of the lightest kind, so that the harsh elision in 2 and second elision in 4 make the stanza unacceptable; see p. 72.

7   The Greater Asclepiad should have a strong caesura after the first choriamb, see p. 63.

8   Only one Lesser Asclepiad in Horace has no caesura: it should not be imitated, see p. 61.

9   There are only a few cases of elision at the caesura in Horace: so the composer should use the licence with reserve, see p. 61.

10   See note on 9, (*ante*).

Chapter Five

An Anthology

« Alle Dilettanten sind Plagiarii. »

Two kinds of Horatian verse have gone to the making of this collection. The first aims at a more or less strict imitation in matter and manner of the Odes themselves: for the most part it is serious in tone, with no tricks about it. The other merely borrows Horatian measures for "odes" which the Venusian bard might have written but for the incontestable fact that he could not possibly have done so.

No attempt has been made to separate these two kinds. Horace himself likes to switch without warning from highfalutin' (real or mock) to homely pedestrian, and there seemed no good reason to depart from this policy of his.

What has been attempted is the entertaining of two different categories of reader. The interest of the classics pundit has been taken for granted, it is to be hoped not too presumptuously. But an attempt has also been made to meet the man-in-the-street half way, and that without any patronising intentions towards his small Latin and less Greek. Fortunately, this is where Horace, of all bards of antiquity, could lend powerful aid. No other could less inappropriately be made a scapegoat for anything done in his name within the scope of an anthology like this. And so it does not matter in the least that some of our contributors have made their Horace write about things that never in fact came the way of the real one, nor ever could. But of one thing we may be sure. Nobody in Elysium will have enjoyed the fun more than he, just as nobody will have been readier to applaud with sincere generosity the skilful imitations here displayed of his own very exacting models.

CONTRIBUTORS TO THE ANTHOLOGY

AUCTOR INEPTUS

W. BEARE, M.A., sometime Professor of Latin, University of Bristol.

W. BONAVIA-HUNT, M.A., brother of the author.

IACOBUS BOROVSKI, Leningrad, U.S.S.R.

A. Y. CAMPBELL, M.A., sometime Professor of Greek, University of Liverpool.

WM. COWPER, English poet (1731–1800)

J. F. CRACE, M.A., sometime Assistant Master, Eton College.

F. R. DALE, D.S.O., M.C., M.A., sometime Headmaster, City of London School.

NAN DUNBAR, M.A., (Glasgow, Oxon., Cantab.) Fellow and Tutor, Somerville College, Oxford.

R. DUNENSIS (Ciesiulewicz), Teacher of Latin, Riga.

W. M. EDWARDS, M.C., M.A., Professor.

A. EUSTANCE, M.A., Head of Classics Department, Wood Green Grammar School, London.

E. O. FURBER, M.A., Senior Classics Master, Pate's Grammar School for Girls.

F. C. GEARY, M.A., Fellow of Corpus Christi College, Oxford.

H. HAMILL, M.A., formerly of the Indian Educational Service.

S. A. HANDFORD, M.A., sometime Reader in Classics, King's College, London.

H. H. HOUSE, M.A., sometime Classical Master at Sherborne and Malvern.

SIR EVELYN HOWELL, M.A., Cambridge.

ANGUS O. HULTON, M.A., Senior Lecturer in Classics, University of Sheffield.

EDWARD HUSSEY, K.S.

SAMUEL JOHNSON ESQ., LL.D., (1709–1784).

F. J. LELIÈVRE, M.A., Senior Classics Lecturer and Tutor, University College, Londonderry.

M. H. LONGSON, B.A., Head of Classical Department, the Edinburgh Academy and for many years contributor to "Punch".

W. S. MAGUINNESS, M.A., Professor of Latin, King's College, London.

T. W. MELLUISH, M.A., formerly Hon. Sec. Classical Association, and Hon. Lecturer, University College, London.

CALLISTO PALUMBELLA, 18th century friar.

E. V. C. PLUMPTRE, M.A., sometime Senior Classical Master Harrow School.

JOHN POLLARD, T.D., M.A., B. Litt., Senior Lecturer in Classics, University College of N. Wales, Bangor.

CHARLES RACE, M.A., Headmaster, City Grammar School, Chester.

L. J. D. RICHARDSON, O.B.E., M.A., Hon. Professor of Classical Literature, Trinity College, Dublin.

W. R. SMYTH, M.A., Lecturer in Classics, University College, University of Wales, Swansea.

LUCY TODD, B.A., formerly Senior Classical Mistress, The High School for Girls, Nottingham.

A. TRELOAR, T.D., M.A., Reader in Comparative Philology, University of New England, N.S.W.

URBAN VIII, Pope (1586–1644).

M. S. WARMAN, M.A., Assistant Master, Harrow School.

E. J. WOOD, M.A., Emeritus Professor of Latin, University of Leeds.

E. C. WOODCOCK, M.A., Emeritus Professor of Latin, University of Durham.

D. E. W. WORMELL, M.A., PH.D., Professor of Latin, Trinity College, Dublin.

HOC·ERAT·IN·VOTIS·MODVS·AGRI·NON·ITA·
MAGNVS·HORTVS·VBI·ET·TECTO·
VICINVS·IVGIS·AQVAE·FONS·ET·PAVLVM
SILVAE·SVPER·HIS·FORET·

I

Ad Lunam

Saepe cur terris pluviam atque nubes
dextera mittit Pater, orbe solis
abdito nimbis, et opus metendi
    laedit iniquus?

sternitur pratum, segetes putrescunt,
per graves humore iacent aristae
debiles campos, modo parca messis
    horrea tanget.

rusticus viso periisse cultu
perditos plorat dubius labores
quem deum quali prece defatiget
    parcere segnem.

unus est horum mihi fons malorum,
quod redit saeclum nova monstra questum
Daedali : sunt qui cupiant volando
    visere lunam.

Luna, iactatis inimica telis,
integro simplex eris usque voltu :
luce vesanos homines maligna
    despicis omnes.

                      L.T.

I

A Very Wet Summer

Why pours paternal Jove with mighty hand
So frequent rain and clouds upon our land,
(The Sun's orb veiled in mist) and, wrathful, spoils
         The Reaper's toils?

The meadow flatted lies, the crops decay,
The feeble ear sinks on the watery clay,
Ruined with moisture; scarcely shall it win
         To gathering in.

The hapless farmer mourns his labours lost
Seeing his hard work all in vain, and tossed
In doubt with what prayers to storm heaven, so slow
         Mercy to show.

These evils to one source the people track;
The age of Daedalus with new horrors black
Returns: some even hope to fly, and soon
         To reach the moon.

Fair Moon, indignant at the missiles driven,
With face unscathed, for ever pure in heaven,
In baleful light disdainful dost thou view
         The crazy crew.

                            L.T.

II

Ad Barbaram

Sunt quos militiae praemia Olympicae
quaesivisse iuvat, seu celeri gradu
triginta stadii circuitus agunt,
seu tundunt pugiles caestibus aemulis
nares oppositas, crurave cruribus
luctantes adhibent. huic placuit iuga,
qua nix candet iners, scandere montium :
illi, si poterit, per medios pilam
postes arte pedis pellere praepetis.
Phoebi iamque sororem ignifero suo
castam percutiunt fulmine Sarmatae
audentes nimium. mox violabitur
sedes caelicolarum et loca siderum
conservata deis. quanta vias vorat
stridendo geminis pulvereas rotis
parvam vecta Monam turba per insulam !
nec spernunt iuvenes stringere fluctibus
suspensi mare, dum stant tabulas super
subnexas crepidis. talia, Barbara,
non curae tibi sunt : perpetuo ambulas.

J.P.

II

To Dr. Barbara Moore

Men there be who love to score
Wins in mock Olympic war,
Some to run a record race,
Some to pound a rival's face,
Or strive limb with limb to seek
Victory. A snowy peak
One will scale, another foot
Flying ball with soccer boot
Through the goal-posts. Much too bold
Russians strike the moon's pure gold:
Soon they'll reach the heavenly seat
Starry realms to mortal feet
Not permitted. Oh, what crowds
Scorch along the island roads
Motor-biking! Nor disdain
Youths to skim the watery main,
Lightly poised upon the waves,
Feet attached to wooden staves . . . .
But of such it's no use talking,
Barbara, while you keep walking!

J.P.

III

Ad Dulce Caput

Reges exitio et regum debentur amici,
      nec suus ingenio
durat honor titulisve decus formaeve venustas ;
      Sol quoque, qui vicibus
tempora disponit certis, iam grandior anno est
      quam tibi, dulce caput,
cum primum occurri ; solvantur cetera, noster
      permanet unus amor ;
non hesternus erat, non crastinus ille novatur ;
      nescit abire fugax,
sit licet in cursu, cui primus et ultimus idem
      stat sine fine dies.

H.H.H.

IV

Lydia, diligebam
te, mihi nec spes aderant, abstinuique voti,
      forsitan et medullis
haereant ignes etiam ; conticui pudore
      aemulus, atque bilem
irritus purgor, studio simpliciore amavi,
      sic tibi dent amator
te deos oro pariter diligat alter olim.

A.T.

III

All kings and all their favourites—
All glories of honours, beauties, wits—
(The sun himself, which makes times as they pass,
Is elder by a year now than it was
When you and I first one another saw)—

All other things to their destruction draw;
Only our love hath no decay;
This no to-morrow hath nor yesterday,
Running it never runs from us away,
But truly keeps his first, his everlasting day.

JOHN DONNE

IV

Я вас любил; любовь ещё, быть может,
В душе моей угасла не совсем;
Но пусть она вас больше не тревожит;
Я не хочу печалить вас ничем.
Я вас любил безмолвно, безнадежно,
То робостью, то ревностью томим;
Я вас любил так искренно, так нежно,
Как дай вам Бог любимой быть другим.

А. С. Пушкин.

V

Latratrix rapido vecta satellite,
venturique tibi nescia funeris,
   quos nunc volveris orbes
     terrae respiciens vices

mutatamque fidem? flevit Horatius
inclusam Danaen carcere aeneo;
   proiecere magistri
     te siccis oculis tui.

atqui seu radiis siderealibus
ictae, sive fame, seu medio aere
   mortem fata pararint
     disrupta tibi machina,

fies nobilium tu quoque nominum;
te quamvis Oriens negligat, hic magis
   nostris laudibus auctam
     emirabitur Occidens.

C.R.

V

To the Russian Space-dog Laika

Barking rapidly at the fellow-traveller
coming nesciently to thy funeral,
whom will you involve in orbits
respecting the vices of earth,
and a change in credit?

Horatius wept.
Danae was enceinte in her ivory tower.
The projects of schoolmasters
would have dried your eyes.

In spite of radio stars and fame
the mortal bronze obeys the smashed machine.

You will join the nominal nobility,
you negligent Oriental ; but to the Magi
our praises shall authorise
an accident à la mode de Marvell.

EZRA POUND [?]

V

Unwitting circler of the sky,
Sputnik-borne Laika, doomed to die,
   Seest thou that Earth is fled,
   And Faith is altered?

Horace had tears for Danae
Pent in her brazen Prison : thee
   Unweeping trainers hurled
   Into another World.

Yet tho' the Fates for thee prepare
Machine disrupt in middle Air,
   Or Hunger end thy days
   Or secret cosmic Rays,

Thou shalt become a noble Name :
Tho' the East spurn thee, here thy Fame,
   Encreased by us the more,
   Shall charm the Western Shore.

ANDREW MARVELL [?]

VI

Ad Beatam Mariam Virginem

Iam toto subitus vesper eat polo,
et sol attonitum praecipitet diem,
dum saevae recolo ludibrium necis
    divinamque catastrophen.

spectatrix aderas supplicio, Parens,
malis uda, gerens cor adamantinum,
Natus, funerea pendulus in cruce
    altos dum gemitus dabat.

pendens ante oculos Natus, atrocibus
sectus verberibus, Natus hiantibus
fossus vulneribus quot penetrantibus
    te confixit aculeis!

eheu![1] sputa, alapae, verbera, vulnera,
clavi, fel, aloe, spongia, lancea,
sanguis, spina, sitis[2] — quam varia pium
    cor pressere tyrannide!

cunctis interea stat generosior
Virgo martyribus : prodigio novo
in tantis moriens non moreris, Parens,
    diris fixa doloribus.

sit summae Triadae gloria, laus, honor;
a qua suppliciter sollicita prece
posco virginei roboris aemulas
    vires rebus in asperis.

                  C.P.

---

[1] The official text of this line reads: *heu, sputa, alapae* . . .

[2] The official text of this line reads: *sitis, spina, cruor* . . . The compiler amended both lines to restore the metre.

VI

Let evening without warning darken the
whole sky and the sun make the astonished
light of day vanish in a flash, as I reflect on
the mockery of that cruel death and the
climax of the divine tragedy.

You, His mother, were there to witness His
sufferings, overwhelmed with grief as you were, but
with a heart that nothing could daunt. Meanwhile
your Son was hanging on the cross of death and in His
agony uttering deep groans.

All torn by the dreadful scourging, His body
all broken with gaping wounds, your Son hung there
before your eyes : with how many needles, as it
were, did this sight pierce right through to
your heart !

Spittle, blows, lashes, wounds, nails, gall,
aloes, sponge, lance, thirst, thorns, blood —
how each of these in its special way oppressed
your heart that loved so well !

The author of the Latin Church hymn which belongs to the Feast of the
Seven Dolours of the Blessed Virgin Mary (15th September), is said to be
Callisto Palumbella, a Servite friar of the 18th century. Much less widely
known than the famous *Ut queant laxis*, it nevertheless strikes me as superior
in literary merit, if not in "piety". Could it be that the composer himself was
more than just officially moved when he penned it? Even the Doxology gets
only a single respectful line to itself, and the stanza ends on a warmly
human note. However small the purely technical skill of the good friar, one
must allow him a distinct talent in the creating of an atmosphere through the
power of a few well chosen words strategically and tactically located.

VII

Ad Crispum

Tertii verso quater orbe lustri,
quid theatrales tibi, Crispe, pompae?
quam decet canos male literatos
    sera voluptas,

tene mulceri fidibus canoris,
tene cantorum modulis stupere,
tene per pictas oculo elegante
    currere formas?

inter aequales, sine felle liber,
codices, veri studiosus, inter
rectius vives; sua quisque carpat
    gaudia gratus.

lusibus gaudet puer otiosis,
luxus oblectat iuvenem theatri;
at seni fluxo sapienter uti
    tempore restat.

                       S.J.

Yet through it all the Virgin stands there,
more courageous than all the martyrs ; for
though each suffering of His was a death-
blow to you, yet by a unique grace you, His
Mother, did not die although transfixed by
each cruel sorrow.

To the most high Trinity be glory, praise
and honour ; whom with earnest and fervent
prayer I ask to be given in life's rough ways
a strength to match the Virgin's constancy.

VII

[This ode, addressed to Crispus, seems to have been composed by Johnson
at Covent Garden during a performance of Handel's *Messiah*, on 8th March
1771. According to Mrs Piozzi who went with him, the Doctor "sat surprisingly quiet" and she flattered herself that he was listening to the music.
But when they got home he repeated the ode which he said he had made at
the oratorio, and asked her to translate it by breakfast time next day.]

*   *   *   *   *

Crispus, what are theatrical shows to you after sixty
years? How ill befits pleasure late in life white-haired
scholars ; are you to be charmed by tuneful lyres, are you to
wonder at singers' airs, are you to run over painted beauties
with connoisseur's eye?

You will live more correctly among your contemporaries,
a free man without gall, among books, a seeker after truth ;
let each man take his own proper pleasures.

The boy delights in games of leisure hours, theatrical
display pleases the youth ; but it remains for an old man to
make wise use of fleeting time.

VIII

Cur litteris me sollicitas tuis
versus iocosos, editor improbe,
    carmenque ter poscens Horati
        par numeris hominem innocentem?

curis onusti num satis, heu satis,
vatum inquietum cogimur in gregem?
    nos rodere ungues, nos capillos
        dilacerare, ferire mensam?

o Musa, semper surda vocantibus!
o verba, nunquam prompta petentibus!
    metrumque fallax et laboris
        plenum opus ingeniumque tardum!

quodsi trecenis versibus in dies
possim immerentem laedere paginam,
    quo fonte ducantur lepores,
        qua mihi materies Camena?

sed tempus urget nos ita garrulos,
dum virgines nos cum pueris manent
    quotidianos ut labores
        undecima repetamus hora.

quis deviam Augen eliciet domo?
"cur lectioni non aderas heri?"
    "devota praeceptis Horati
        cum socio calidum bibebam."

W.B.

VIII

What? On the telephone again,
Reprobate editor? In vain
You look for light Horatian song
From one who never did you wrong.

Have I so little else to do
That I can be a poet too?
Bite nails, thump roll-top desk and tear
In composition's throes my hair?

O Muse, so chilly when I woo you!
O words so scarce when I pursue you!
O metre, hammered out again!
O general sluggishness of brain!

But even if I had the power
To scrawl three hundred lines per hour,
Where find a theme for sportive verse,
When Muse her treasure won't disburse?

But time is pressing while I'm prating:
I mustn't keep my classes waiting:
The eleventh hour is drawing near;
Great George's muted boom I hear.

"Where's Auge? Who will fetch her, pray?"
"Where were you, Auge, yesterday?"
"Horatian-fashion—what more clerkly?—
I with a friend was in the Berkeley".

W.B.

IX

Ad Fuscum

Fusce, Pontilis subiture Ludi
lubricos casus, elementa prudens
pauca ludendi bene, pauca mecum
    disce licendi.

auctio dum fit, numerare oportet
puncta ; neve ultro, nisi forte divi
plura viginti dederint, duabus
    incipe Clavis.

cum caves idem stolidaque opimas
praeteris chartas taciturnitate,
iure te grandes fugiunt triumphi,
    iure minores.

re semel gesta bene, ne tumescas :
tunc opus freno tibi, tum periclum est
volneris ; quin et subito repertus
    illicitator

duplicat poenas vafer hostis auctas.
stare conventis moneo ; et quod audes
quidquid est, recte tabula notatam
    consule summam.

exitus ludens reditusque apertos
provide ; sero sapis impeditus,
sed reviviscens ferat usque puppim
    spes prope mersam :

IX

Faced with the snares of Bridge you need
A guide to bidding and to play:
Attend then, if you will, to what
          I have to say.

The auction open, count by points
What fate has dealt you: while a sum
Of twenty for "Two Clubs" is deemed
          A minimum,

If with misguided pawkiness
You pass a splendid hand, you'll see
Slams, grand and small, elude your grasp
          Deservedly.

But vulnerable (game in hand)
Then, Fuscus, temper pride with care;
Then most, with so much more to lose,
          The foe beware,

Doubling the bid he's pushed you to.
Stick to conventions, and before
You bid, religiously consult
          A well-kept score.

In play watch entries, nor too late
Find dummy's hand blocked from your own;
And if you'd parry all attempts
          To get you down,

saepe seu caecas poteris latebras
Regis infesti procul augurari,
seu catus Scyllae medium et Charybdis
    presseris hostem,

victor emerges. properare noli,
ne procax legem violes sequendi et
iussus errorem revocare solvas
    lugubre damnum.

neve post mortem male distributas
increpes chartas nimiove amantem
Psychicae Vocis socium Nigraeve
    retia Silvae.

quisquis acceptos socio triumphos
imputat cunctasque sibi ruinas,
gloria tutus caret invidenda et
    servat amicos.

                  M.S.W.

               X

Aegre ferenti verbera filiae
dantique poenas flagitii pater
   "nolim", inquit, "ignores flagella
    me magis excruciare quam te".

plorare virgo desinit ilico :
"si vera dicis, plura libet mihi
   perferre," respondet, "neque istum
    cura mei teneat lacertum."

                  W.S.M.

At times finesse a missing King
By leading through the likelier hand;
At others, properly applied,
      A "squeeze" will land

Your contract. Follow suit with care,
Nor blindly rush to your design;
Gratuitous "revokes" incur
      A swingeing fine.

Losing, blame neither Blackwood nor
Bad distribution for your fall,
Nor partner's gross addiction to
      The "Psychic Call",

But blame yourself; and if you win
Give him the praise though undeserved:
Forgo the glory and ensure
      A friend preserved.

x

Father, chancing to chastise
  His indignant daughter Sue,
Said, "I hope you realise
  That this hurts me more than you".

Susan straightway ceased to roar;
  "If that's really true," said she,
I can stand a good deal more;
  Pray go on, and don't mind me."
        Ruthless Rhymes for Heartless Homes

XI

In Diem Natalem Horati

Insonat laetis Helicon choreis,
tibiae certat lyra non silenti,
concinit clara melos ad sorores
    voce Thalium.

illius sacris properans honorem
Lesbios qui primus adire fontes
ausus est adfertque novo decore
    carmina nobis,

ipse cui lauroque hederaque cingit
tempora et frontem Patareus virenti
quique natales decies peregit
    rite ducenos,

semper et florens valida iuventa
spernit immanis metuenda regis
sceptra, dum caelum superat profundum
    laude perenni.

quin, age, et nostros Borealis aurae
flamine ambustos patiare flores
in tuam necti nitidam coronam,
    suavis Horati.

               I.B.

XI

На день рождения Горация

Празднуют сегодня свой праздник Музы,
Флейт всяких с лирами слышны звуки,
Помню голос свой обращает звонкий
  Талия и сестры.

В честь того, кто первый сумел присвоить
Стихотворной грубой латинской речи
Эллинских стихов красоту достойно
  С новым напевом.

И кого за то Аполлон цветами,
Лавром и плющом увенчал — не вянет
Тот венок, и в третье вступает слово
  Тысячелетье.

Угрожать не смеет им царь подземный
Тем жезлом, который так страшен смертным
Победил ты смерть и достигнул неба
  Вечною славой.

Так позволь и нам, дорогой Гораций.
Твой блестящий лавром венок и миртом
Северных цветов, обосвеченных вьюгой
  Веткой украсить.

XII

Non tantum reficit membra sopor mihi,
quantum sol rediens, cum tua non semel
    obversetur imago,
        dum somnis oculi vacant.

cura utcunque mihi missa, Licymnia, est,
menti continuo gaudia tu refers :
    si sublime voluto,
        occurrit tua sanctitas.

scrutanti penitus vera latentia
vitae certa mihi forma tui nitet :
    Arcturus velut aequor
        immotus varium regit,

sic menti domina es blanda meae levi,
libertate licet sic fruar unica :
    si sic regna gubernes,
        tollatur vitium et dolor.

A.T.

XII

I cannot raise my eyelids up from sleep,
But I am visited with thoughts of you;
Slumber has no refreshment half so deep
As the sweet morn which wakes my heart anew.

I cannot put away life's trivial care,
But you straightway steal on me with delight;
My purest moments are your mirror fair;
My deepest thought finds you the truth most bright.

You are the lovely regent of my mind,
The constant sky to my unresting sea;
Yet, since 'tis you that rule me, I but find
A finer freedom in such tyranny.

Were the world's anxious kingdoms governed so,
Lost were their wrongs, and vanished half their woe.

LAURENCE BINYON

XIII

Ad Numisium

Mercator, Numisi, nomine sub notho
nummos et lapides Coaque tutius
vectas : sit numeris apta Lyce meis,
      urit me penitus Chloe.

inter femineas illius arculas
plectrum dulce meum et charta poematis
melliti iacuit, cum dedit haec mihi
      signum : "tange canens lyram!"

dum testudine, dum laudis idoneae
canto voce Lycen non sine questibus,
responsum ex oculis intima pars mei
      reginae nitidis petit.

haec formosa rubet, contrahit altera
frontem, me in trepidos visa movent modos :
collectis et ait Mater Amoribus :
      "arte ut dissimulant rudi!"

                            A.I.

The merchant to secure his treasure,
Conveys it in a borrowed name;
Euphelia serves to grace my measure,
But Chloe is my real flame.

My softest verse, my darling lyre
Upon Euphelia's toilet lay—
When Chloe noted her desire
That I should sing, that I should play.

My lyre I tune, my voice I raise,
But with my numbers mix my sighs;
And while I sing Euphelia's praise
I fix my soul on Chloe's eyes.

Fair Chloe blushed; Euphelia frown'd:
I sung and gazed; I played and trembled;
And Venus to the Loves around
Remark'd how ill we all dissembled.

                              MATTHEW PRIOR

XIV

Salvete, salvete, Helladis insulae,
quondam calores qua feriit lyris
   Sappho, vigescebant et artes
      pacis honos pariterque belli,

qua Delos orta est non sine Apolline,
vos sol inaurat perpetua face;
   sed praeter aestatem rapaci
      cetera deperiere fato.

prospectat agros mons Marathonios,
unde ille pontus cernitur; hic mihi,
   dum saecla volvebam priora,
      Graecia compedibus soluta

iam stare visa est, nec poteram amplius
servire Persarum insiliens rogo:
   sedebat in saxo tyrannus
      unde patet Salaminis aequor;

subter iacebant innumerae rates,
gentesque totae quas numeraverat
   surgente sub Phoebo cohortum
      quantula pars abeunte restat!

                    L.T.

XIV

The Isles of Greece, the Isles of Greece!
  Where burning Sappho loved and sung,
Where grew the arts of War and Peace,
  Where Delos rose, and Phoebus sprung!
Eternal summer gilds them yet,
But all, except their Sun, is set.

*   *   *   *   *

The mountains look on Marathon—
  And Marathon looks on the sea;
And musing there an hour alone,
  I dreamed that Greece might still be free;
For standing on the Persian's grave
I could not deem myself a slave.

A King sate on the rocky brow
  Which looks o'er sea-born Salamis;
And ships, by thousands, lay below,
  And men in nations; all were his!
He counted them at break of day—
And, when the Sun set, where were they?

                                    LORD BYRON

XV

Auratus huius noster Eques[1] Domus,
Orator idem Publicus et Stilus,[2]
    Maiorque,[3] Procurator,[4] unus
        iam Senior Socius,[5] Robertus,

quondam Decanus[6] qui iuvenes manu
lasciviores rexit amabili
    (ut nullus unquam post et ante—
        dent Carolus[7] veniam et Cinaethus ![8]),

iam iam sua edit *Carmina*.[9] cedite,
prisci scholares ; cedite, quot prius
    versus dederunt *Hermathena*,[10]
        Kottabos,[11] *Hesperidum Susurri*.[12]

                                L.J.D.R.

An ode written on receipt of the news that Sir Robert Tate's *Carmina Dublinensia* would appear shortly.

xv

Sir Robert, dear knight of this House, both Public Orator and College Pen, and Major, Proctor, now Senior Fellow too, sometime Dean who with charitable hand controlled wanton youths (as none ever before and after — by leave of Charles and Kenneth), is on the point of publishing his *Odes*. Make way, scholars of old; make way, all verses formerly offered by *Hermathena, Kottabos* and *Hesperidum Susurri*.

---

1   K.B.E., 1920
2   Public Orator (and 'College Pen'), 1914–52, see *Orationes et Epistolae Dublinenses*, 1941.
3   Major, Dublin University Contingent, O.T.C., 1912 (and its commander until disbandment in 1920).
4   Senior Proctor, 1941.
5   Co-opted Senior Fellow, 1941.
6   Junior Dean, 1919–31.
7   Charles Rowe (Junior Dean, 1942–3).
8   Kenneth Bailey (Junior Dean, 1931–42).
9   *Carmina Dublinensia*, 1943; 2nd ed. 1945.
10 *Hermathena*, twice yearly, 1874 to present day.
11 *Kottabos*, once a term, 1869–95.
12 *Hesperidum Susurri*, 1867.

XVI

Ad Neoteddiam

Ubi saltant per Alhambram, excitus ictu puer aeris
Eduardensis amicas tremulis odit et horret
      genuum motibus usas.

cata virgo, fera feles, socios mittit in altum et
cito volvit resupinos triplici aestu Furiarum
      veluti turbine raptos.

neque desunt ibi nuptae, manus expers hymenaei;
sibi crines ita nodant ut equorum fluitantes
      imitentur bene caudas.

ego ludam pede agresti, iocus inter rabiosos
nimis aptus, mea lux, quem levis aegre tolerabis
      tenebris obvia Phoebe?

A.E.

XVI

Ode to a Teddy Girl of the 1950's

When all over the Alhambra girl-friends join the lively
[dancing,
teddy-boy in hate and horror, mad with beat of brassy
sees their knees go rock-'n'-rolling.   [trumpet,

Clever hep-cat, each a wild cat, sends her partners sprawling
[skyward;
back they tumble, quick she rolls them gripped as if by wild
with the brio of three Furies.   [tornado

Brides unbridled all abound there, band that knows no bond
[of Hymen;
locks are drawn in knots all tightly, locks that make uncanny
of the flying tails of horses.   [semblance

Shall I sport like plodding peasant, ready butt of rock-'n'-
[rollers,
I whom you, light-footed darling, hardly suffer without
[flinching,
Phoebe face to face with shadows?

A.E.

XVII

Ad Acmen

Acme, plus nimio ne doleas memor
absimus quoties alter ab altera ;
   sic nos arte benigna
     prudens vult dirimi deus,

dum sensim educat ut ferre libentius
discamus teneros per monitus diem,
   vita cum semel acta
     leto dissociabimur.

nimirum ille cavens, in male providos
ne tam maesta dies durius incidat,
   quae tristi super omnes
     nos formidine commovet,

hac arte erudit, hac edocet in dies
suetosque instituit discidium pati,
   ne tam flebilis horae
     incautos timor opprimat.

J.F.C.

XVII

Earl Bristol's Farewell

Grieve not, deare love, although we often parte,
But know that Nature gently doth us sever,
Thereby to traine us up, with tender arte,
To brooke that day when we must parte for ever.

For Nature doubting we should be surprised
By that sad day, whose dread doth cheefly feare us,
Doth keepe us dayly schooled and exercised,
Lest that the fryghte thereof should overbeare us.

ANON.

XVIII

Regali solio fortis Iberiae,
Hermengilde, iubar, gloria martyrum
    Christi quos amor almis
      caeli coetibus inserit,

ut perstas patiens, pollicitum Deo
servans obsequium, quo potius tibi
    nil proponis, et arces
      cautus noxia quae placent.

ut motus cohibes pabula qui parant
surgentis vitii, non dubios agens
    per vestigia gressus
      quo veri via dirigit.

nullis te genitor blanditiis trahit,
non vitae caperis divitis otio
    gemmarumve nitore
      regnandive cupidine.

diris non acies te gladii minis,
nec terret perimens carnificis furor;
    nam mansura caducis
      praefers gaudia caelitum.

nunc nos e superis protege sedibus
clemens, atque preces, dum canimus tua
    quaesitam nece palmam,
      pronis auribus excipe.

sit rerum Domino iugis honor Patri,
et Natum celebrent ora precantium,
    divinumque supremis
      Flamen laudibus efferant.

POPE URBAN VIII

XVIII

Valiant Hermengild, shining light of Spain's royal house
and glory of martyrs whose love of Christ has won them a
place in the gracious company of heaven, how staunchly you
persevered in keeping that service you promised to God,
which was the most cherished of all your designs, and carefully kept at arm's length things that please but are sinful.
How well you curbed those impulses that provide fuel for
wrongdoing, firmly planting your steps on the path where
the way of truth directed! By no blandishments did your
father move you, neither were you taken in by the ease of a
life of luxury or by the sheen of jewelry or by the ambition
of kingship. Not by the dread threats of a sword-blade, not
by the rage of a death-dealing butcher were you terrified;
for you put the permanent joys of heaven far above the
fleeting ones of this life. Now from your heavenly place on
high be kind and protect us; and while we sing of the reward
you have won by your death, incline your ears to our prayers.
Let there be everlasting honour to the Father, Lord of all
things; may the lips of your suppliants extol in song the Son,
and glorify the Holy Spirit with the highest praises.

*　　*　　*　　*　　*

Note: Urban VIII, the last and perhaps the most vigorous of the so-called
Humanist popes of the Renaissance, was responsible for the revising of the
Hymnal of the Roman Breviary. The Old Hymnal, according to the human-
ists, was a tasteless thing, its Latin inelegant and barbarous. This revision is
now generally admitted to have been a great mistake. "Ambrose and
Prudentius took something classical and made it Christian; the revisers and
their imitators took something Christian and tried to make it classical.
Accessit Latinitas, discessit pietas" (*Hymns of the Roman Liturgy*, by the Rev.
Joseph Connelly, M.A.).

The above hymn is given here not for any special intrinsic merit, but rather
as an indication of an interesting reactionary phase in the development
of the Latin church hymn.

XIX

"In Submersionem Navigii cui Georgius Regale
Nomen Inditum."

Plangimus fortes—periere fortes—
patrium propter periere litus,
bis quater centum subito sub alto
    aequore mersi.

navis innitens lateri iacebat,
malus ad summas trepidabat undas,
cum levis funes quatiens ad imum
    depulit aura.

plangimus fortes—nimis, heu, caducam
fortibus vitam coluere Parcae,
nec sinunt ultra tibi nos recentes
    nectere laurus,

magne, qui nomen licet incanorum
traditum ex multis atavis tulisti—
at tuos olim memorabit aevum
    omne triumphos.

non hiems illos furibunda mersit,
non mari in clauso scopuli latentes,
non fissa rimis abies, neque atrox
    abstulit ensis.

navitae sed tum nimium iocosi
voce fallebant hilari laborem,
et quiescebat calamoque dextram im-
    pleverat Heros.

XIX

Every schoolboy and schoolgirl knows "Toll for the brave".[1] Those who write Latin verses will be interested to see how William Cowper deals with his own spirited and familiar poem in a free Sapphic rendering. Even a superficial knowledge of Horatian art and practice will be enough to show them what a mediocre job the poet, turned Latinist, makes of it on the whole. A false quantity, a line that doesn't scan properly, jerky parentheses, Adonic verses containing elisions, and even strained Latin as such — these are things that will endear him to every lower Fifth struggler.

And, by the way, historians too could complain that Cowper does but scant justice to the facts. The disaster itself occurred on the 29th August 1782, on a Thursday morning. At that time the *Royal George* was undergoing a refit and a partial careening at Spithead, just off Portsmouth. To enable the carpenters to do repairs below the water-line on the port side, she was deliberately heeled over by having her 108 guns, or most of them, run over to starboard. So it only needed the "land-breeze" to tip her right over beyond the safety angle. But the shocking truth behind the news only came out at a court-martial which was held a few days later. For it was then proved that the ship had been on her last legs structurally, her timbers decayed, her planks ready to fall apart from the holding pegs, her entire hulk rotten and collapsing in pieces under the combined weight of the guns and some 1200 human bodies on board.

---

[1] First words of "Loss of the *Royal George*".

vos quibus cordi est grave opus piumque
humidum ex alto spolium levate,
et putrescentes sub aquis amicos
    reddite amicis.

hi quidem—sic dis placuit—fuere;
sed ratis nondum putris ire possit
rursus in bellum, Britonumque nomen
    tollere ad astra.

WM. COWPER

XX

De Feminae Fide

Stellam praecipitantem excipe de polo,
immortale deum fac pereat genus;
undas siste manu rite volubilis
    motusque Oceani ratos.

telluris mediae viscera perfora;
hesternus revocet praeteritas dies
horas, ver hiemem tempore non suo
    laetis velet honoribus;

vel flammam mihi tu divide in uncias,
vel tu flare retro coge Favonios:
tum demum in vario pectore feminae
    certam reppereris fidem.

S.A.H.

So much for—

> "Her timbers yet are sound,
>   and she may float again" *etc.*

> *sed ratis nondum putris ire possit*
> *rursus in bellum* . . . .

xx

Catch me a star that's falling from the sky,
Cause an immortal creature for to die;
Stop with thy hand the current of the seas,
Pierce the earth's centre to th' Antipodes;
Cause Time return and call back yesterday;
Clothe January like the month of May;
Weigh me an ounce of flame, blow back the wind;
Then thou hast found faith in a woman's mind.

ANON. (17th CENTURY)

XXI

Reddat Lyaeus numen; ego Evius
unus vocabor; scilicet hic, nefas,
 arcebit a regno bibentum
  terque quaterque capaciorem?

mundum universum di recreent mero,
vinosus aer ut simul additis
 tellure vinosoque ponto
  suppeditet mihi vina soli.

A.Y.C.

XXI

Cedas remittens imperium mihi,
Lenaee; vini sum deus unicus.
 certare dignarisne mecum
  qui decies supero bibendo?

mundum creetis, caelicolae, novum
vinique plenum; sit nihil insuper;
 sit pontus et tellus et aer
  tota merum mihi destinatum.

D.E.W.W.

XXI

A Drinking Song

Bacchus must now his power resign—
I am the only God of Wine!
It is not fit the wretch should be
In competition set with me,
Who can drink ten times more than he.

Make a new world, ye powers divine!
Stock'd with nothing else but Wine!
Let Wine its only product be,
Let Wine be earth and air and sea—
And let that wine be all for me!

HENRY CAREY (1693?–1743)

[*Note:* Interest attaches to these versions not so much for what they are as for
the fact that each is the work of one of two most distinguished classics,
Professors Campbell and Wormell, who independently of one another
happened to find themselves engaged in working the same original material,
no doubt both many years ago.]

XXII

Ponti profundis clausa recessibus,
strepens procellis, rupibus obsita,
    quam grata defesso virentem
        Skia sinum nebulosa pandis !

his cura, credo, sedibus exulat ;
his blanda certe pax habitat locis :
    non ira, non moeror quietis
        insidias meditatur horis.

at non cavata rupe latescere,
menti nec aegrae montibus aviis
    prodest vagari, nec frementes
        e scopulo numerare fluctus.

humana virtus non sibi sufficit,
datur nec aequum cuique animum sibi
    parare posse, ut Stoicorum
        secta crepet nimis alta fallax.

exaestuantis pectoris impetum,
Rex summe, solus tu regis arbiter,
    mentisque, te tollente, surgunt,
        te recidunt moderante fluctus.

                                        S.J.

XXII

["I am inclined to think", writes Boswell in the *Tour*, "that it was on this day (Sunday, 5th September 1773) he composed the following Ode upon the *Isle of Sky*, which a few days afterwards he showed me at Rasay". Boswell also records the alterations made by Johnson in verses 2 and 15–16 respectively. It appears that in the MS of stanza 1 Johnson originally had *imbribus invida* and *uvida nubibus*, but deleted both in favour of *rupibus obsita*: and in the fourth stanza he had written but struck out

parare posse, utcunque iactet
grandiloquus nimis alta Zeno]

* * * * *

Locked in the deep recesses of Ocean, howling with gales, defended by rocks, how welcome to the weary, cloudy Skye, you open your green breast!

Care, I believe, is a stranger to these parts: surely grateful peace lives in these parts; no anger, no grief plans treacherous attack in quiet hours.

But it is useless for the mind diseased to hide in the hollow of a rock or to wander on pathless mountains, or to count the roaring waves from a cliff.

Human virtue is not self-sufficient, nor is it given to each man to procure peace of mind for himself in accordance with the false and over-subtle doctrine of the Stoic sect.

Of the emotion of the passionate heart, O King supreme, Thou alone art Lord and Master; the passions of the mind rise at Thy command and fall back at Thy command.

XXIII

Euro tremendam nuntius ocior
defert anhelans rem Capitolio,
    quae vera compagem columnae
        totius imperiumque franget.

fertur Sygambris noster in ultimis
stativa miles praesidia occupans
    sentire non parvis pruinis
        esse pedes penetratus ambos.

vultus viriles deiciunt humi et
castrensis escae dulcia respuunt;
    et contubernales cohortis
        post tacitos sedet atra Cura.

dux ipse verbis exposuit suis
causam malorum: "castra diu carent
    formae puellarisque tactus
        indiciis, quibus orba pubes

taurinam apud se militiae crepat
partem, neque hostis Sarmatici minas
    arcere, nec tuto per auras
        dirigere Icarios volando

currus valebit: fronte domestica
sit aequa virtus!"—numquam alias dato
    dimovit obstantes Catones
        consilio rigidosque mores.

iam quinque lectae de popularibus
praestant puellis se per Ionicos
    motus theatralemque mimum
        photographis simul exhibendas:

XXIII

Thus Jones Minor obliges:-

Swifter than the East Wind the panting messenger reports a fearful thing to the Capitol, which being true will break the framework of the whole column and the Empire. Our soldiery occupying static garrisons among the distant Sygambri is said to be feeling itself penetrated as to both feet by no small hoar-frosts. Their manly countenances they cast on the ground; they spit back the sweets of camp food; and behind the silent mess-mates of the cohort sits Black Care. The leader himself has explained in his own words the cause of the evils:-

"For a long time the camp lacks indications of
girlish beauty and touch, deprived of which our youth
keeps harping on the bullish part of military service
in its midst: nor will it be able to keep off the
threats of the Sarmatic enemy, nor safely direct Icarian
chariots by flying through the breezes. O for an equal
courage on the home front!"

With a plan never before given he has moved aside the obstructive Catos and rigid manners. Now five chosen ones from the popular girls offer themselves to be exhibited together in photographs during Ionic dances and a theatrical show.

By imprinting red mouths on Kodakian films, each the mark of her little lip, they have sent to the tottering heroes tablets thus mindful of love. May these stars, having been hung up, raise the sad minds of the fighting man!

"Not without Gloria dancing shall this wall, o comrades, hold the transparent Marlene — this wall, which guards the curved flank of the chaste Monica. Here, here, place the others, whether Diana with a raised leg or whether Phyllis with the projecting breastplate pleases more." Hope having been restored to you, neither do you — while a Marxian satellite hangs over and threatens — scorn vital statistics, o boy, nor dancing shows.

*   *   *   *   *

[*Note*: A press report gave it that morale having collapsed at an R.A.F. unit in a remote part of the globe its cause was traced to the complete absence of "pin-up's" in the crew-room. It appeared from the report that matters were only put right and the fighting spirit of the men restored after certain measures had been taken, as described in the above ode.]

ora imprimendo Kodakiis rubra
chartis, labelli quaeque notam sui,
   misere ad heroas labantes
      sic memores tabulas amoris.

haec astra maestas militis erigant
suspensa mentes : "non sine Gloria
   saltante Marlenam, sodales,
      hic vitream paries habebit,

curvum pudicae qui Monicae latus
custodit : hic, hic ponite ceteras,
   seu crure sublimi Diana,
      sive magis placet eminenti

thorace Phyllis." spe tibi reddita
nec, dum satelles Marxius imminet
   instatque, vitales figuras
      sperne, puer, neque tu choreas.

A.I.

XXIV

Khushhal Khan
Warrior and Poet (1613–1689 A.D.).

Note: Khushhal Khan, hereditary chief of the Khatak tribe of Pathans, was born at Surai in the Peshawar Valley and lies buried at the same place. On his tomb, which is shaded by the chenar trees that he loved, is inscribed the best remembered of his verses :-

"My sword I girt upon my thigh
    To gird our nation's ancient fame;
Its champion in this age am I
    The Khatak chief, Khushhal my name."

For the first half of his long life Khushhal enjoyed the favour and in some degree the friendship of the Mogul Emperor Shah Jahan, whose feudatory he was and to whose state he did some service. But in 1658 Aurangzeb succeeded to the throne having defeated and deposed his father. With that Khushhal's fortunes began to decline, and in 1664 he was arrested, clapped in irons and sent down into Hindustan, where he spent five weary years in captivity. Having somehow procured his release he laid himself out for revenge, and began to play a part not unlike that of William Wallace or Owen Glendower. The rebellion which he fomented by his pen and furthered by his sword can be counted as not least among the causes that on the death of Aurangzeb brought about the dramatic downfall of the great Moguls, and that in turn opened the way for the East India Company to become the Paramount Power in India.

Khushhal sang of love and wine as well as of war and of the chase in which he took great delight. He sang, too, of the mystery of human destinies and of the relentless march of time, and his psalms proclaim his earnest faith in one God, beneficial but inscrutable. Beauty in all its forms he loved. As he himself recorded–

"Let old Khushhal confess
    Two things I prize In me mine eyes
    In all the world beside Where they have loveliness espied,
    I prize that loveliness."

One form of loveliness that delighted his heart as well as his eyes was the loveliness of his native country Khorassan, with its distant snows, its rugged peaks and its fertile valleys, where running water — skilfully applied — rewards the garden, and the grateful shade of trees, in whose branches birds sit and sing — all in contrast to the arid flatness of Hindustan, the land of his

xxiv *(cont.)*

Ad Ministrum

Sit comes gratus mihi, sit diota
cum rosa multa veteris Falerni :
ver sine his odi ; cyathos, minister,
    prome capaces.

tibiae mixti citharaeque cantus
quid docent, quid nos procul audientes?
"nescit exactos iterare cursus
    mobilis hora ;

nec semel lapsam revocare possis,
si petas : vitae spatium licet sit
dulce, nil prodest tamen hoc caducum et
    futile donum.

num tibi urgenti properabit aetas,
num retardanti pede lentiore
cedet? heu saevum precibusque inexo-
    rabile tempus !

quotquot arserunt pueri et puellae
mutua flamma, cito tempus omnes
ferreum occidit." citius, minister,
    funde liquorem.

E.B.H.

captivity. In the prose narrative with which the cantos of Lalla Rookh are
interspersed, Moore mentions "the rich valley of Hussun Abdaul which had
always been a favourite resting-place of the Emperors in their annual migration
to Kashmir". There the Emperor Jahangir, Shah Jahan's father, had caused
a garden to be made and it is this garden with its chenar trees that on the long
road from Delhi northwards first apprises the traveller that Hindustan is
behind him and Khorassan in front. Elphinstone's description of it was the
source of Moore's inspiration. In such a garden — for it is not unique — the
scene of this little ode is set.

XXIV (cont.)

Roses, Wine—a friend to share:
Spring sans wine I will not bear;
Abstinence I do abhor—
Cup on cup, my Saki, pour.
Hark the lute and pipe! Give ear.
What says music to our cheer?
"Time once flown returneth never;
Idle moments, gone for ever.
Would'st recall them? Call in vain.
Life, our mortal life, hath sweetness:
As its sweetness, so its fleetness.
Count it nothing: 'tis no gain.
Doth time tarry for thy prizing?
Or make speed for thy despising?
Time hath many a lover slain:
Time is heedless, time is heartless."
Saki, fill and fill again.

KHUSHHAL KHAN[1] (translated by
Sir Evelyn Howell).

[1] The distinctly Horatian tang of Khushhal's verse I have already commented on in G & R viii 1961 184–7, in a paper entitled *Khushhal Khan
Togatus*. The Editor of *Greece & Rome* has kindly consented to the
reprinting of material from this article here and on pp. 256, 257.

XXV

Ad Pegasum

O propulse novum, Pegase, per polum,
cui, dum cauda fluit flatibus igneis,
    prisci natus Apollo
        fit dux undecimus dei,

lictis Castalio fonte sororibus,
sic audax amitam visere Cynthiam,
    dic quos aethera nautas
        visuros ferat alveus.

ut Troianus equus ventre suo duces
fudit Graiugenas, unde per editum
    funem sic inimicam
        terram lapsa petit manus.

expertusne vias Armipotens latet
caeli sidereas? qui peragrat polum
    Collinus prius illic?
        illic stridulus Aldrinus?

quos omnes moneo cum semel ex equo
fortes exierint, ne quis inhospitum
    dum cratera pererrat
        Tranquilli Maris inscius,

si fors ante oculos Endymion toro
Lunae iunctus erit, sollicitet deam,
    neu Lunae latus atrum,
        dum caeco pede decidit,

XXV

To Pegasus, New Style

O Pegasus, driv'n o'er uncharted skies,
   whose tail streams out afar with jets of fire,
whose bridle-rein even now Apollo plies,
   eleventh son of ancient godly sire,

Leaving his sisters at Castalian spring,
   his father's sister, Moon, to visit bold,
what astronauts within art sheltering?
   say, what sky-watchers does that belly hold?

As once the Trojan Horse poured forth from womb
   Greek chiefs, who thence by rope put out from side
to soil unfriendly, foes they knew not whom,
   a band that blindly searched, did downward glide.

Does Armstrong lurk within, long skilled to probe
   the starry ways of heaven? O, tell me, does
Collins there hide, who erstwhile ranged the globe?
   hides there brave Aldrin, whom his friends call Buzz?

All whom I warn, as soon as from the Horse
   they boldly venture forth, that none there be
wending across some crater drear his course,
   or blindly ranging o'er the Tranquil Sea,

To vex the goddess, should his eyes chance meet
   Endymion locked in Moon's embraces tight.
o never let a faller's groping feet
   upon the darker lunar surface light!

attingat ; canibus nam periit suis
Actaeon sibi quod viderat obviam
   casu membra Dianam
     nudam. dum vagus impiis

aversam pedibus conteris heu deam,
pendendum quod erit supplicium tibi
   danti partibus ictum
     Phoebes posterioribus?

T.W.M.

XXVI

Rugosa quamvis displiceat mea
frons intuenti, Lydia, non minus
   instante signabit senecta
     sollicitam tibi ruga frontem.

longo venustas tempore disperit :
signo notabunt omnia lugubri
   anni recedentes, genisque
     deripient roseis honorem.

atqui superstes nescioquid manet
huius venusti, Lydia, corporis,
   quo fretus elusi valebo
     ferre minas animosus Orci.

olim nitebunt perpetuis tua
dilecta quondam lumina laudibus
   nec mille post annos hebescent
     carminibus celebrata nostris.

F.C.G.

Actaeon by his own fierce hounds was rent,
  though only chance had brought him to the place;
and bore through Dian cruellest punishment
  for gazing on her naked, face to face.

Woe, if when goddess's face be turned away
  thine impious foot to bruise her, Wanderer, starts!
what penalty wilt thou perforce then pay,
  planting a kick on Phoebe's hinder parts?

T.W.M.

XXVI

Marquise, if now upon my face
  Some wrinkles show, remember only
The same will mar your comely grace
  When you are old and you are lonely.

Time spares no beauty. Year by year
  He marks with his fell sign abhorrèd,
And he will blanch your roses, dear,
  As he has wrinkled all my forehead.

Yet have I something that is fair
  To leave undimmed when I've departed,
Something that makes my spirit dare
  To meet old Time and leave him thwarted.

Those eyes that once were dear to me
  May shine with an undying glory,
And in a thousand years may be
  Still bright because I tell their story.

WILFRID THORLEY (after Corneille)

XXVII

Num meis currit biiugis aratrum
quod manu certa per agros regebam?
num, mihi ut vivo, crepitant habenis
    aera vibratis?

"nunc pedes pulsu resonant equini et
lora tinnitu crepitant aeno:
nil novi, si te quod arare noras
    occulit ipsum."

dic an agresti iuvenes palaestra
fluminis ripam celebrent, et acre
robur ostendant, mihi dum iacenti
    membra quiescunt.

"strenui dedunt studio virili
corpora et florent viridi iuventa,
qualis in silvis abies et alto
    vertice pinus."

mente contenta mea Pyrrha vivit,
Pyrrha quam tanto gemitu reliqui?
an dies maestos agit et dolendo
    fessa recumbit?

"scilicet laetam gerit illa mentem
nec cubat tristi dolitura lecto:
mitte iam curas, age, tu profundum
    carpe soporem."

XXVII

"Is my team ploughing,
    That I was used to drive,
And hear the harness jingle,
    When I was man alive?"

Ay, the horses trample,
    The harness jingles now;
No change though you lie under
    The land you used to plough.

"Is football playing
    Along the river shore,
With lads to chase the leather
    Now I stand up no more?"

Ay, the ball is flying,
    The lads play heart and soul;
The goal stands up, the keeper
    Stands up to keep the goal.

"Is my girl happy,
    That I thought hard to leave,
And has she tired of weeping
    As she lies down at eve?"

Ay, she lies down lightly,
    She lies not down to weep:
Your girl is well contented,
    Be still, my lad, and sleep.

quid? tuosne artus iuvenalis ardor
firmat exili mihi denegatus?
tune quam nostrum melius cubile es
    vespere nactus?

"est mihi in lecto bene, qua paratum est
quicquid optarent iuvenes, amice:
mortui solor viduam; illa quae sit
    quaerere noli."

F.R.D.

XXVIII

Hortuli praesens nemorisque custos,
Faune—nam tu scis placuisse nymphis—
virgines quaero quot in hoc solebant
    ludere saltu.

quo fugit Chloris numerosa, cuive
flava resplendet Damalis? quod altum
callidam Lyden utriusque linguae
    detinet antrum?

nonne dilectae redeant alumnae
cantibus semper choreisque amicae?
trade, qua possim revocare pulchras,
    Faune, cicutam".

at mihi ridens deus: "huc redire
non datur", dixit, "semel evagatis:
disce et, o iam nunc properantis horae
    praeda, monere."

F.J.L.

"Is my friend hearty,
        Now I am thin and pine,
And has he found to sleep in
        A better bed than mine?"

Yes, lad, I lie easy,
        I lie as lads would choose;
I cheer a dead man's sweetheart:
        Never ask me whose.

                        A. E. HOUSMAN

XXVIII

To a Faun
(On an Urn in the garden of Bedford College, London
University)

"Garden protector, patron of grove
        Delightful to nymphs, Faun—
For you know how to charm them—all the girls
I seek, who used to play upon this lawn.

Where's Chloris fleeing with her fading music?
        Who sees the gleam of gold—
Damalis's golden hair? And Lyde skilled
In both the tongues is prisoned in what deep hold?

Surely the fair would return? Garden Faun,
        Give me the flute whose voice
Recalls; and favourite pupils—ever the friends
Of song and dance—will all again rejoice."

The god was laughing: "No return for those
        Who go their different ways.
My warning heed: for now the victim's you;
On you the hastening hour this moment preys."

                        Transl. MARY OAKES

XXIX

Ad Titum

Tellurem Phaëthon exsciderat rotis
ni fulmen citius Iuppiter anxius
misisset; puerum qui temerarium
    dat leto, dat opem suis.

fratrem nunc ululant Heliades suum,
secure cisium qui regat, increpant,
qui cena rediens 'Da, puer et viae!'
    clamet, potus equos agat.

cuius vix patiens saeva Britannia,
qua castella ferunt barbara per suos
multum posse, vetat quemlibet ebrium
    nutans dirigat essedum.

saccum nam statuit lex ibi iudicem,
Bacchum, si fuerit pars animae, reum,
qua sufflet titubans Automedon datam
    vesicam, iubet ut vigil.

crystallique rubent, indicium nocens,
os circum tubuli, dum pater evolat,
ut fugit Bromius carcere Pentheos,
    digna indigna ferens deus.

te nuper biiugos dum, Tite, per vias
imprudens agitas, undique fluctuans,
et tecum Clymenen quae sedet, uvidum
    ne pergas prohibet vigil.

XXIX

To Titus

With chariot Phaëthon the world had rent
Had troubled Jove a quicker bolt not sent;
The god that gave to death a headstrong boy
Assistance timely to his people lent.

Sun's daughters mourn their brother, sad threnode,
Chide carefree drivers who no danger bode,
The driver drunk, who as he leaves the feast
Asks for another cup to pledge the road.

Such brooked not savage Britain, as they say,
Where barbarous castles o'er their own held sway,
And wielded power, forbidding any sot
To steer a lurching car upon its way.

There Bag is judge—for so the statute saith—
Bacchus the felon, be he linked with breath
With which the staggering Jehu must inflate
The proffered skin if Law so ordereth.

Dark flush the crystals—O the damning sign!—
About the mouthpiece ere the God of Wine
Flies, as the Thunderer fled from Pentheus' jail,
Enduring unmeet sufferings, though divine.

Thee, Titus, late along the road out flat,
Mad driver hurling car this way and that,
Thee stopped a policeman and forbade proceed,
As drunk, while Clymene beside thee sat.

qui saccum nimii porrigit indicem
vini, flare iubens, scilicet ut dei
tu fias bibuli proditor halitu :
    contra nobile tu refers—

"si sic flare deos fas homines foret,
flaret Pierius Naevius Evium.
evoe, Bacche ! piis non ego te meis
    labris expulero deum !"

quae dixisse tamen paenituit brevi ;
libertate cares, deliciis, rotis,
odit te Clymene ; te peditem facit
    lex et carceris incolam.

frenos lippus erus ne teneam madens,
mavult ipse deus credere lyncibus.
cur auriga merum, potor amet rotas ?
    aut temo iuvet aut cadus.

T.W.M.

Held out the bag, as witness to the truth
Of wine excessive, bade thee blow, forsooth,
To make thy gasps bewray the thirsty God—
Yet thy reply befitted noble youth.

"If it were right that man exhale god so,
Bard Naevius a Bacchic gale would blow;
My pious lips shall n'er have blasted forth
Heaven's son. I'd rather "Bacchus!" call, "Evoe!"

Words soon alas! to bring their bitter rue.
Thou'rt reft of freedom, love and chariot too.
Thee Clymene now hates, pedestrian made
By law, in prison and with time to do.

I'd ply no reins, blear after many a draught;
Bacchus lets sharp-eyed lynxes steer his craft.
Why seek the driver wine, why drinker wheel?
Choose this or that, wine-cask or chariot shaft.

                    T. W. MELLUISH

XXX

Ad Murem

Pelle qui parvus nitida pavere
promptus es, quid tam trepidante cursu
me fugis? vano quatitur timore,
    Mus, tibi pectus,

si truci credis stimulo minaces
nos secuturos: homo enim tyrannus
omne quae vivum prius obligabant
    foedera rupit,

hostis et muri metuendus ipse
iure nunc, eheu, videor; sed ambo
nonne terreni breve pauperesque
    degimus aevum?

saepe te furto rapuisse frustum
non nego: victu tibi quis carenti
parcus e tanta dare messe raras
    nolit aristas,

parte cum maiore bearit illum
Faustitas largum? tua nunc ruinam
dat casa exilis pariesque in omnes
    spargitur auras,

nec novus restat viridantis herbae
caespes ut possis renovare tectum,
nec procul distat referens December
    frigora ventis.

XXX

To a Mouse

[On Turning her up in her Nest with the Plough,
November 1785]

Wee, sleekit, cow'rin', tim'rous beastie!
O, what a panic's in thy breastie!
Thou need na start awa sae hasty,
    Wi' bickering brattle!
I wad be laith to rin an' chase thee,
    Wi' murd'ring pattle!

I'm truly sorry man's dominion
Has broken nature's social union,
An' justifies that ill opinion
    Which mak's thee startle
At me, thy poor earth-born companion,
    An' fellow-mortal!

I doubt na, whyles, but thou may thieve;
What then? poor beastie, thou maun live!
A daimen-icker in a thrave
    'S a sma' request:
I'll get a blessin' wi' the lave,
    An' never miss 't.

Thy wee bit housie, too, in ruin!
Its silly wa's the win's are strewin'!
An' naething, now, to big a new ane,
    O' foggage green!
An' bleak December's winds ensuin',
    Baith snell an' keen!

ante visisti segete arva falces
flava nudantes rapidumque inertis
impetum brumae, Boreanque molli
    tegmine falsus

usque vitabas ibi cum, frequenti
quae tibi morsu steterat, tremendo
perscidit cellam tenuem fragore
    vomer iniquus.

iam domo pulsus profugusque rupta
irritam spectas operam, pruinae
frigus et durae subiturus acres
    grandinis imbres.

an putas mentem tibi inesse frustra
providam soli? cata cogitemus,
in vicem gaudi veniunt utrisque
    saepe dolores.

tu tamen prae me caput es beatum,
te nihil tangit nisi cura praesens;
me retro spectare piget, futuri
    me timor angit.

                       N.D.

Thou saw the fields laid bare an' waste,
An' weary winter comin' fast,
An' cozie here, beneath the blast,
    Thou thought to dwell,—
Till, crash! the cruel coulter past
    Out thro' thy cell.

That wee bit heap o' leaves an' stibble
Has cost thee mony a weary nibble!
Now thou's turn'd out, for a' thy trouble,
    But house or hold,
To thole the winter's sleety dribble,
    An' cranreuch cauld!

But, Mousie, thou art no thy lane,
In proving foresight may be vain;
The best laid schemes o' mice an' men,
    Gang aft a-gley,
An' lea'e us nought but grief an' pain
    For promis'd joy.

Still thou art blest, compar'd wi' me!
The present only toucheth thee!
But, och! I backward cast my e'e,
    On prospects drear!
An' forward, tho' I canna see,
    I guess an' fear.

ROBERT BURNS

XXXI

Quo, Musa, tendis? tristitiam mihi
arcessis? apta carminibus lyra
   imponis antiquam iocosis
      fervidus ut moduler querelam?

frigescit aer, nox tenebris tegit
terram, quieto labitur alveo
   dum Rhenus, accendit cacumen
      puniceis radiis Apollo.

considit illic crinibus aureis
virgo renidens, cui species nitet
   miranda sublimi, comasque
      pectinibus decorans et auro.

splendor comarum fulget et aureus
cultus refulget; carmina non prius
   audita dum cantat modisque
      mirificis capit audientes.

audit magister navis et angitur,
defixus haeret nec videt ut minax
   praerupta saxorum coronet
      spuma; trahit miserum puellae

cantus, puellam suspicit impotens
montemque summum: praecipiti ruunt
   in saxa Sirenis tenore
      navis et ipse modis revinctus.

A.T.

XXXI

Ich weiß nicht, was soll es bedeuten,
Daß ich so traurig bin;
Ein Märchen aus alten Zeiten,
Das kommt mir nicht aus dem Sinn.

Die Luft ist kühl und es dunkelt,
Und ruhig fließt der Rhein;
Der Gipfel des Berges funkelt
Im Abendsonnenschein.

Die schönste Jungfrau sitzet
Dort oben wunderbar,
Ihr goldnes Geschmeide blitzet,
Sie kämmt ihr goldenes Haar.

Sie kämmt es mit goldenem Kamme,
Und singt ein Lied dabei;
Das hat eine wundersame,
Gewaltige Melodei.

Den Schiffer im kleinen Schiffe
Ergreift es mit wildem Weh;
Er schaut nicht die Felsenriffe,
Er schaut nur hinauf in die Höh.

Ich glaube, die Wellen verschlingen
Am Ende Schiffer und Kahn;
Und das hat mit ihrem Singen
Die Lore-Ley getan.

H. HEINE

XXXII

Ad Doctorem Vtriusque Linguae

Mitte neglectos, Licini, Camenae
conqueri lucos veterumque mores,
parcior quod iam tibi praebet aurem
    mane iuventus.

turba dum crebro studet apparatu
nosse quod pondus proprium sit aeri,
quive frigentis lateant Galaesi
    mole calores.

non leves curas nimium frequentis
pastor accepit gregis : huic diurnos
cum tulit coetus et acerba rauci
    proelia ludi,

durior restat series laborum
nox et horrendis operosa chartis :
te quies matura vocat novello
    non sine libro.

desipit vano bona qui deorum
dona metitur numero : biformi
gloriam aeternam peperit magistro
    rarus Achilles.

M. H. L.

XXXII

To a Classical Schoolmaster

Nay, honoured mentor, cease this dull complaining
   Of Art and Wisdom driven from the land
Because the virtues of your proffered training
   Attract so sparse a band;

What time the throng, in all their massed depravity,
   With tube and balance tirelessly compete
To wrest from copper his Specific Gravity,
   From Ice his Latent Heat!

Who rules a mob may bid farewell to quiet;
   The big battalion brings a wealth of care.
What vocal hordes, what angry scenes of riot
   The hapless man must bear!

What reams of paper, hungry for correction,
   Demand his labours ere the night be fled—
While you resume some fable of detection,
   And seek the timely bed!

Then prate no more of numbers, worthy mentor:
   Not thus the bounties of high Heaven are weighed.
A few good pupils won their peerless Centaur
   A crown that shall not fade.

M. H. LONGSON

XXXIII

Iam Sol ab ortu iecit in aetheris
cratera rubram lumine tesseram,
    gaudetque flammantem Diei
        Rex laqueum iaculatus arci,

gratum elocuta mane clientibus
Bacchi ferarum Matre cupidinum,
    "potate mortales ! diebus
        inserui geniale vinum."

cantare credas Atthida sic rosae
quae pulsa nimbi verbere palleat,
    "ne decoloreris, bibenda est
        adsidue medicina rubra."

mane hauriendum fer, puer, huc pede
laeto Falernum ; dic feriens melos
    plectro quot hi menses tyrannos
        abstulerint minuente Phoebo.

decede nulli, reice gratiam
seu fiat hostis dirior Hercule
    seu forte Lucullo sodalis
        divitiis meliorque donis.

haec sola nacto, caespitis angulum,
plectrum, puellam, vina, satis mihi
    lucri sit in praesens ; quod ultra est
        debeat Elysium volenti.

de farre panem vasque capax mihi
pernamque si des et comitem Chloen
    inter recumbenti ruinas,
        tam bene non epulere, Caesar !

XXXIII

The sun has cast the noose of dawn upon the roof; the Kaikhosrau of day has cast the bead of rosy light into the cup of Heaven.

Drink wine, for Love's cry at the hour of morn has cast the proclamation "Drink!" among the days.

The cloud washes the dust from the rose-garden's cheek; the nightingale cries to the pale rose, as so it seems, "Ever must one be drinking wine!"

'Tis the time of the morning-draught, O boy of happy foot; play a melody and bring forward the wine: this coming of June and going of December has carried off to the dust hundreds of thousands of Jam (shyds) and Kai (khosraus).

Lower not thy neck, though the adversary be Rustum-i-Zal; take no favour, though the friend be Hatim of Tai.

A cup, an idol (fair) and a lute on the meadow's marge: these three are my cash-in-hand; take, if thou wilt, thy credit-paradise.

If one may have a loaf of wheat-flour, a two-maund of wine, and a thigh of lamb, seated with a heart's darling in a ruined palace — that is a pleasure that is not the attainment of any Sultan.

The translation by Prof. A. J. Arberry from the Persian of the original is published with his kind permission.

dulce est, ut aiunt, Elysium ; puto
dulces racemos : prende quod hic datur
   spe plebis eluta—memento
      tympana dulce procul sonare !

noctu, priusquam te dolor opprimat
o stulta, vinum ferre iube rubens ;
   aurone te finxit Prometheus
      quam fodiant positam ligones?

Tellus ut antiquum hospitium est, ubi
Lux invicem et Nox dant stabulum iugis ;
   molesve semeso tyranni
      strata cibo tumulisque multi.

ne quicquid herbae ripa dat hispidae
spernas ! prioris pulvere fac satum
   lanugine ex molli genarum
      gramen Hamadryadis fuisse.

qui sint dolores cras fuge pendere !
pone in lucro iam nunc data ; cras pedes
   tellure delapsi sequemur
      saecula quotquot abhinc profectos.

adversa passus flamina, temporis
momenta carpas prospera ; Fors tibi
   nunquam vacillans nil favoris
      alterius vice largiatur !

florent ut herbae, cum pluit, uvidae
nobis rubenti sic opus est mero :
   quis cernet ex nostris virentes
      ossibus et reputabit herbas?

They tell me that Paradise with houris is delightful : I say the grape's juice is delightful ; take the cash-in-hand and wash thy hands of the credit, for to hear drums from afar is delightful.

Ere thy sorrow surprises thee by night and carry thee away, speak idol, that they may bring the rosy wine ; not gold art thou, O foolish one, that men should lay thee in the earth and dig thee up again.

This ancient hostelry named Earth is the resting-place of the piebald (steed) of dawn and nightfall ; it is a feast left over by a hundred Jamshyds, it is a grave that is the couch of a hundred Bahrams.

Ev'ry grass that has ever been on the bank of a stream has been, so to say, the down on the cheek of one of faery temper ; see that thou settest not thy foot contemptuously upon the grass, for that grass has been from the dust of a tulip face.

O friend, come, let us not consume to-morrow's grief, and let us count for gain this one moment of cash-in-hand ; to-morrow when we pass out of this ancient tavern, we shall be step in step with those gone a thousand years ahead.

Arise ! indulge not in the sorrow of the passing world ; sit down and pass a moment happily ; if there had been any fidelity in Fortune's temper, never would the turn have come to thee from others.

The cloud has come and wept over the grass ; one must not live without crimson wine. This grass, upon which we gaze to-day—for whom shall our dust provide grass to gaze upon ?

labrum premebam vivere longius
ardens doceri; labra premens mea
   sic clam susurravit culullus,
      "nos similis societ cupido!"

spectare Thressae lumina deviae
sparsoque mundam rore libet rosam,
   ne frigus infandum revolvas
      deliciis modo restitutis!

uno Dolorem vase cecidero,
dives duobus ducere Thyiadas
   ausim; ter, uxores, valete,
      caeca Fides Ratioque sicca!

quid "esse vel non" sit facie scio,
re cuncta "subter vel super"—at probro
   sit scire—num scivi quid usquam
      re superans facieve Bacchum?

potum et ferentem vas umero senem
vidi ex taberna: "te pudeat," madens
   inquam, "Deorum!" "Quid quod," inquit,
      "pocula Di peperere? pota!"

gaude repletis ebrius amphoris
Thressamve iuxta si breve tu sedes;
   nil cuncta fient—nil es, Omar;
      te recolens nihil esse, gaude!

pro calculis nos trans tabulam movet
tellure factam saeva Necessitas,
   vitaque deludit necisque
      dein alium ex alio dat arcae.

I laid my lip against the pitcher's lip in the extremity of desire that I might seek from it the means of long life; it laid its lip upon my lip, and said secretly — "I too was once like thee. Consort with me awhile."

Upon the cheek of the rose the Nauruz dew is sweet; at the meadow's marge the face of the heart's delight is fair; of the winter that is past, whatever thou sayest, 'tis not sweet — be happy, speak not of winter, for to-day is fair.

I will slay Sorrow with a cup that holds one maund, I will enrich myself with two bumpers of wine; I will triply divorce Reason and Faith, then I will take to wife the daughter of the vine.

I know the outward shape of "not-being and being"; I know the inward of all that is high or low; for all that, may I be ashamed of my knowledge if I know of any rank beyond drunkenness.

Last night, drunken, I passed by the Tavern and saw an old man drunk, with a jar on his shoulder. I said, "Why art thou not ashamed before God?" He replied, "God is gracious. Drink wine."

Khayyám, if thou art drunk with wine, be happy; if thou hast sat for a moment with an idol, be happy; the end of everything is nothingness, consider that thou art nothing, and — while existing — be happy!

We are playthings, and Heaven is the player: we play our little game on the board of existence, we fall back one by one into the box of non-existence.

en, huc et illuc ceu pila cursitas
ictus flagello ; nil ais ; advenis
   iactatus—ut iactaris, istae
     Tergeminae tua fata norunt !

Supreme, nutu cuncta movens tuo,
seu vita seu mors exitus est, valet
   plus murmur hoc tecum tabernae
     voce pia sine te sacelli.

nuper vagatus fictilium fabri
visi tabernam, qua duo milia
   collata vasorum fuere et
     labra loqui potuere partis,

nam poculi vox, crede mihi, querens
non ante visum me subito rogat
   "is vasa qui vendit coempta
     vel fabricata—ubinam locorum est ?"

quassetne potus particulas faber
vasis ?—tot artus membraque tenuia
   quis iunxit impendens amorem ?
     quae manus haec furiosa fregit ?

cum mors supinum sub pede vulserit
me ceu volucrem, vas modo pulvere
   fingas, odoratus Falernum et
     forte vigens Acheronta rumpam !

praebe Lyaeum quo facies mea
pallens rubescat ; cum perii, comes,
   haec lauta Lenaeo liquore
     pampineis tege membra lignis.

Whirling like a ball before the mallet of Fate, go running right and left, and say nothing ; for He that hurled thee into the chase, He knows and He knows, and He knows.

If I should speak secrets with Thee in Taverns, better than I should say prayers without Thee in the prayer-niche ; O Thou first and last, beside Whom all else is naught, if Thou wilt consume me, or if Thou wilt do me cherish !

Last night I walked into the workshop of a potter ; I saw two thousand pots, vocal and silent.

Suddenly one of the pots lifted up its voice and cried, "Where is the potter, the pot-buyer and the pot-seller?"

The particles of a goblet joined together no drunkard thinks it right to shatter ; so many delicate heads and feet, heads and hands, by whose love were they joined together? By whose hate were they shattered?

When I lie down under Death's feet as a bird plucked by his hand — beware ! make not my clay into aught but a bowl ; methinks when the wine's perfume comes to me, I shall live.

Comrade, make me my provender of wine and make this amber cheek like the ruby ; when I die, wash me with wine and make my coffin of the timber of the vine.

heu, ver iuventae fugit, adest hiems ;
cantoque versum carminis ultimum :
   quando vel advenit iuventa
     laeta citis abiitve pinnis?

rerum potitus dummodo sim Deus
hoc omne tollam de medio genus
   ficturus integro proboque
     commodius magis atque cordi.

conviva, mirans ora sodalium
pulchra et iocosas colloquii vices,
   cum Chia promentur, precare
     pro misero Styga me bibente !

W.B.-H.

XXXIV

Quae tibi poscam superos, Georgi,
dona, cui solem furibundus urget
iam Leo et natale reversa tempus
     sidera dicunt?

non cupis tellus quod avara condit,
non quod ex Indis reparatur oris,
nec quod et ponti generat nitescens
     unda refusi.

Gratias semper facilesque Musas
diliges horasque coles quietas :
hae tibi sint, hae pretiosiores
     usque vel auro.

A.O.H.

Alas, the scroll of my youth has been rolled up and the spring of life has turned to winter; that joyous bird whose name was youth, alas, I know not when it came or when it departed.

If I had hold of heaven like God, I would remove this Heaven from the midst, and would make another Heaven in such wise that the noble man should easily attain his heart's desire.

When, comrades, ye come meeting together and gladden your hearts with one another's beauty — when as the Saki takes in hand the Magian wine, do you in your prayers be mindful of me.

OMAR KHAYYÁM
(transl. A. J. Arberry)

XXXIV

What, George, for you shall be my prayer to heaven,
While 'gainst the Sun the fierce Lion makes his way,
And now the stars revolving bring again
      Your natal day?

You seek not what the miser earth conceals,
Nor what of wealth on Indy's shores men gain,
Nor what with shining wave creates anew
      The ebbing main.

Always the Graces and the gentle Muse
You love; you love the quietly passing hour:
May these be yours, may these remain—than gold
      A richer dower.

XXXV

Tu quae timorum reicis impetum et
curas sedentes post equitem nigras
    depellis, aeterno saporis,
        Herba, tui capior lepore,

seu me sub ortu pallidulo iuvas,
seu prandii post tempora non minus
    iucunda, seu summas sub umbra
        vesperis illecebras ministras.

atqui veneni deripitur tui
guttis duabus vel minus, ut ferunt,
    aelurus ad larvas ut exstet
        nil nisi quod veribus rotetur.

sic increpant te iam medici : "picem
si quis cylindro e fumifero imbibet,
    exilis in formam lacertae et
        ingenium prope simiarum

tabescet ; amens adsiduo suam
mox in maritam verbere saeviet,
    vitaque defunctus probrosa
        perfodiet iugulum ipse cultro."

hos tam malignos Dis ferat ! est mihi
multus sodalis qui bene cum sua
    uxore vicinisque vivit
        ac tubuli redolentis aurae

XXXV

Ode to Tobacco

Thou who when fears attack
Bidst them avaunt, and black
Care, at the horseman's back
   Perching, unseatest;
Sweet, when the morn is grey;
Sweet, when they've cleared away
Lunch; and at close of day
   Possibly sweetest:

I have a liking old
For thee, though manifold
Stories, I know, are told
   Not to thy credit;
How one (or two at most)
Drops make a cat a ghost—
   Doctors have said it:

How they who smoke fusees
All grow by slow degrees
Brainless as chimpanzees
   Meagre as lizards:
Go mad and beat their wives;
Plunge (after shocking lives)
Razors and carving knives
   Into their gizzards.

Confound such knavish tricks!
Yet know I five or six
Smokers who freely mix
   Still with their neighbours;

iussu maritae post solidum diem
indulget, et si noxia felibus
    tu grata es humanis, quis usum
      deneget, Herba, tui vaporis,

si continenter sumitur? occupa
testam tabaci, Postume; tu novum
    succende, Pomponi, cylindrum
      Fumifer ut celebretur Auctor.

E.O.F.

XXXVI

Ad Erycum

Miserorum est modo ludo dare amorem, neque fumum
bibere herbae, neque sedem variari patientes
    ferulae verbera longae.

tibi pensum Gulielmus, puer audax, tibi capsam,
numerorumque, Eryce, atrox studium aufert, catapultae
    fabricator male tutae,

simul hora schola dicta pueros fudit in urbem,
iaculator superans vel Baliares, neque feli
    neque vitro sine noxa.

catus idem puer hortum comitatus rapientum
grege malis spoliare, et celer arbustum agitando
    pira ramo excutere alto.

T.W.M.

Jones—(who I'm glad to say
Asked leave of Mrs. J.)—
Daily absorbs a clay
    After his labours.

Cats may have had their goose
Cooked by tobacco-juice;
Still why deny its use
    Thoughtfully taken?
We're not as tabbies are:
Smith take a fresh cigar!
Jones the tobacco jar!
    Here's to thee, Bacon!   C. S. CALVERLEY

XXXVI

'Tis the dreariest fool who loves only his school, and never
              [desires to inhale
Tobacco-leaf smoke, never suffers the stroke of a long
      Describing designs on his tail. [pedagogical flail
But William the bold little thirteen-year old makes satchel
              [and homework to fade,
And, Eric, your chum's making hay of your sums, those
             [horrible studies that jade;
    A catapult deadly he's made.
For when the school's whistle at hour of dismissal decants
            [on the City its brats,
Superlative shots who at Bisley win pots—he knocks them
            [all into cocked hats,
    A terror to glass and to cats.
The same has a knack with a following pack the garden to
            [strip of its crop;
Of apples the mob someone's orchard will rob, and shaking
            [the trees to their top
    Soon catch all the pears as they drop.   T.W.M.

XXXVII

Mortuum flet silva Linum, Linumque
pastuum caulis loca flent relictis ;
ille sed vino Stygialis implens
    pocula regis

Ditis ad mensas statuetur aulae,
qua cient nullae numeros volucres,
nec solent agni teneri protervo
    ludere saltu.

tempore haud ullo poteris redire
deserens Orcum, nisi commovebis
forte Plutonis miserandus atri
    corda superba,

vel deae natam Cereris, Sicana
valle carpentem nova serta florum,
quam Stygis Pluto rapuit sub undas
    captus amore.

audiet lenis dea supplicantem,
osculis mulcens dominum rogabit,
vallibus donec stabulisque ademptos
    reddat amores.

mollibus divam numeris preceris,
lacta nec mittas dare multa divae
mellaque, et tristes referas sacrato
    carmine versus.   E.H.

This Sapphic version is reproduced untouched as Edward Hussey wrote
it as an Eton schoolboy of but 14 years of age.

XXXVII

Dead is Linus—him the grove,
Him the pleasant pastures mourn
And the shepherd-cotes forlorn;
But he standeth by the board
In the Stygian hall abhorred,
Pouring cups for the grim king
Where no merry birds do sing,
Nor the frolic lambkins play.
Linus wilt thou come again?
Canst thou melt the cold disdain
Of black Dis, or haply move
Her who smote his soul with love,
Plucking flowers in Enna's dale?
She, I trow, will heed your tale,
Soothe her lord with kisses soft,
Till he yield, and how and croft
Welcome their lost darling back:
Hymn her softly with no lack
Of milk and honey, and your verse
In sad and solemn strains rehearse.

XXXVIII

Ad Licinium

Rectius ludes, Licini, neque ictu
semper obliquante pilam secando
nec fera fines magis ad sinistros
    arte trahendo.

saepius clava temere heu rotata
vel parum caute capite allevato
caespites tantum removebis ipsumve
    aera caedes.

quisquis attonsi mediocritatem
diliget campi neque quaeret herbis
asperis sphaeram neque trux in alta
    tundet arena.

providus metae viridi propinques,
fortis appare fovea retentus
improba; nam si putidam malignus
    scindere chartam

Iuppiter cogit, tibi mittet idem
forte victrices aquilas avesque;
neve contemnas bona quae satelles
    claviger offert.

victor et posthac rediens triumphos
largiter donis celebrabis amplis
Liberi mecum, totidemque sumes
    pocula victus.

E.V.C.P.

XXXVIII

"How to succeed at golf?" here's my advice;
Lest you go out of bounds beware that slice:
And let me tell you, friend, it doesn't pay
Wildly to pull your shots the other way.
But if the club you rashly swing around,
Or fail to keep your head towards the ground,
Nothing but divots will reward your care,
Or else you'll find that all you've hit is air.
The middle of the fairway, that's the mean
To follow always: then you won't be seen
Looking for lost balls somewhere in the rough,
Or, bunkered, slogging blindly in a huff.
When near the green then ever careful be,
But brave when trapped: you somehow may get free.
And though one day Fate seems unduly hard,
Making you end in tearing up your card,
Another day perhaps she holds in store
Birdies and eagles to reduce your score.
Nor rudely spurn—it's neither wise nor nice—
The caddy-offered club or good advice.
And afterwards when homewards you've returned,
We'll share the bottle you've so justly earned:
For if you've won, we'll toast the winning score:
And if you've lost, you'll need it all the more.

E.V.C.P.

XXXIX

Ad Grosphum

Grosphe, tranquillum tegit hoc sepulchrum
patris et nati pariter iacentis
ossa cum saxo peritura, quorum
    vivida virtus

usque durabit. quod adulta cunque
persequi debet probitas, in illo
cerneres, quicquid fugere; hic suorum
    vota fefellit,

magna promittens iuvenis; sed ambo
Mors tulit, non plus miserans procella,
poma quae perfecta novasque gemmas
    perdidit aeque;

nosque maturis truculenta primum
fructibus saevo spoliavit ictu,
nunc futurorum cupidis bonorum
    praeripit usum.

S.A.H.

XXXIX

Epitaph upon Robert Huntingdon and Robert his son.

This peaceful Tomb does now contain
Father and Son together laid;
Whose living virtues shall remain
When they and this are quite decay'd,
What Man should be, to Ripeness grown,
And finish'd Worth should do, or shun,
At full was in the Father shown.
What Youth could promise, in the Son.
But Death, obdurate, both destroyed,
The perfect Fruit and op'ning Bud.
First seiz'd those Sweets we had enjoy'd,
Then robb'd us of the coming Good.

WILLIAM CONGREVE

XL

Genius Loci

Imber ut saevit niveus forasque
comprimit terras hiemale frigus!
intus at festo calet in cubili
    mense Decembri.

ecce festivus rubeo colore et
somnifer tectum maculat caminus;
sibilant vasis nisi qua liquores
    omne silescit.

hic super lectos quasi Lar benignus
sede sublimi sedet atque velo
vitreo tectus puer et corona
    tempora cinctus

despicit sanctus, nitidamque vestem
splendet indutus, manus altera orbem
sustinet, supra pueros quietos
    porrigit unam.

numen obscuras velut inter aras
solus apparet radiis coruscis,
et suos fratres tegit usque solis
    divus in ortum.

nunc inauditum, quasi dormientum
spiritus, totas volitat per aedes
numen aeternum puerisque castis
    complet amicum.

nil mali praesente deo secundo
laedat infantes: bene dormiamus:
hic adest; divo bona nos favente
    fata sequentur.

XL

L'Enfant Jésus de Prague

Il neige. Le grand monde est mort sans doute. C'est
décembre.
Mais qu'il fait bon, mon Dieu, dans la petite chambre !
La cheminée emplie de charbons rougeoyants
Colore le plafond d'un reflet somnolent.
Et l'on n'entend que l'eau qui bout à petit bruit.
Là-haut, sur l'étagère, au-dessus des deux lits,
Sous son globe de verre, couronne en tête,
L'une des mains tenant le monde, l'autre prête
A couvrir ces petits qui se confient à elle,
Tout aimable dans sa grande robe solennelle
Et magnifique sous cet énorme chapeau jaune,
L'Enfant Jésus de Prague règne et trône.
Il est tout seul devant le foyer qui l'éclaire
Comme l'hostie cachée au fond du sanctuaire,
L'Enfant-Dieu jusqu'au jour garde ses petits frères.
Inentendue comme le souffle qui s'exhale,
L'existence éternelle emplit la chambre, égale
A toutes ses pauvres choses innocentes et naïves !
Quand il est avec nous, nul mal ne nous arrive.

nos habet somnus, sed equi sigilla
mira Troiani tamen atque pupae
gaudium restant puerile ; claudunt
    vela fenestras :

et foris nocte in nivea canora
voce proclamat vigil urbis horas ;
in toro somnis puer excitatur
    laetus amoeno,

somnio qui sentit adesse amicum
seque dormire, et relevat lacertum,
tentat expergi reciditque fessus,
    murmurat ore.   E.C.W.

XLI

Quicumque inermes armiferis meas
dux obsidebis militibus fores,
    si quando virtuti studebas,
        incolumem dominum tuere :

aequo rependam munere gratias,
benignitatem dum celebro tuam,
    terraque diffundens marique,
        solis ubi calet aura, nomen.

tu ne Camenae sedibus impium
intende telum ; victor enim domos
    vastante Thebanas ruina,
        Pindaricis Macedo pepercit

tectis : valebant Cecropidae suas
defendere arces exscidio gravi,
    tristes Oresteae sororis
        carmine dum geminant dolores.   F.C.G.

On peut dormir ; Jésus, notre frère, est ici.
Il est à nous, et toutes ces bonnes choses aussi :
La poupée merveilleuse, et le cheval de bois,
Et le mouton, sont là, dans ce coin tous les trois.
Et nous dormons, mais toutes ces bonnes choses sont à nous !
Les rideaux sont tirés . . . Là-bas, on ne sait où,
Dans la neige et la nuit sonne une espèce d'heure.
L'enfant dans son lit chaud comprend avec bonheur
Qu'il dort et que quelqu' un qui l'aime bien est là,
S'agite un peu, murmure vaguement, sort le bras,
Essaye de se réveiller et ne peut pas.

PAUL CLAUDEL

XLI

Sonnet : 1642
("When the assault was intended to the city".)

Captain, or Colonel, or Knight in arms
　　Whose chance on these defenceless doors may seize,
　　If deed of honour did thee ever please,
Guard them, and him within protect from harms.
He can requite thee ; for he knows the charms
　　That call fame on such gentle acts as these,
　　And he can spread thy name o'er lands and seas,
Whatever clime the sun's bright circle warms.
Lift not thy spear against the Muses' bower :
　　The great Emathian conqueror bid spare
The house of Pindarus, when temple and tower
　　Went to the ground ; and the repeated air
Of sad Electra's poet had the power
　　To save the Athenian walls from ruin bare.

JOHN MILTON

XLII

Sigulda

Si, mi care, cupis regionem noscere, Poldi,
       in Latvia pulcherrimam,
tum mecum vehere in vicum, cui pulchra Sigulda
       ab incolis nomen datum est:
altis in ripis fluvii, quas Gauia revellit—
       est omne flumen Latvicum—
antiquas turres castellorumque ruinas
       spectabis et saltus boum.
tu nitidas pinges ripas a colle Turaedae
       specumve magnum Gutmani,
ast ego Vergilii propter te scripta libenter
       legam sub umbra frondium.
tu pones aprica locis cum semper opacis,
       ut omnia in terra vides,
me delectabunt animus mentesque poetae
       et rura descripta ac labor.
in tabula formam naturae reddere largae
       coloribus multis petes,
verbis quae scripsit vates pedibusque studebo
       illustris ad gentem suam.
inde novus nobis quaerendus collis amoenus—
       mutare sedes utile est—
ibimus ad dextram, qua celsior usque Crimulda
       regnat super comam arborum.
tu propere facies picturam frondis opimae
       et tortuosi fluminis,
his ego conabor patienter pangere versus,
       sequens poetarum pedes.
cumque reverterimus naturae vespere pleni
       sero manentem nos domum,

XLII

Sygulda

Jeśli, mój drogi Leopoldzie, chcesz poznać krainę
    najładniejszą w Łotwie,
to jedź ze mną do okolicy, zwaną przez lud miejscowy
    ładna Sygulda.
Z wysokich brzegów rzeki, które Gauja podmyła
    (cała rzeka płynie w Łotwie),
będziesz oglądał starożytne wieże i ruiny zamczysk
    oraz pastwiska trzód.
Ty będziesz malował piękne brzegi z góry Turaidy
    lub wielką Gutmanowska grotę,
ja zaś obok ciebie będę chętnie czytał Wergiliusza
    w cieniu zieleni drzew.
Ty będziesz kreślił jasne i zawsze cieniste miejsca,
    jak zwykle rozróżniasz na ziemi,
mnie zaś będzie porywał duch i myśli poety,
    opisy łak i wiejskich prac.
Ty na płótnie będziesz się starał odtworzyc piękno
    przyrody rozmaitymi kolory,
ja znów będę badał zdania i wiersze, jakie ułożył
    sławny wieszcz dla swego narodu.
Następnie pójdziemy na inne piękne wzgórze
    (pożytecznie zmienić pobyt)
pójdzmy na prawo, gdie zawsze wyższa Krymulda
    góruje nad zielenia drzew.
Ty szybko nakreślisz obraz bogatej zieleni
    i rzeki krętej brzeg,
a ja tu sprobuję cierpliwie ułożyc wiersze
    na wzór starożytnych poetów.
I gdy przyrodą nasyceni wrócimy późnym wieczorem
    do czekającego nas domu,

tum noster paries picturas parvus habebit
    tua arte crescens iam novas,
versibus atque meus paucis augebitur audax
    libellus in mensa gravi.

R.D.

XLIII

E quo prodigio nascitur hic fremor?
num possit fieri Motor ut opprimat
    Bus me nunc peditem? scilicet indicat
      Bum Motorem odor ac bombus atrocior.
Sacra forte Via perve Suburam eo,
sicut mos meus est: corda metus mihi
    Bi Motoris edit, Bi timor occupat;
      Motorique querens terque quaterque Bo
clamo, ne subita Bo nece prorutus
a Motore cadam—namque quid interest
    fias *casus* uter, dummodo vivere
      nobis des hodie? quae fuga victimis,
quae, Motor Be, patet? parce, precor precor.
sic frustra cecini: Bi magis et magis
    Motores coeunt, innumerabilis
      Motorum omne forum copia Borum habet.
tot Motoribus ut Bis superabimus
cincti nos miseri? sancte Diespiter,
    Motores, age, nos protege Bos in hos!

A.I.

wówczas nasz niewielki pokój ozdobi się nowymi obrazami,
    rosnąc twoją sztuką farb,
lecz i mój śmiałego tworu zeszyt na poważnym stole
    zbogaci się wierszami.

ROMAN CIESIULEWICZ

XLIII

What is this that roareth thus?
Can it be a *Motor Bus?*
Yes, the smell and hideous hum
indicat Motorem Bum!
Implet in the Corn and High
terror me Motoris Bi:
Bo Motori clamitabo
ne Motore caedar a Bo—
dative be or ablative
so thou only let us live:—
Whither shall thy victim flee?
Spare us, spare us, *Motor Be!*
Thus I sang; and still anigh
came in hordes *Motores Bi,*
et complebat omne forum
copia Motorum Borum.
How shall wretches live like us
cincti Bis Motoribus?
Domine, defende nos
contra hos Motores Bos!

A. D. GODLEY

XLIV

Ad Ibycum

Lignorum putrium perfide venditor,
cum primum icta tibi Pontica nobilis
silvae progenies concidit, Ibyce,
    non feci querimoniam,

quamvis multimodis sollicitudines
mentem concuterent; ut decuit virum,
fugi quaerere cur merx tibi sordida
    auro esset pretiosior,

immundum redolens : non male pertinax
mirabar nebulas cur vomeret graves ;
cur longis pluviis robora panderes,
    ustum ceu lasanum lavans.

sed iam criminibus me gravioribus
tu cogis querulam fundere neniam :
quid putere querar ligna madentia,
    quae ne suppeditas quidem?

F.C.G.

XLIV

To my Wood Merchant

When first upon my hearth to blaze
    Your precious trees were slain,
Though sore perplexed in sundry ways
    I did not once complain.

I bore it as a brave man should,
    Nor clamoured to be told
Why such a common thing as wood
    Should ask the price of gold;

Nor why it had to smell so strong
    And breathe so foul a smoke,
Nor why you left it out so long
    (Like frying pans) to soak.

But now a fault more irksome yet
    Forbids me to be dumb:
Malodorous, expensive, wet—
    It doesn't even come!

                M. H. LONGSON

XLV

Ut si quis olim per fretorum angustias
      vindex furoris Persici
nunc vivus hic maneret, aspectu dolens
      sua minoris Graeciae,
sic tu, Canare, iunioribus senex
      nobis verendus interes,
mox transituri pars relicta saeculi,
      heros et heroum comes.
nutricum ab ore parvulo primum mihi
      te contigit cognoscere
mirabilis dum panditur, semper nova,
      tuae iuventae fabula.
Thesei labores Herculisve crederes
      audire : "nauta ille e Psyra
sescenta pondera hosticarum navium
      uno ipse vectus lembulo
fecit favillas" : audienti vix minor
      mihi videbaris deo.
cum venit aetas firmior—mansit tamen
      puerilis admiratio—
quam me iuvabat paginas evolvere
      tuam loquentes gloriam !
sequebar ubicunque aequoris per ambitum
      tu, numen infestum maris,
molis tremendas impari certamine
      victor dedisses ignibus.
omnes in oras magna virtutis tuae
      dilata sunt praeconia,
tua et tropaea audire gestientium
      fervebat expectatio ;
tu sicut aquila ab edito cacumine
      fulmen citatum deferens

XLV

ΠΡΟΣ ΤΟΝ ΚΑΝΑΡΗΝ[1]

Ὡς λείψανον εἰσέτι ζῶν μεμακρυσμένων χρόνων,
ὡς τμῆμα ἔργου εὐκλεοῦς τῶν εὐκλεῶν προγόνων,
μὲ λύπην τὴν σμικρότητα τῆς νῦν Ἑλλάδος καθορῶν,
οὕτω καὶ σὺ παρίστασαι ἐν μέσῳ μας, Κανάρη,
σημεῖον μέγα γενεᾶς, ἥτις σχεδὸν ἐφθάρη,
ἥρως ἡρωϊκῶν καιρῶν.

Νήπιον ἔτι ἤκουον, ἑκάστοτε ἀλλοῖον,
ἀπὸ τὰ χείλη τῶν τροφῶν τὸν σύγχρονόν σου βίον,
ὡς βίον ἥρωός τινος ἢ ἡμιθέου παλαιοῦ·
μ' ἔλεγον «ναύτης τῶν Ψαρῶν εἷς μόνον μὲ ἐν πλοῖον
σωρείας ἀπετέφρωσε τρικρότων γιγαντείων! »
κ' ἴσος μ' ἐφαίνεσο θεοῦ.

Ἀνέγνων νέος ἔπειτα μὲ ἔκπληξιν παιδίου
τὰς πράξεις τοῦ γονίμου σου καὶ εὐκλεοῦς σταδίου.
Σὲ ἠκολούθησα παντοῦ τὰ βήματά σου εὐλογῶν.
ὁπότε περιέτρεχες τοῦ πόντου τὰς ἐκτάσεις,
καὶ τρίκροτα μὲ λέμβον σύ, ὁ δαίμων τῆς θαλάσσης,
ἔκαμες θύματα φλογῶν.

Τὸ ὄνομά σου πανταχοῦ ἀπέστελλεν ἡ φήμη·
ἡ οἰκουμένη ἄφωνος ἀνέμενεν, ἑτοίμη
πάντα σου νέον θρίαμβον νὰ χαιρετίσῃ μὲ χαράν.
Ὡς ἀετός, καταπεσὼν ἐκ κορυφῶν ὑψίστων,
ἐν μέσῳ στόλων ἔπιπτες ἐξαίφνης πολυΐστων
ἐκλέγων πλοῖον ὡς βοράν.

[1] Kanaris, the fire-ship hero of the Greek War of Independence (1821–30) was born in 1790 and died in 1877. Vyzandios was born in 1841.

densa inter armamenta classium ratem
    flammis legebas pabulum.
saepe, ut per undas visa nocturnas procul
    nova emicare fulgura
latusque ad aures quasi tonitrui fragor
    vocesque desperantium,
dixit tabernae litoralis incola
    "cremat Canares hosticam"!
vorabat aequor carbasa, antennas, trabes,
    clarorum et artus satrapum.

W.M.E.

XLVI

Diffugere pili, vitreos mea tempora vincunt
    Bandusiae latices.
mutat Cura vices, mutat medicamina tonsor
    immodicis pretiis.
unguinis infusi lente labentia mentum
    flumina praetereunt.
iam glomerata ruit, iam lubrica gutta decentem
    commaculat tunicam.
visa repercussi capitis me ludit imago,
    spem neque dat speculum.
sacculus effudit nummos; nunc qualis ut ante
    sto nisi pauperior.
tonsori meritas, comites, imponite poenas!
    vellite quemque pilum!

H.H.

Ότε εἰς νύκτα ζοφερὰν ἐν μέσῳ τῶν κυμάτων
ἀντήχουν αἴφνης γοεροὶ ὀλολυγμοὶ θυμάτων,
κ' ἔβλεπον λάμψιν ἀστραπῆς κ' ἤκουον κρότον κεραυνῶν,
ἔλεγον τρίκροτον κανὲν θὰ καίη ὁ Κανάρης . . .
Κ' ἡ θάλασσα κατέπινεν ὅπλα, ἱστούς, κιδάρεις,
        πασσάδων πτώματα κλεινῶν.

                        Ἀλέξανδρος Βυζάντιος.

XLVI

My hairs have scattered,
My temples outshine Bandusia's fountain.
Anxiety goes through each varying season,
The barber goes through each varying treatment
And charges excessively ; pours on his unguent
Which flows past my chin ; and languid the streams then
That gather, and downwardly run as they clot, and
My best shirt is spattered.
The glass reflects a face that mocks,
And only brings despair.
I've showered cash, I'm still the same
Except my purse is bare.
Friends, give the barber his deserts
And tear out every hair !
                        Transl. MARY OAKES

XLVII

Albius Albo

Quondam otiosus vespere dum Viam
Sacram pererrabam aut oculo vago
 captare tentabam puellas,
  adstiterat Cypris ambulanti.

tunc illa : "quid tu, dedecus o meum,
frustra vagaris, cui toga decolor,
 cui spurca, cui non lauta vestis
  pulvere colluvieque sordet?

non his puellas illecebris trahes :
nunc aspice *AESTUM* vi magica mea
 tironis instantes ad usus
  pyxide sic habili paratum.

infunde lymphis non calidis nimis :
spumam videbis crescere qua togam
 merses profunda ; confricandi
  nullum opus est tibi nec laboris.

mox dum per horae dimidium aut minus
labro Falernum purpureo bibis
 limosa perpurgabit *AESTUS*
  sponte sua maculasque tollet.

splendere miro conspicies togam
candore ; quin et pulchrior evenit
 iam comparari nuper emptae
  digna : sed et medicata fuco

XLVII

As I was strolling down the street
Winking at the lassies neat,
Venus suddenly beside me
Stood and with suspicion eyed me.

Says she: "Rascal, what's your plan?
Why disgrace me, beastly man?
Look at all those spots and dirt—
Your toga's filthy, so's your shirt.

What girl would throw a glance at you?
Now here's the cure, my magic brew,
A box of T—— in handy pack:
It's instant too—you need no knack.

With tepid water mix it well,
And watch the bubbles start to swell;
Then let your toga soak—no rubbing,
You won't believe this—nor hard scrubbing.

Titulus de toga candida BT: de uenere et spuma marina FM, Y a m.2
varr. lectt. et doctorum conii. 2 uagas *cd, Heinsius, Orelli* 3 puellos *hic et
in* 9 *Fürchtenkampf perperam* 4 obstitit, heu! Venus osculanti *AYCampbell*
10 *mire discrepant inter se renascentis aeui codd.,* OMO (N), OLAM *et sim.
legentes (an pretio adducti?)* Nunc Persil exit *Housman dub.* 14 fumum ...
surgere *Hieronymus de Bosch, quo probato* quo .... profundo *legendum* 17
horae anni] *Housman* 18 labris ... purpureis *Bentley*; 'quis enim uno labro
bibisse auditur?' 19 rimosa F, *quo probato* consutabit *Jortin* despurcabit *Fea:*
detergebit *Ognissanti de Voto, lingua latina invita* 22 fuscior *g, Housman* 25
deterget aestus *de Voto* 27 primo *ab:* privi *d, Housman* 28 lavandi *florilegium
Mancuniense.*

AESTUS novabit, cum Tyrius color
clavusque latus, concilii decus,
   prisco refulgebunt nitore :
     tempus adest hodie probandi !"

W.R.S.

XLVIII

Anni nox erat ultima,
Romae cum Boreae mira per asperum
   fulsit stella gelu polum,
florem et gemma rosae pandit amabilis
   album, gaudeat ut dies
unus per nivium tempora frigida.
   heu, stella in tenebris perit :
unum cum viguit laeta diem, fugit
   quo cunctae fugiunt, rosa.
sed lux nunc etiam splendida per nives
   e stella procul enitet,
perque annos niveae spirat odor rosae.

E.J.W.

Now go away and have a drink
(One two or three); while in the sink
T——'s magic action (no arm achin')
Removes those stains of egg and bacon.

You'll find besides that it adds brightness
Even to most perfect whiteness:
Your toga'll come out good as new.
But T—— is good for coloureds too:

Your reds and purples, green and yellow
Stripes, and pastel colours mellow
Will gleam and shine with brightest ray—
Go and try a box today!"   w.r.s.

XLVIII

A wonderful Star shone forth
From the frozen skies of the North
Upon Rome for an Old Year's Night.
And a flower of the dear, white Rose
Broke in the season of snows
To bloom for a day's delight.

Lost is the Star in the night,
And the Rose of a day's delight
Fled "where roses go",

But the fragrance and light from afar
Born of the Rose and the Star
Breathe o'er the years and the snows.

ANDREW LANG
(On the birthday of Prince Charles
Edward, 31st December 1720).

Beatus ille qui velut Laertius
    heros revectus est rate
cursu secundo, sive velleris potens
    audax Iason, doctior
prudentiorque redditur penatibus.
    at ipse quando patrium
exul revisam sordidum fumo focum?
    agrosque quos non praedio
mutem Sabinos Africo? patrum mihi
    quae facta sedes est manu,
praestat superbum gloria palatium :
    non gratiora marmora
mihi renident rusticae quam tegulae :
    amoeniorne praefluit
Aniensis amne turbido Tibris pater?
    Lucretilisque me capit
aura salubri dulcior caloribus
    Palatioque suavior.

A.T.

Reprinted with the permission of the Editor of *The College Courant*.

XLIX

Heureux qui, comme Ulysse, a fait un beau voyage,
Ou comme celui-là qui conquit la toison,
Et puis est retourné, plein d'usage et raison,
Vivre entre ses parents le reste de son âge !

Quand reverrai-je hélas, de mon petit village
Fumer la cheminée? et en quelle saison
Reverrai-je le clos de ma pauvre maison,
Qui m'est une province, et beaucoup d'avantage?

Plus me plaît le séjour qu'ont bâti mes aïeux,
Que des palais romains le front audacieux ;
Plus que le marbre dur me plaît l'ardoise fine ;

Plus mon Loyre gaulois que le Tibre latin,
Plus mon petit Lyré que le mont Palatin,
Et plus que l'air marin la douceur angevine.

JOACHIM DU BELLAY

L

Ad Philippum

Philippe, bene te novimus quo rectior
    non alter est mortalium,
non aequior, nec diligentius prece
    deos fatigat sedula.
sed imbuisti caede fraterna manus
    et Marte adortus impio
patrem tenebas arce captivum senem
    dum vita erat superstiti.
quid fronte tactum milies fanatica
    solum, quid insana fame
retractus umbilicus ad spinam valet,
    quid talis ostentatio,
si facta dictis aequa non adiunxeris
    bonamque non servas fidem?
serpens decore pellis externo nitens
    intus venenum ac fraudem alit.
stat fortibus res gesta pro facundia,
    stat lingua pro telo tibi.
his te, Philippe, versibus fideliter
    ut in tabella ponimus;
quem si scelestum nostra non tanget manus,
    at hoc precamur "o Pater,
damnent Philippum iudices summa die
    summo dolore Tartari!"

E.B.H.

L

A Hymn of Hate

Aurang, full well I know him. So just he is, so fair,

Precise in all observances, punctilious in prayer.

But he slew his own blood brothers in fratricidal strife,

Gave battle to his father and imprisoned him for life.

The devotee a thousand times may brow to earth incline,

Or by repeated fasts may bring his navel to his spine ;

But if his acts mate not with speech to further good intent,

His posturings are profitless, his fasting fraudulent.

The outward of the snake is fair, and glossy is her skin ;

But venom lurks behind her lips and treachery within.

The valiant speaks but little, and by deeds his praise is sung ;

The coward and the braggart make sword-play with their
tongue :

My words reveal to him who reads a portrait of Aurang.

My hand can never reach him. But hear me, Lord, I pray :

To Aurang, Lord, be merciless on thy great Judgement Day !

KHUSHHAL KHAN
(transl. E.B.H.)

LI

Ad Lycen

Flatu nox queritur culminibus, stirps Minyeidum
per lunam volitant, fusca polum nubila navigant,
bubonis strepitu fur trepidat, pulla canum deae
noctis vis ululat—sacra, Lyce, iam Lemures agunt.
nam cum silva fremit flaminibus, stagna tegit vapor,
busto e marmoreo proveniunt ossa iacentium,
quae rictu patulo rite petunt festa fugacia et
intempesta, brevi cantus avis quae premet, orgia.
hinc mas umbra sua cum domina sub tumulum fugit,
malis quisque macris basia dat, dicit "Ave!" gemens,
dum laetos sonitus aes vigilum noctivagum efferet,
intempestaque erit nox iterum festaque Manibus.

T.W.M.

LI

Song (*Sir Roderic Murgatroyd*)
from "*Ruddigore*"

When the night wind howls in the chimney cowls, and the
      bat in the moonlight flies,
And inky clouds, like funeral shrouds, sail over the
      midnight skies—
When the footpads quail at the night-bird's wail, and
      the black dogs bay at the moon,
Then is the spectres' holiday—then is the ghosts'
      high noon!

As the sob of the breeze sweeps over the trees, and
      the mists lie low on the fen,
From grey tomb-stones are gathered the bones that once
      were women and men,
And away they go, with a mop and a mow, to the revel
      that ends too soon,
For cockcrow limits our holiday—the dead of the night's
      high noon!

And then each ghost with his ladye-toast to their church-
      yard beds takes flight,
With a kiss perhaps on her lantern chaps, and a grisly
      grim "good night";
Till the welcome knell of the midnight bell rings forth
      its jolliest tune,
And ushers in our next high holiday—the dead of the
      night's high noon.

W.   S.   GILBERT

LII

Ad Paetum

Optimum si quid dare vis amico,
nil aquam praestat gelidam, sed istum
largus indigno mihi cur honorem,
      Paete, reservas?

principes lymphis, domini fruantur
fontibus ; Chium bibere aut Falernum,
quod mihi praebes, satis est vel uvae
      musta Sabinae.

H.H.H.

LII

Cold water is the best of gifts
    That man to man can bring ;
But what am I that I should have
    The best of everything?

Let princes revel in the springs,
    Peers with the pump make free ;
For whisky, wine, or even beer
    Are good enough for me.

ANON.

NON OMNIS MORIAR

ODES
III·XXXVI

SELECT BIBLIOGRAPHY

The Works of Horace, ed. by E. C. Wickham. Oxford Clarendon Press. Vol. i (ed. 3 1896).

Horace, *Odes and Epodes. A Study in Poetic Word Order.* Ed. by H. D. Naylor. CUP 1922.

Q. Horatius Flaccus, *Oden und Epoden*, 8. Aufl. erkl. von A. Kiessling, erneuert von R. Heinze, mit einem Nachwort und Bibliogr. Nachtr. von E. Burckh. Berlin Weidmann 1955.

Bo, D., *Lexicon Horatianum.* 2 vols. Olms Hildesheim 1965, 1966.

Cooper, L., *A Concordance of the Works of Horace.* Washington 1916. (Reprinted 1961: W. Heffer & Sons, Cambridge).

Staedler, E., *Thesaurus Horatianus.* Akademie-Verlag Berlin 1962.

Axelson, B., *Unpoetische Wörter. Ein Beitrag zur Kenntnis der lateinischen Dichtersprache.* Lund Gleerup 1945.

Bellinger, A. R., *The Lesser Asclepiadean Line of Horace. YClS* xv 1957 101–9.

Blackett, J. P. M., *A Note on the Alcaic Stanza. G & R* iii 1956 83–4.

Büchner, K., *Studien zur römischen Literatur.* Band III: *Horaz*, Wiesbaden 1962.

Burck, E., *Horaz. Die Musik in Geschichte und Gegenwart* vi 1957 707–11.

Campbell, A. Y., *Horace — a New Interpretation.* London, 1924.

Collinge, N. E., *The Structure of Horace's Odes.* London OUP 1961 (repr. 1962).

Enk, P. J., *De Symmetria Horatiana. Mn* iv 1936/7 164–72.

Fraenkel, E., *Horace.* Oxford: Clarendon Press 1957.

Heinze, R., *Die lyrischen Verse des Horaz.* Verlag Adolf M. Hakkert: Amsterdam, 1959.

Heinze, R., *Vom Geist des Römertums*, 3. erweit. Aufl. Teubner Stuttgart 1960.

Mackail, J. W., *A Lesson on an Ode of Horace. CR* xxxv 1921 2–7.

Moritz, L. A., *Some 'Central' Thoughts on Horace's Odes. CQ* xviii 1968 116–31.

Muller, F., *De Horatianis Metris deque eorum usu Poetae animi habitui respondente. Mn* iv 1936/7 114–28.

Pasquali, G., *Orazio Lirico.* Firenze: Felice le Monnier 1920.

Perret, J., *Horace.* Hatier Paris, 1959.

Postgate, J. P., *Notes on the Asclepiad Odes of Horace. CQ* xvi 1922, 29–34.

Prakken, D. W., *Feminine Caesuras in Horatian Sapphic Stanzas. CP* xlix 1954 102–3.

Rose, H. J. and H. Pritchard-Williams, *Interlinear Hiatus in the Odes of Horace*. CR xxxvii 1923 113–4.

Rotsch, L., *Zur Form der drei Horaz-Oden in Asclepiadeus maior (I xi, I xviii, IV x)*. *Gymnasium* lxiv 1957 89–98.

Skutsch, O., *Rhyme in Horace*. *BICS* xi 1964 73–8.

Sonnenschein, E. A., *The Latin Sapphic*. CR xvii 1903 252–6.

Staedler, E., *Über den Gebrauch vielsilbiger Wortbildungen bei Horaz*. *Glotta* xxvii 1938/9 199–206.

Thompson, E. S., *The Latin Sapphic*. CR xvii 1903 456–8.

Verrall, A. W., *The Latin Sapphic*. CR xvii 1903 339–43.

Wilkinson, L. P., *Accentual Rhythm in Horatian Sapphics*. CR liv 1940 131–3.

Wilkinson, L. P., *Horace and his Lyric Poetry*. 2nd ed. CUP 1951 (also available as a CUP paperback).

Wilkinson, L. P., *Golden Latin Artistry*. CUP 1963.

Wille, G., *Singen und Sagen in der Dichtung des Horaz*. *Eranion Festschrift für H. Hommel* 1961 169–84.

INDEX

Abstract nouns   45, 90, 113, 119, 123 *et al*

Accentual stress *vs* metrical ictus   29 *sqq*

Addressee   40–1, 77–9, 96, 107, 121 *et al*

Adjectives,   see *Epithets, Horatian*

Adonic verse-line   46, 48 *sqq* and see *Further Notes* on Sapphics

Adverbs   44, 110 *et al*

Alcaeus   20, 22, 41

Alcaic metre and ode structure   47, 52–61, 82, 130 *et al*

Anacrusis   52

Anaphora   46, 53–4, 114, 119, 128 *et passim*

Andrewes, Horace's imagery   97n1

Arberry, Prof. A. J.   xvi, 217

Archaic words, use of by Horace   42

Arion story (Ovid)   12

Aristotle   37

Asclepiad metres and ode structure   61–74

Ateius Capito, antiquarian   37

Athens, Horace and   8, 26, 37

Atque, Horace's use of   45

Augustus (Octavian)   37, 94

Aulos (and see *Tibia*)   10 n1, 17 *sqq*

Axelson, B.   41 n3

Balanced Decoration (and see *Epithets, Horatian*)   42, 44, 88, 99, 103, 107–110 *et passim*

Barbitos   21

Beare, Prof. W.   34, 160–1

Bellinger, A. R.   42, 61 n1

Bentley   97

Blake, Wm. ('Whether on Ida's') Alcaic version   111–2

Bonavia-Hunt, W. (brother of author)   xv, 52 n1, 216 *sqq*

M. Bonnafé, A.   137

Brahms   99

Büchner   39–40

Bunting, Basil   1 n1

Burlesque, suitability of Alcaics for   53

Caesura   31, 47 *et passim,* and see *Further Notes* on Sapphics, Alcaics, Asclepiads

Calverley, C. S.   129, 227–229

Carmen Saeculare   6 *sqq*, 8, 10 n1, 13, 17, 27–29, 31 *sqq*, 48, 50, 56, imaginary melody for   32–37

Carmina Dublinensia   120 n1, 174

Catullus   xi, 31, 46, 140

Causals in Horace   45

Chia, musical girl friend of Horace   16

Chloe, musical girl friend of Horace   3, 11, 16, 85

Choir trainer &c.   11, 14

Choriambic words   61 *sqq* and see *Further Notes* on Asclepiads

Chorda   17, 23–4

Christie, J. T., demonstration   131
   sqq

Cicero   19, 30, 43

Cithara, see *Lyre*

Cleopatra   92 *sqq*, 127

Concessives in Horace   46

Concords   42, 43, 51, 88 *et passim*
   and see *Further Notes* on
   Sapphics, Alcaics, Asclepiads

Concrete nouns   45, 102, 123 *et al*

Conjunctions in Horace   45–6 *et al*

Connexion of thought   44–5 *et al*

Consonants, bunching of, to be
   avoided   53, 78, 90–1 *et al*

Continuity in diction   108, 120–1,
   125–127 *et al*

Cory, W. J.   77

Cribs   77, 79, 82, 121

Cowper, Wm. (Sapphic version of
   hymn)   121–3

Cybele   7, 18, 19

'Dashes', un-Horatian use of   127

De la Mare, drafts & versions of
   Occluded   135–6

Delphic Hymn   8

Diaeresis   47, 54–7, 63, 94, 130
   and see *Further Notes* on
   Sapphics, Alcaics, Asclepiads

Diction   41 *sqq*

Diminutives in the Odes   41

Dissyllables, caution for students   55

'Donec gratus' (III ix),
   comments on   7, 99, 100 n3

Double negative turn   127

Dudley, Prof. D. R.   100 n3

Elgar, Sir Edward   8 n1

Elegiac verse   75

Elision   48–9, 58, 65 *sqq*, and
   see *Further Notes* on Sapphics,
   Alcaics, Asclepiads

End-stopping see *Further Notes*

Enjambment   39, 40, 59, 96, 118
   et passim, and see *Further Notes* on
   Sapphics, Alcaics, Asclepiads

Epithets, Horatian   87, 88, 89
   sqq, et al

Euphony   2, 43, 53–4, 90

Exercises for students   137 *sqq*

Expressive technique, varieties of
   116 *sqq*

Ferguson, Donald   36

Flaccus – not QHF – musical
   composer   27–8

Fraenkel, Prof. E.   3 n2, 4 n2,
   12–15, 16, 20, 21 n1, 24,
   28 n1, 32 n2, 86 n2

Further Notes on Sapphics   47 *sqq*

Further Notes on Alcaics   54 *sqq*

Further Notes on Asclepiads   61 *sqq*

M. Gagé   10 n2

Gemination, in the Odes   128–9

'Gentleman's education' in Horace's
   day   8 n1

Glyconic verse   61, 63–5 *sqq*
   and see *Further Notes* on
   Asclepiads

Goethe on Horace's 'frightening
   realism'   88

Gosling, W. G.   100 n1

Gow, Dr. J. G.   20, 27, 50 n1

Gravitas, Horace can lay aside   53

Gutturals, see *Consonants, Euphony*

Handel, G. F.   9

Heinze, R.   3, 30, 41

Henderson, Isobel, musicologist 9, 32, 36
Herrick, Robert, Latin versions of his poems 81, 103 *sqq*, 107, 109, 128–9
Hexameter verse 5, 17 *sqq*, 62
Hexasyllabic words 41, 57
Hiatus 49, 59 n2, 66, 72, 99 *et passim*
Housman, A. E. 18, 201–3
'Hypothetical ass', wholesale purchaser of harps 5, 27

Iam, Horace's uses of 44, 123
'Impossible' working material 120–1
Inflected language, by-products of 43
Ionic Metre 39
Iullus, Mark Antony's son 4

Johnson, Wm., stopping in Sapphic version 130

Kalidasa (Meghaduta) 83
Kaiser, L. M. 85 n1
Knox, Mgr R. xiv, 77

L, repetition of, denoting water 118
Landor, W. S. *Resignation* (Sapphic version) 114
'Leaden' Latin versions 102–3
Lear, Edward, 'The Owl & the Pussy-cat' version 118, 120
Lee, A. G. a demonstration 135
Lesbian foot 10, 30, 32, 34
'Lex Meinekiana' 38, 39 *sqq*, 85
Licymnia, musical girl friend of Horace 16
Livius Andronicus, composer 6
Livy, historian 6, 9

Lucie-Smith, Edward 1 n1
'Lyre' in Horace's works 2–3, 12–15, 23, 25, 26, 17 *sqq* (technical detail), *et al*

Macleane, Rev. A. J. 7 n2
Marisa, song of 99
Meghaduta 83 n2
Metrical scheme 46, 52, 61 and see *Further Notes* on Sapphics Alcaics and Asclepiads
Michie, James 124–5
Modes, ancient musical (Dorian, Lydian, Phrygian) 18, 36–7
Modi 4, 27–8
Mommsen 9, 32 n2
Moritz, L. 78 n1
Munro, H. A. J. 76–8, 80–4
Muses 4, 19–21
Music, technical details 17, 18 music-words in Horace 4 *sqq*
Musical notation 33

Nam &c. in Horace 45–6, 105
Naylor, H. Darnley 44
Newbolt, Sir Henry 120 n1
Newman, Cardinal J. H. ('Lead, Kindly Light') Sapphic version 115–6
Nisbet, regrettable views on "Donec gratus" (III ix) 99
Numeri 28 n1

Onomatopoeia 115–118
'Opposition, the' 1, 2–5, 6, 11, 12, 15, 19, 21, 23–5
Order of words in Horace 44
Ordinary words, Horace's use of 41, 113

Oribasius, on reading aloud   91 n1
Ovid   xiv, 12, 15, 16, 24 n1,
                                28 n1

'Padding,' Horace suspected of   87
Page T. E.   27, 88
Parentheses   50 *sqq*, 60, 61,
                      127–8, *et al*
Pasquali   11 n1, 42 n2
M. Perret, J.   6 n3
'Persicos odi' (I xxxviii) set to
    music?   7 n2
Personification in the Odes, 45, 90
                              et al
Pherecratean verse 61, and see
    Further Notes on Asclepiads
Phyllis, musical girl friend of Horace
                              4, 11
Pianoforte in the vestry   14
Pindar   8, 37, 86 n1
Piso, Horace's advice to   22
Platnauer, M.   45 n
Plato   29
Plectrum   4, 52 n2
Polysyllabic words 41, 47, 54, 94
Postgate, Dr. J. R.   21, 70
Prepositions in Horace   45
Proper Names   45, 80, 89, 113,
                      119, 129 *et al*
Propertius   15, 16
'Pyrrha' Ode (I v)   99 *et al*

Quintilian   5, 19 n2, 35, 43 n1
Quatrain (see stanza)   39, 86 *et al*

Rand, E F , *Horace by Heart* 86 n1
Reading aloud (the Odes) 3, 4, 91–2
Repeated words, (see also *Anaphora,
    Gemination*)   43, 116–18

Rhyme, use and avoidance of in the
    Odes   42, 51 (f) 52, 66, 68,
    and see *Further Notes on
    Sapphics, Alcaics, Asclepiads*
Richardson, Prof L. J. D.   50 n2,
                              174
Rogers, Samuel (*A wish*)   120 n1
Roman liturgy (Sapphic hymns) 33
                              n1
Roman music and instruments   7,
                      9, 10, 17
Rome, noises in the city of   25–6
Royal College of Organists (R.C.O.)
                              XIV

Sachs, Curt   36
Sapphic metre and ode structure
    29 *sqq*, 46–52, 131 *et al*
Sappho   22
Sargent, Sir Malcolm   13
Saturnian measure   52
Scabellum   9–10
Schiller/Schubert—what was set to
    what?   23
Schmidt, Dr. J. H. H.   52 n2
Scott, Sir Walter, 'Breathes there
    a man' (Alcaic)   118
Sense pause   46, 50, 56 *et passim*
Sibilants   53, 98, 116–7 *et al*
Skutsch, Prof. O.   42
Socrates, lyre-playing of   5 n1
Sound effects   43, 90 *et al*
Specialities, Horatian   108, 114–5
                              et al
'Square-cut' stanzas   107–109, 122
                              et al
Staedler   41
Stanford, Prof. W. B.   8 n2
Stanza   39 *sqq*, 71, 95 *sqq et al*
Stopping 59, 108, 121, 130 *et passim*

Structure of the Odes   85 *sqq* and
    see *Sapphic, Alcaic, Asclepiad*
    metres
Subject matter   47, 53, 67–9, 72,
    74, 85, 120 *et al*
Suetonius   14
Superlative form of adjj. in the Odes
    45, 103, 110, 127
Swinyard, Lawrence   117
Syllabic distribution, variety of 54,
    94, 108, 112
Symmetry in structure of the Odes
    85–88
Synaphea   49, 59, 70, 72

Taj Mahal not a British Rail station
    99
Tape-recorder   4, 91, 92
Tate, Sir Robert (*Carmina
    Dublinensia*)   120, 174–5
Tennyson's *Vision of Sin*, versions
    77–81, 125
Terence   10 n1, 27, 134
Testudo   7, 17 *sqq*
Themistocles   8 n1
Tibia   17, 19, 21 *et al*
Trochee   48, 52, 140 *et al*

Un-Horatian versifying   102 *sqq*
Unknown names (in the Odes)   100

Varieties of Expressive technique–
    see *Expressive technique*
Verrall, theories on Sapphics verse 30
Virgil   41, 71, 89, 113
Vocabulary   79 *sqq et passim*

Watson, Sir Wm.   88
Waugh, Evelyn   xiv, 85
Weak caesura   see *Caesura*
Wickham   97 n2, 100
Wharton, E. R.   131
Wilkinson, L. P.   13–118, quoted
    extensively throughout the book
Wilamovitz   3
Winnington-Ingram, R. P.   36
Wood, Prof. E. J.   xv, 252–3
Word order, Horatian   44
Word usage, Horatian   44 *sqq*
Worst Sapphic verse ever?   78

XVviri sacris faciundis   11, 37

Zosimus   14